Reflective Teaching of Geography 11–18

Also available from Continuum:

Reflective Teaching of Geography 11–18

Continuum Studies in Reflective Practice and Theory

Graham Butt

 continuum
LONDON • NEW YORK

Continuum
The Tower Building
11 York Road
London SE1 7NX

370 Lexington Avenue
New York
NY 10017-6503

www.continuumbooks.com

First published 2002

British Library Cataloguing-in-Publication Data
A catalogue record for this book is available from the British Library.

ISBN: 0-8264-5267-1 (hardback)
   0-8264-5268-X (paperback)

Typeset by YHT Ltd, London
Printed and bound in Great Britain by MPG Books Ltd, Bodmin

For Mum
1930–2002

CONTENTS

CHAPTER 1

Geography, initial teacher training, standards and research

What is taught in the schools, in a sense, codifies our accepted knowledge and, in a large degree, the teacher is thus the custodian of the truth.

(David Stoddart, 1988)

1 | AN INTRODUCTION TO INITIAL TEACHER TRAINING

Initial teacher training (ITT) has, over recent years, undergone a series of reforms aimed at making the preparation of new teachers for the teaching profession more accountable. Whilst the explicit purpose of such reforms is stated as being the improvement of the quality of the training (or, more correctly, the *education*) of beginning teachers, other intentions are also apparent. Not least amongst these is the desire of the government to closely regulate and control the training process. As part of the reforms the location for much of the training, supervision and assessment of trainees shifted in the 1990s away from its traditional place in Higher Education Institutions (HEIs) and into partnership schools. Although the results have been largely beneficial for all concerned, issues still exist for many schools concerning the effect on their own students of greater contact with trainees, the time implications for mentor teachers involved in ITT, and the scale of financial transfer to schools for their part in the training process (Barker *et al.*, 1995).

During the 1990s, new pathways within ITT were created, designed primarily to meet the need to train some 25,000 new teachers for English and Welsh schools each year. Many potential trainee teachers could not commit themselves to a 'traditional' full time, one year, postgraduate course of training, hence the development of innovative training courses following 'non standard' routes. Faced with a crisis of teacher supply at secondary level, particularly within shortage subjects such as English, Mathematics, Sciences, RE and ICT, governments have also recently provided various financial incentives to train. It is perhaps significant that teacher supply in geography became such an acute problem in the late 1990s that it too was designated as a shortage subject, with trainees eligible to apply for financial awards under the Secondary Shortage Subject Scheme (SSSS) if they could prove severe financial hardship. Faced with a continuing and severe recruitment problem the government announced that all trainees on Postgraduate Certificate of Education (PGCE) courses would become eligible for a £6000 training salary for the first time in 2000.

Since 1994, the Teacher Training Agency (TTA) has overseen all aspects of teacher training in England and Wales, replacing the Council for Accreditation of

Teacher Education (CATE) established in the early 1980s. This government appointed body is charged with the responsibility of improving the quality of all training routes into the teaching profession, as well as monitoring aspects of the continuing professional development of teachers. The TTA funds providers of ITT and, on the basis of three yearly inspections of their courses by OFSTED/HMI, decides upon the number of trainees to be allocated to various subjects in different training institutions. The Department for Education and Skills (DfES) acts as a further 'gatekeeper' for the recruitment of new teachers into the teaching profession, as well as taking responsibility for education in schools, colleges and universities.

At the culmination of ITT, successful trainees are awarded Qualified Teacher Status (QTS) by the DfES following recommendations made by their training institutions. This permits the Newly Qualified Teacher (NQT) to start teaching in a maintained state school. QTS becomes a permanent award following the successful completion of an induction period of not less than one year within a school. As stated above, the training routes towards the achievement of QTS in England and Wales are numerous – at undergraduate level trainees may take a BA or BSc in Education (with QTS) over a three- or four-year period. This is the main route into primary teaching and combines subject and professional studies with practical teaching experience within schools. At postgraduate level the most common route, followed by around 95 per cent of trainees, is the one-year Post Graduate Certificate of Education (PGCE) studied after the successful completion of an undergraduate degree in an area relevant to the phase and subject one wishes to teach. Other routes into teaching exist, such as the modular PGCE, distance- and employment-based routes, and school-centred (or SCITT) schemes. These can be part- or full-time courses and may not have to comply with all the requirements which other ITT courses must meet. At the time of writing these requirements state that secondary trainees in the core subjects (English, Mathematics and Sciences) must follow their own subject-based National Curricula for ITT, that an ICT in ITT National Curriculum should be studied by all trainees, that all courses must comply with specifications on standard course length and the amount of time trainees spend in schools, and that courses should address a set of Standards for the assessment and eventual award of QTS (TTA, 2001a). The centrality of partnership arrangements between schools and HEI providers is also clearly stated.

QTS is therefore an essential qualification for anyone who wishes to enter teaching in a state maintained school. All entrants to the profession must also be graduates and have successfully passed a Numeracy, Literacy and ICT Skills Test before they are permitted to start their induction year. These criteria do not apply to people wishing to teach in non state-maintained schools, such as independent and public schools, City Technology Colleges and post-16 colleges – for these institutions can employ whoever they wish as teachers. Nonetheless, the possession of QTS is preferred and few new teachers in non-maintained schools and colleges gain access to their posts without this award.

2	THE NATURE OF PARTNERSHIP

A cornerstone of most ITT courses is the fact that they are based on a partnership between the training institution and schools. Recent legislation has strengthened the requirements on partnerships to clarify their procedures for quality assurance, including the necessity to comply with stated criteria for the selection of partner schools (TTA, 1997). Schools wishing to become involved in ITT must demonstrate high standards of general educational provision, as evidenced by recent OFSTED reports, test and examination results. Where schools fall short of these criteria, but still wish to be partners in the training of new teachers, it is expected that HEIs will offer additional support to ensure that the training provided by these schools is of a high standard.

All secondary PGCE courses are 36 weeks in length, with 24 weeks being spent in schools (although a trainee's former experience of working with students in schools, or other settings, may count towards these totals). It is therefore essential that the professional training for QTS is closely planned and administered by an effective partnership between the central provider and its partner schools. Most partnerships are built upon common assumptions about the ways in which beginning teachers should be trained. They are therefore often characterized by all, or many, of the following elements (Trend, 2000, pp. 8–9):

- trainees are active participant learners, working alongside experienced teachers in schools and tutors in the HEI;

- trainees learn through structured reflection on their experience, with assignments designed to reinforce and enhance such learning;

- trainees undertake significant periods of university-based work, involving a range of activities designed to develop their knowledge and understanding and their professional skills in teaching;

- trainees undertake sustained periods of school-based work, with support and guidance from school-based mentors who have themselves been trained in the scheme by university staff;

- during periods of school-based work, trainees maintain links with university staff through Link Tutors and University Visiting Tutors, although the main responsibility for professional support resides with the school-based mentors;

- during the school-based work there is no sacrifice of quality for the sake of quantity. There is no 'throwing in at the deep end' on any mistaken understanding that trainees learn by such an experience. Trainees are inducted into the profession systematically so that their professional skills are developed in a planned and structured way. All parties are required to make explicit the processes by which an inexperienced teacher can learn from an experienced one. This places a heavy but crucial responsibility on the experienced teacher (mentor) to explain and justify the activities observed by the trainee;

- university and partner schools maintain close and regular contact with each other at a variety of levels, both in strategic planning and in day-to-day operational matters.

Mahony and Hextall (2000) capture the essence of training within a partnership when they describe it as being 'a process through which practitioners develop an underlying knowledge, principles and values base, acquire an expanding repertoire of potential strategies from which to choose, and can justify and defend their choices as being appropriate for particular contexts and purposes' (p. 2).

3

The assessment of the professional competence of trainees against the QTS Standards is undertaken by a variety of agents (mentors, university tutors, external examiners) drawing upon a wide range of evidence (lesson plans, reflective lesson evaluations, formal assignments, additional activities, progress reports against Standards, teaching file, action plans, targets achieved, etc.). The Standards, which are applied for assessment purposes during the period of training, serve two functions (as do the mentor and tutor). First, they are the foundation on which to build formative guidance and advice for trainees on a day-to-day basis – the Standards can therefore be used to help trainees to learn and develop as beginning teachers. Second, they are the means by which trainees are summatively assessed at the end of their training – in effect they provide the final assessment 'yardstick' against which to measure professional competence. This summative use of the Standards is not unproblematic. For example does 'ticking off' a particular Standard, observed being 'achieved' by a trainee in the context of a particular class in a particular school, mean that the trainee has now securely gained that Standard and no longer needs to revisit it during their period of training? What constitutes 'achievement'? Can attainment of the standards be considered in a 'yes/no' fashion? The importance of professional judgement within the interpretation, application and assessment of the Standards becomes immediately apparent.

3 THE ROLE OF THE MENTOR

The importance of the partnership between schools and universities in ITT has already been stated. Much of the focus of the day-to-day training of beginning teachers falls upon the mentor teachers in partnership schools – experienced teachers trained by a university or other provider to guide, advise, supervise and assess trainees during their period of ITT. This role has developed significantly, such that mentors in geography education might now be expected to:

- assist in the interviewing and selection of appropriate trainee teachers;
- assist in the development of the geography ITT course;
- provide an introduction for trainee teachers to their school and geography department, and the observation, planning, teaching, assessment and evaluation of geography lessons;
- provide a suitably balanced timetable of geography lessons for trainees to teach, reflecting the age and ability range of the school;
- observe lessons taught by the trainee and provide feedback;
- set targets within (weekly) mentor meetings;
- liaise with university tutor(s) regarding the progress made by trainees;
- provide formative and summative assessment of the progress of trainees during teaching placements, including making recommendations on the award of provisional QTS;
- assist in the delivery of university-based elements of the geography ITT course.

The mentor teacher has assumed a more important and diverse role in the initial training of teachers over the last decade. Apart from the expectation that mentors are good role models for newcomers to the profession, they also have complex responsibilities involving supporting, advising and ultimately assessing trainees' competence to teach. In addition they must make sure that trainees are aware of school and departmental policies and practices, ensure access to other staff and provide examples of various teaching and learning strategies that trainees might use within geography education (see Ellis, 1997).

Practical activity 1.1

The preceding section of this chapter discusses recent developments in ITT, the nature of training partnerships, and the role of the mentor in schools.

Discuss what role you think higher education institutions (HEIs) should play in the training of new teachers. In particular, what should be the function of university based tutors in the preparation of beginning teachers?

4 | WHAT ARE STANDARDS?

The term 'standard' has been used already in this chapter in relation to the training and assessment of beginning teachers, but what does the word mean? Any consideration of 'standards' within education must first begin with a definition of the term. Standards are established by professionals within a particular field to define levels of performance and/or quality. Educational standards are not immutable and some are regularly contested, having been created by professionals who may themselves disagree on what actually constitutes a verifiable standard. However, there is probably a more marked agreement about those standards which have been created by professional educators than those which have been imposed upon education either by the government, or by one of its appointed bodies. Thus, within education, standards are no longer created and assessed through common agreement between educationists and fellow professionals, but increasingly through the imposition of certain ideals or measures by external agencies. These agencies may also be employed to provide evidence of the attainment of such standards. For example, within both schools and HEIs the standards of performance of teachers, tutors, students and trainees are (supposedly) verified by the use of inspections conducted by OFSTED/HMI. The TTA also collects and publishes performance data from ITT providers on an annual basis, focusing on quality indicators such as the entry qualifications of trainees, ethnic and gender mix on courses, and completion and employment rates.

The QTS standards can be seen as statements against which individual trainees can monitor their achievements and set targets for future work, as well as providing a professional measure of their attainment and expertise. They therefore serve both a formative and a quality assurance function. By using the standards as criteria against which attainment is assessed a number of benefits can accrue for initial teacher training. The standards provide a focus on a range of different qualities and abilities that beginning teachers must possess and attempt to define each of the factors essential to effective teaching and learning. By so doing they aim to list all of the essential attributes of a NQT. They also enable providers to create a framework for reporting progress and attainment towards the achievement of QTS and help to establish an overall national standard for this award.

However, like any criterion referenced system of assessment, standards can only become commonly accepted following their interpretation and application by the professionals who use them. It is the tutors and mentors who have to determine the levels of performance necessary to 'achieve' the standards and who must act as responsible 'gatekeepers' for the profession. They must only allow through those new teachers who have reached at least a basic level of professional competence. Obviously those involved in the training process should have a shared under-standing of what the standards mean in the context of the particular schools in which the trainees are placed. Every school and every classroom is different, making the application of a single interpretation of each standard *out of context* virtually impossible.

4.1   The standards for the award of Qualified Teacher Status

Courses of initial teacher training in England and Wales currently exist within a statutory framework which presents a number of standards which trainees must 'demonstrate' before they can be awarded Qualified Teacher Status (QTS). The standards and requirements for ITT are currently stated in a relatively concise document (TTA, 2001a), which is accompanied by a more expansive Handbook of non-statutory guidance (TTA, 2001b). At the time of writing the standards were subject to a phase of consultation following the revision of Circular 4/98 *Teaching: High Status, High Standard* (DfEE, 1998a) – the standards document previously used for the award of QTS.

Circulars express directives concerning current government policy towards education and are issued through the DfES by the Secretary of State for Education. The 'new standards' circular replaces all the previous circulars concerning ITT in England and Wales (Circulars 9/92 (DFE, 1992a), 14/93 (DFE, 1993a), 10/97 (DfE, 1997a) and 4/98 (DfEE, 1998a)) – the frequency of revision of these circulars illustrates the rapid nature of change in education and highlights the recent gov-ernmental interest in teacher training. Although none of the circulars concerning ITT make specific reference to geography some higher education institutions have reworked the training standards to make a geographical component explicit to trainees.

Circular 4/98 had been 'a complex document, hard to assess, repetitive, and daunting for its users, including trainees'. Some training providers even felt that it had 'reduced the professionalism of teaching' (TTA, 2000, p. 4). However, there was support for the overall achievements of this circular, particularly with refer-ence to its focus on pedagogy and the attention it gave to assessment and target setting within ITT. As a consequence the 4/98 standards were streamlined and restructured, rather than rejected, with particular attention being paid to those standards which had previously proved un-manageable, prescriptive or repetitive. More expansive exemplification of the standards and non-statutory guidance on ITT was also provided in the Handbook produced to accompany the new stan-

dards (TTA, 2001b). This Handbook contains examples of the range of knowledge, understanding and skills that trainees need to demonstrate for the award of
QTS; a code of practice on assessment; and guidance on ITT partnerships. The
overall intention of any set of training standards is to make sure that at the point of
entry to the profession 'each new teacher has a good foundation of knowledge and
understanding, is able to perform as a skilled teacher and can operate within a clear
framework of professional values and practice' (TTA, 2001a, p. 3).

4.2 Assessment of standards

The ease with which ITT standards can be assessed is usually a major signifier of
their acceptability to both trainees and providers. In this respect the 4/98 standards
proved to be unmanageable, forcing providers into assessment practices which they
knew to be either invalid or anti-educational – as 'atomistic' statements of
attainment the standards reflected an assessment problem previously experienced
within the National Curriculum in the early 1990s. Teaching is such a complex
activity that trying to reduce it down to a series of separate standards is always
something of a fruitless exercise; it therefore follows that assessing teaching
competence in this way is also flawed. This point was partly acknowledged within
Circular 4/98, which considered that the assessment of teacher professionalism
implied:

> more than meeting a discrete set of standards. It is necessary to consider standards as a
> whole to appreciate the creativity, commitment, energy and enthusiasm which
> teaching demands, and the intellectual and managerial skills required of the effective
> professional.
>
> (DfEE, 1998, quoted in Trend, 2000, p. 10)

As a result, a more holistic approach was adopted towards the formulation of
standards in the revised document (TTA, 2001a), involving either a clustering,
simplification or selection of statements from the previous standards. The standards are written as outcome statements which set out what a NQT must know,
understand and be able to do to be awarded QTS.

Assessment problems were generally felt to have been made worse in the 1990s
by the imposition of a three yearly ITT inspection cycle by OFSTED/HMI. Any
attempts that HEIs made to 'cluster' standards to make them more manageable –
often on the advice of the TTA itself – were effectively negated by HMI's insistence
that there should be evidence that every single standard had been assessed for each
trainee. In this way the 'tick box' mentality of assessment had actually been
encouraged by HMI, rather than questioned. This problem has been addressed in
part by revising both the standards for ITT and the inspections procedures in
tandem.

During the creation of the current standards the key role of schools in ITT
partnerships was again highlighted. Providers are aware that whatever future
changes are made to the standards for ITT, great care is needed not to disturb or
damage effective, but often fragile, partnership arrangements. An important truism
is regularly restated: schools do not have to work in partnership with HEIs and do
not have to take part in any aspect of ITT. Although, from the providers' perspective, schools are a vital component of ITT, the focus of schools' work is *not*
dominated by teacher training, but by the education of students. Schools therefore

require incentives to take part in training, be they financial or professional (for example, the fact that OFSTED inspections of schools note positively any involvement in ITT). The TTA review of Circular 4/98 (TTA, 2000, p. 5), in a section on HEI/school partnerships, noted the difficulties that many schools faced with respect to ITT when it stated that:

> Several respondents, mainly providers, drew attention to practical difficulties: these included the planning of courses; funding (and guidance about the distribution of resources); the turnover of schools in partnership, and the problems of maintaining suitable subject placements; the amount of time trainees are expected to spend in schools, and its definition; the complexity and cost of training mentors and of providing school-based quality assurance. Some felt that the Circular and the prospect of ITT inspection were daunting for prospective partner schools (TTA, 2000, p.5).

4.3 Composition of the standards for Qualified Teacher Status

The standards for the award of Qualified Teacher Status (TTA, 2001a) are expressed under three headings:

1. Professional values and practice

2. Knowledge and understanding

3. Teaching

    3.1 Planning, expectations and targets

    3.2 Teaching strategies

    3.3 Monitoring and assessment.

    3.4 Class management and inclusion.

The standards are generic, cover a range of essential knowledge and expertise, and lay particular emphasis on (TTA, 2001a, p. 5):

- subject knowledge;
- understanding of the high standards expected of pupils;
- the principles and practice of entitlement and inclusion for all pupils;
- planning and teaching to clear objectives and setting pupil targets;
- the core pedagogical skills of interactive teaching, differentiation and assessment of learning;
- principles and practice in the Foundation stage;
- the National Strategies in Key Stages 1, 2 and 3
- the expansion and flexibility of provision for 14–19-year-olds;
- effective class organization and behaviour management;
- support for pupils with Special Educational Needs and those learning English as an additional language.

The *main* requirements within the standards for teaching geography at secondary level are listed in Figure 1.1.

The current standards are, in some respects, curiously worded. Their purpose is to provide an explicit and assessable collection of statements of trainee performance; nonetheless the language in which some are written invite various interpretations of meaning and intent. What *is* clear is that they are not contestable – they are presented as assertions, rather than statements to be investigated or debated by trainees and providers. Difficulties are further compounded because the standards, and Handbook, give no guidance as to how they are to be successfully achieved within a 36-week course.

Some mentor teachers and tutors involved in the initial training of teachers have argued that many of the standards are still too demanding for beginning teachers and are more appropriate for practitioners who have been teaching for some years. It has also been argued that although the standards provide a 'code of proficiency', and can be used by beginning teachers to frame their progress towards becoming the kind of teacher they wish to be, they are lacking in at least two respects. First, they are written at a general level, whereas teachers need more specific individualized guidance if they are to improve. Second, they are rather bland and soulless, giving little encouragement to the beginning geography teacher (or teacher in any other subject) to show a real 'spark' (Lambert and Balderstone, 2000). These criticisms may represent considerable (and perhaps unrealistic) expectations of any official standards devised as generic statements covering the essential knowledge and expertise expected of beginning teachers. However some ITT courses have, in the past, either added to the standards, or restructured them into a more usable format, in an attempt to make them more user friendly or customized to subject requirements. If one refers to the 'additional standards' applied to the PGCE Geography course at the Institute of Education, University of London (see Lambert and Balderstone, 2000, p. 406) one can see that beginning teachers in geography might also be encouraged to ensure that:

- their teaching of geography is topical and enquiry led;
- geographical study occurs at all spatial scales;
- economic, social, environmental, and political aspects of geography are promoted;
- spiritual, moral, social and cultural development of pupils occurs through geography;
- geography addresses the concerns of young people;
- citizenship and sustainability are themes that geographers should study;
- democratic learning which fosters autonomy and responsibility is encouraged.

5 | THE NATURE AND VALUES OF TEACHING

A major omission from previous ITT standards was any statement of the importance of the professional values of the teacher and of the teacher's role within

Standards for the Award of Qualified Teacher Status (TTA 2001a)	Rationale
1. Professional values and practice	• high expectations of pupils and respect for their cultural, religious and ethnic backgrounds • committed to raising pupils' educational achievement • treat pupils with respect, consistency and consideration • demonstrate and promote positive values, attitudes and behaviour • communicate sensitively and effectively with parents and carers, recognizing their rights, responsibilities and interests • contribute to/share responsibility in the corporate life of school(s) • support the roles of other professionals • take increasing responsibility for own professional development • use research, inspection and other evidence to improve their teaching • aware of legal frameworks of teachers' employment and conduct
2. Knowledge and understanding	• of geographical principles, concepts and skills (to degree level) • of pupils' typical questions and misconceptions • of cross-curricular expectations of the National Strategy for KS3 • of national qualifications framework 14–19, and of geography's contribution to this • passed QTS skills tests • competent users of ICT with respect to teaching geography • of national statutory requirements/ frameworks/guidance/syllabuses/schemes of work • of the *Three principles for inclusion* (NC Handbook) • of National Curriculum assessment of geography, national qualifications (general and vocational), statutory arrangements for reporting pupils' progress • can access, understand and interpret NC Programmes of Study in geography and levels of attainment; examination criteria for public examinations in geography • of expectations, progression, typical curricula and teaching in key stages from, and to which, pupils transfer • of SEN Code of Practice

	• understand how pupils' learning is affected by their physical, intellectual, social and emotional development
3. Teaching 3.1 Planning, expectations and targets 3.2 Teaching strategies 3.3 Monitoring and assessment 3.4 Class management and inclusion	• have high expectations of pupils and use these to set clear teaching objectives and targets • plan lessons/sequences of lessons taking account of assessment and supporting pupils' needs • select and prepare appropriate resources • plan for the use of ICT in teaching geography • participate in, and contribute to, teaching teams • plan fieldwork • identify levels of attainment of pupils learning English as an additional language (EAL) (with the help of an experienced teacher) • build successful relationships with pupils, set high expectations, establish a purposeful learning environment • teach the knowledge, understanding and skills relevant to the geography curriculum in its specific phases • use ICT effectively in teaching geography • provide opportunities for pupils to develop key skills • teach clearly structured lessons, with clear learning objectives; employ interactive methods and group work • differentiate according to pupils' needs • promote active learning and independent learning strategies • provide homework • take account of pupils' varying interests, experiences and achievements • teach across age and ability range • use/devise monitoring and assessment strategies • monitor/assess so as to give immediate and constructive feedback to pupils • use assessments to enable pupils to reflect on their own learning • accurately assess pupil progress using geography NC level descriptions/criteria from national qualifications (with guidance from an experienced teacher if necessary) • use school/classroom data on pupil attainment by gender and ethnic group • use assessment data to support specific pupil's learning (with guidance from an experienced teacher if necessary) • record pupils' progress systematically

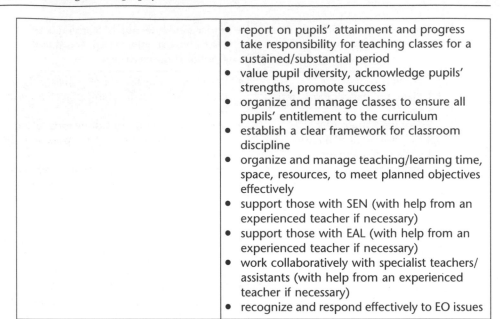

- report on pupils' attainment and progress
- take responsibility for teaching classes for a sustained/substantial period
- value pupil diversity, acknowledge pupils' strengths, promote success
- organize and manage classes to ensure all pupils' entitlement to the curriculum
- establish a clear framework for classroom discipline
- organize and manage teaching/learning time, space, resources, to meet planned objectives effectively
- support those with SEN (with help from an experienced teacher if necessary)
- support those with EAL (with help from an experienced teacher if necessary)
- work collaboratively with specialist teachers/ assistants (with help from an experienced teacher if necessary)
- recognize and respond effectively to EO issues

Figure 1.1   *The main requirements for teaching geography at secondary level*

society. The values dimension became central to the review of Circular 4/98 with the addition of a new section of standards under the heading of 'Professional Values and Practice' (TTA, 2001a) in line with the Professional Code of the General Teaching Council (GTC). The introductory section of the standards document (p. 4) also provides a strong rationale for the professional expectations of teachers. Together with the additional notes for guidance in the Handbook (TTA, 2001b) trainees are now given a better indication of the professional role of the teacher as one which is not only personally rewarding, but also hugely responsible and privileged. Education is a major factor that shapes our society for the future – a point which is now more fully acknowledged within the standards themselves, although there should perhaps still be greater recognition that teachers need to be energetic, dedicated, intellectually able, committed and skilled in a variety of ways. Any circular which sets the standards for beginning teachers should aim to establish the range of characteristics and qualities teachers should possess. Therefore some statement in the standards about the abilities of teachers to think critically, to foster their own as well as other's intellectual development, to show capacities of good judgement, and to have a possible commitment to lifelong learning might be included. If such values were made even more explicit they could form the basis for the construction of all the standards for ITT and would provide an important indication of the professional pride that should accompany the trainee teacher in his or her development. It was, in effect, a *vision* of education which was perceived to be lacking in the 4/98 standards.

Curiously neither the new standards (TTA, 2001a), nor those of Circular 4/98 which they replace, make many statements about the *purpose* of ITT, or of the *principles* which should underlie it. The section titled 'Requirements for the Provision of Initial Teacher Training' (TTA, 2001a, pp. 16–19) is functional rather than explanatory, although in some ways this may be advantageous as providers are given more freedom to devise courses to suit their local conditions as a result.

Projecting forward to try to consider what might be the requirements for ITT in the future is always difficult. The new standards will not be able to predict what the teacher who trains in five years' time will require with respect to their professional knowledge, understanding and skills – however, providers are constantly faced with addressing such issues and therefore need a set of standards flexible enough to incorporate change. Projections of the future need to encompass a variety of potential shifts – such as the continuing development of ICT within the process of teaching and learning, and the need for beginning teachers to be increasingly adaptable and flexible in their use of learning technologies. Given current recruitment difficulties, and the need to attract teachers from wider afield, the new standards might also make reference to where the expected intake of trainees might come from.

6 A BRIEF DISCUSSION OF EDUCATIONAL IDEOLOGIES

But what sort of teachers do we want in our schools? And what sort of educational philosophies, values, beliefs and ideologies should trainee teachers experience or aspire to? An important consideration within any form of education, be it of pre-school children or post graduates who are training to teach, is the educational ideology in which their learning occurs. These ideologies have developed over time to represent the application of various beliefs, values, traditions and cultures within the education process. The expression of such ideologies are worth considering and juxtaposing to give an impression of the foundations from which educational aims, and their resultant curricula, are derived. In geography education it is rare to find teachers or departments that function from only one ideological stance, as the range of resources, specifications and teaching materials which they use (each developed and influenced to some extent by different educational ideologies) often reflect a mélange of influences.

It is useful to start by looking at Skilbeck's (1976) definition of four major educational ideologies, as outlined below:

1. *Classical Humanism* – education is visualized as a process of handing on cultural heritage, traditional values and subject knowledge. This ideology is sometimes viewed as being narrowly elitist and overly academic.

2. *Progressivism* – often child centred, with childhood seen as an important stage in development in itself rather than merely being a stage before adult life. Discovery learning and providing children with educational choices and options are seen as being important within this approach.

3. *Utlitarianism* – the purpose of education is primarily seen as the preparation of children for a useful life in society. This is often narrowed into an expectation that schools should instruct and train children for employment and for the advancement of the state's economy. By doing so, it is argued, education will bring wealth and happiness to the individual through consumerism.

4. *Reconstructionism* – education is seen as a vehicle for reconstructing society along more fair and just lines. The aim is for the individual to achieve the means to live harmoniously within society. This ideology focuses on moral and social values as well as highlighting the means to change society.

One danger with stating educational ideologies in such an abbreviated form (as they have been above) is that they can be applied as a shorthand to narrowly classify certain types or phases of schooling, often in a biased and negative way. For example the classical humanist ideology is often applied to describe independent and grammar schools whose academic education best serves the 'more able' child; progressivism has become associated with changes in primary schooling in the 1960s and 1970s; utilitarianism, with its emphasis on vocationalism, has been linked to education for employment for 'less able' children; whilst reconstructionism has been tied to the wider educational aims associated with comprehensive schooling. These oversimplified applications have a political expression as well, with classical humanism and utilitarianism being broadly associated with the political Right, and progressivism and reconstructionism with the Left.

Naish (1996a) describes these ideological notions as 'competing tensions' in the context of geography education, which he believes are strongly influenced by epistemology (that is, the thinking about the nature of knowledge and how it is created). In essence, he sees these tensions as being between:

- political and economic forces or pressures versus idealistic philosophical ideas;

- the call for an emphasis on basic skills, vocationalism and instrumentalism, versus the view of education as humanitarian, liberal and progressive, of intrinsic value in its own right rather than seen as preparation for the future;

- the elitist view of education versus the egalitarian;

- academic versus child-centred education;

- traditional versus progressive approaches; and

- didactic teaching versus enquiry learning.

Other educational ideologies exist which, to some extent, mirror those of Skilbeck's. For example Miller (1983) outlines the following ideologies: traditional knowledge based teaching, teaching for enquiry and decision making, and teaching for social transformation; whilst Kemmis *et al.* (1983) describes educational ideologies which have a vocational/neo-classical orientation, liberal/progressive orientation, and socially critical orientation. These ideological traditions have been explored by geography educationists over recent years with particularly useful contributions being made by Walford (1981), Naish (1996a), Slater (1995) and Fien (1999).

Practical activity 1.2

Consider Naish's list [above] of 'competing tensions' within geography education.

Choose two or three of these 'tensions'. Think about the impact that each element might have on the geography curriculum for secondary schools if it were to become dominant within education.

Which of the elements do you think are important within learning geography? To what extent should the 'ideal' geography curriculum try to balance all of these elements?

CONCLUSION

One of the main purposes of this book is to impress upon the beginning teacher that education is, in essence, a scholarly and research-based profession. Geography teachers, at whatever stage of their professional careers, regularly need to reconsider their thinking about teaching and learning in geography – to do so they must access current research into geographical education, which they can then relate to their own particular context. It is therefore apparent that educational research should have an impact upon practice within schools as well as influencing the ways in which teachers are trained. Roberts (2000a, b) argues that interest in teaching as a research-based profession is not new, citing teacher research projects of the 1970s and 1980s such as the Humanities Curriculum Project (Stenhouse, 1970) and Ford Project (Elliot and Adelman, 1976). More recent publications, such as the Teacher Training Agency's (TTA) policy statement 'Teaching as a Research-based Profession' (TTA, 1998) and the DfEE's report 'Excellence in Research in Schools' (Hillage *et al*, 1998), simply build upon this tradition. Current thinking favours the use of research evidence, particularly that which is gathered within the classroom, to support the development of innovative teaching practice – both for the experienced and the beginning teacher (see Barratt Hacking, 1998, Slater, 1996b, 1998; Naish, 1996b).

The standards for initial teacher training (TTA, 2001a), along with those which they replace (DfEE, 1998a), still do not place much emphasis on the use of research by beginning teachers. Indeed only one of the 56 standards makes a direct reference to educational research. This states that, when assessed, those trainees to be awarded Qualified Teacher Status (QTS) must be able to demonstrate that they:

> are able to improve their own teaching, by evaluating it, by learning from the effective practice of others and by using *research*, inspection and other evidence
>
> (TTA, 2001a, p. 8, emphasis added)

This is built upon within the non statutory guidance by statements that those to be awarded QTS should:

- maintain an active interest in current research developments in their subject, phase, sector or specialism

- demonstrate the ability to interrogate research, inspection or other data and form accurate conclusions about the extent and limits of findings.

> (TTA, 2001b, p. 13)

Although these statements are welcomed the trainee teacher is only really required to monitor or keep abreast of some recent research in geography, geography education and pedagogy – he or she is hardly encouraged to see teaching as a profession in which research findings are significant, either to the process of learning to teach or to professional development. Research is therefore still presented as something that the trainee should refer to, rather than actively engage in.

Nonetheless, within geography education the importance of a research perspective for the beginning and experienced teacher is growing. Professional associations, such as the Geographical Association (GA), are now promoting current research findings into geographical education in the form of short monographs for the classroom practitioner. The 'Theory into Practice' series, which started in 1999,

15

seeks to enable geography teachers to access research findings on a variety of issues which could be related to their own context. In addition a variety of recent publications and articles underline the significance of research evidence in supporting the professional development of effective geography teachers (Gerber, 1996; Williams, 1996; Kent, 2000; Roberts, 2000a, b).

CHAPTER 2

Developments in geography and geography education since 1970

From being a collection of travellers' tales, cosmography and some informational bric-a-brac, [geography] has matured into a major school subject at all levels, passing through several stimulating intellectual debates on the way, and gaining something of lasting value from each of them. Its place in the curriculum of schools, once unimportant, is now established, though not secure.

(Walford, 2000, p. 296)

INTRODUCTION

This chapter explores the development of geography, geography education and curriculum theory in England and Wales over the past 30 years. It culminates in an analysis of the aims of geography education, placing them into the context of the teaching of geography in schools at the start of the twenty-first century. What emerges is a curriculum story which reflects a growing political involvement in the structuring of the school curriculum, where geography in education has at times lost status and curriculum 'ground', but still remains a statutory requirement of state education. It must be remembered that geography, as a non core subject within the National Curriculum, has to guard against 'curriculum complacency' – that is, any notion that the subject has a place *by right* within the school curriculum. Unlike English, Mathematics and the Sciences, the hold that geography has on its curricular position in many school timetables at Key Stage 4 and beyond is not assured. It therefore requires the advocacy of geography teachers in schools, as well as national professional organizations such as the GA and Royal Geographical Society with the Institute of British Geographers (RGS-IBG), to support its tenure. This advocacy became increasingly political towards the end of the last century as a result of the growing involvement of central government in education matters.

The teaching of geography in schools, like the teaching of all other subjects, has been influenced by a variety of factors over the years – the prevailing philosophies of education, the existing paradigm of geography in higher education, the economic climate and the political complexion of the government of the day (Butt, 1997a). In their commentaries on the development of geography as an academic subject both Gregory (1978) and Goodson (1983) highlight the primary concern of many geographers as being their subject's survival, rather than its intellectual progression, during much of the last century. Adopting such a focus is obviously damaging to the ongoing curriculum development within the subject and, to some observers, comes dangerously close to opportunism (Smith, 1973).

1 | GEOGRAPHY IN EDUCATION

The period from 1970 to 2000 has witnessed substantial changes in geography as a subject in schools and universities. At the same time shifts have also occurred in curriculum theory and practice, and in party political involvement in education in England and Wales. Geography education in schools has faced the challenge of reacting to substantial curriculum changes occurring 'around' it, whilst also developing as a subject from 'within' largely through a series of curriculum development projects in the 1970s and 1980s. These projects have had a lasting effect on both the substance of, and the approach to, geography teaching in schools at all levels.

Many writers have chronicled the events which have influenced the development of geography education in recent years. For a fuller exploration of these matters it is advisable to refer to the following sources: Binns (1996), Boardman and McPartland (1993a, 1993b), Butt (1996, 1997a), Naish (1996a, 2000), Walford (1996, 1997, 1998), Graves (1997), Rawling (2000a, 2000b).

1.1 1970 to 1980

Naish (2000) describes the period from 1970 to 1980 as one of 'laissez faire' with respect to curriculum decision making. The decade followed an 'expansive' period in the late 1960s when geography, and other curriculum subjects in secondary schools, addressed the demands of creating a meaningful curriculum for candidates sitting the new Certificate of Secondary Education (CSE) introduced in 1965. This examination brought the prospects of certification to substantially larger numbers of children than had previously been served by the more challenging Ordinary, or O level, examination. This stimulus for curriculum development in geography was also enhanced by the work of the Schools Council, which established three major geography projects in the 1970s. These projects have influenced the teaching of geography up to the present day. Nonetheless, Graves (1975) refers to the period immediately after 1965 as one of 'crisis in geographical education in Britain' (p. 61) due to the large-scale developments in academic geography, advances in educational theory, and changes to the structure of secondary schooling at the time. It was, in many respects, a period of some confusion regarding the overall philosophy and direction of geographical education.

The 1970s saw increasing numbers of candidates choosing to opt for geography at CSE, O and A level in England and Wales. During this period there was a gradual development of new syllabuses which reflected the advances of the 'conceptual revolution' that had occurred within academic geography in the 1960s. The substantial influence of examination syllabuses on what is taught in the classroom is well documented. It was therefore mainly as a result of syllabus changes that the ideas of the conceptual revolution were spread widely amongst geography teachers and their students, towards the end of the decade. Needless to say many teachers were resistant to change and preferred to maintain their attachment to the regional geography paradigm of the past, only altering their approach when revisions of examination syllabuses forced them to do so. Regional geography, which often exhibited a descriptive and idiographic rather than analytic stance, came under increasing pressure to change towards more scientific, nomothetic and predictive enquiries during this time. Researchers in geography were largely concerned with developing the explanatory nature of their subject, often incorporating hypothesis testing, modelling and the use of statistical sampling in their attempts to gather empirical data to use within spatial analysis. Some of the main instigators of change in schools were the geographers who had recently completed their degrees and initial teacher training in institutions which embraced the so called 'new geography' and wished to see its concepts incorporated into the school geography curriculum. Such adjustments were supported by events such as the Madingley Conferences and resultant publications such as *Frontiers in Geographical Teaching* (Chorley and Haggett, 1965) through which academics and teachers combined to promulgate the new ideas. During this period of reformation many geography departments in secondary schools exhibited a strange amalgam of geographies being taught to different ages and abilities of students, with regional approaches often maintained within the lower school and more conceptual and quantitative approaches at post-16 level.

Inevitably the swing towards quantification saw compensating movements by some academic geographers away from the increasingly scientific approaches adopted within their subject. Welfare geographers were concerned with how inequalities within space could be resolved (Smith, 1977), whilst other geographers adopted more radical stances, concentrating upon the political and decision making processes which affect space and place (Harvey, 1969, 1973). Behavioural and Humanist geographers reacted to the excesses of law producing geography by returning to idiographic approaches which placed a greater focus on *why* people make particular decisions concerning spatial questions. Such changes at the research frontiers of geography required translation into the context of geography education in schools (Naish, 2000). Interestingly, given the somewhat piecemeal ways in which the study of geography had developed within schools and universities in the United States after the Second World War, it was the American High School Geography Project (HSGP, 1971) which initially stimulated change in geography education in English and Welsh secondary schools. HSGP conveyed some of the new ideas of the quantitative revolution to schools and revealed how geography teachers might incorporate new thinking into the school geography curriculum.

The major curriculum development projects in geography which began within this period, under the auspices of the Schools Council, were Geography for the Young School Leaver (GYSL), Geography 14–18 (Bristol Project), and Geography 16–19 (see Boardman, 1988; Tolley and Reynolds, 1977; and Naish *et al.*, 1987). These projects were largely based within higher education institutions (HEIs), but could only progress satisfactorily with significant input from practising geography teachers. The combination of ideas from geography educators in secondary and higher education created a potent mix; it ensured that the emerging geography curricula reflected changes from the academic frontiers of the subject, from innovative curriculum theory and from a realization that geography should serve as a *medium* for the education of young people, rather than necessarily being an 'end in itself'. The overall aim was that geography education within schools should not only furnish students with relevant knowledge and understanding, but also a range of skills and an appreciation of their own, and other people's, values and attitudes. Importantly, from the perspective of the dissemination of their curriculum ideas, each of the projects were linked to their own external examinations. Naish (2000) visualizes this period of educational change as one in which the geography teacher was cherished as a school-based curriculum developer, a situation which was to dramatically alter with the introduction of the National Curriculum at the end of the following decade.

1.2   1980 to 1990

The decade from 1980 to 1990 saw the increasing centralization and politicization of the school curriculum, culminating in the passing of the Education Reform Act (ERA) in 1988. The period of 'laissez faire', when Local Education Authorities (LEAs) and teachers largely determined *what* was taught and *how* it was taught, was over. However, some would later question the extent to which secondary school curricula in the 1970s were actually open to change by teachers, given the strong influence exerted by examination board syllabuses on the post-14 curriculum.

Debate over whether schools in England and Wales should follow a National Curriculum had occurred for a number of years before the passing of the ERA. Some writers focus upon James Callaghan's speech at Ruskin College, Oxford in 1976 – upon which he intended to launch a 'Great Debate' about education – as a significant milestone towards centralization, although the resulting national debate was actually something of a damp squib. Over the next few years the Department of Education and Science (DES, 1980, 1981) and HMI (1977) edged towards the idea of a National Curriculum; disappointingly the references to geography within these publications were minimal (see Walford, 1997). However, it was not until a Conservative government under Margaret Thatcher achieved office that any of the political parties became heavily involved in reforming the educational system in England and Wales.

During the 1980s the geography curriculum in many schools was generally well planned, with teaching and learning activities in geography being more diverse than in previous decades. In addition, the use of fieldwork had increased, largely encouraged by examination syllabuses which made primary data collection and analysis part of an assessed coursework component. However, the content and teaching methods used in geography teaching varied greatly from school to school. Most schools adopted a framework of both systematic themes and topics, illustrated by case studies taken from around the world, or combined systematic and regional approaches to geography. The selection of places, topics and teaching styles within each geography department varied considerably, depending on the way in which the subject was organized, the nature of teacher preferences, the geography GCSE syllabus studied and the levels of departmental resourcing.

What was to emerge from this decade was the first National Curriculum in Geography (DES, 1991). In essence it represented a disappointing return to the informational and utilitarian traditions of the subject from much earlier in the century; a 'restorationist' curriculum revealing the influence of New Right thinkers in the development of the National Curriculum (Rawling, 2000b). Geography had won the 'status battle' by achieving its place in the curriculum, but had lost the broader educational and ideological arguments about what the subject should be and how it should contribute to the education of young people. The structure of the Geography National Curriculum (GNC) also largely inhibited the role of teachers in school-based curriculum development (Rawling 2000c).

1.3   1990 to 2000

The National Curriculum had recognized the importance of geography as a foundation subject for the education of children from ages 5 to 16, but presented a statutory curriculum that many geographers found limiting and backward looking. Produced in less than a year by a high profile Geography Working Group (GWG), who were deliberately kept isolated from their own subject community, the result was to sap the morale of geography teachers and educationists (Butt, 1997a). With its Programmes of Study, five Attainment Targets and 183 content-laden State-ments of Attainment, the Geography National Curriculum which emerged from the 1991 Statutory Order (DES, 1991) was not an attractive prospect for teachers or students. Both with respect to the kind of geography it espoused and the assessment difficulties it presented, this was a disappointing curriculum document. The starting premise of the GWG, which took a deficit view of school geography and its content – particularly with respect to children's 'place ignorance' – gave little credence to curriculum advances made within the subject during the previous twenty years. The lack of opportunities for skills development, or possibilities for affective education through geography, were serious flaws in the GNC, as was the lip service it paid to the role of enquiry learning. These drawbacks were soon officially recognized (see NCC, 1992b; OFSTED, 1993a, b, 1996, SCAA 1997a) and provided an impetus for the geography curriculum to undergo more radical revisions than those experienced by other subjects during the subsequent reviews of the National Curriculum for England and Wales.

Although the Geography National Curriculum exhibited some of the most severe problems of any of the subject curricula it was certainly not unique. It very quickly became apparent that the whole National Curriculum would need to be reviewed and revised to eliminate the difficulties presented by its size, inflexibility, assess-ment structure and content overload. Sir Ron Dearing was invited to undertake the review, which proved to be only the first of a series of reviews he would co-ordinate into the National Curriculum, post-16 education and eventually higher education. Rawling (2000b) identifies three distinct phases of curriculum policy making during this decade, labelling them the period of 'political control of the curriculum content' (1988–93), of 'pragmatic accommodation and negotiation' (1993–7) and of 'less ideology and more control' (from 1997 onwards). During each of these phases the GA, RGS-IBG and Council of British Geographers (COBRIG) cam-paigned for the voice of geographers to be heard concerning the need for major structural changes to be made to the GNC.

Following the Dearing Review (1993–5) the second version of the Geography National Curriculum was published in January 1995 (DfEE, 1995b). It represented a considerable step forward in terms of reducing the geographical content of the curriculum and improving the manageability of teacher assessment, through the introduction of level descriptions. As a minimum entitlement this slimmer, simpler and more pragmatic curriculum gave geography teachers greater freedom to include other dimensions of geographical learning into their teaching and to develop aspects of values work, enquiry learning, and political literacy. However, as a slimmer version of the original GNC, the revised version still contained much of the New Right's emphasis on content, which was still firmly embedded within the geography curriculum.

Unfortunately, from a geographer's perspective, one aim of Dearing's Review of the whole National Curriculum was to create additional timetable space for secondary schools – this was largely achieved through making foundation subjects (such as geography and history) optional at Key Stage 4. This return to optional status for geography post 14, as experienced in most schools before the National Curriculum, was a significant weakening of geography's curriculum presence. When combined with a later disapplication of the subject from Key Stages 1 and 2 (between 1998 and 2000) the effect was to reduce the original statutory requirement to learn geography from ages 5 to 16 to an entitlement to study geography for only three years at lower secondary level. Although primary schools were encouraged to reintroduce the teaching of geography in 2000, following the launch of the National Literacy and Numeracy strategies at Key Stages 1 and 2, by this time the subject's hold within many primary schools had become tenuous. Even the introduction of the third Statutory Order for geography had little impact at this level (DfEE/QCA, 1999a)(see Chapter 3).

Geography has therefore been accurately described by Rawling (2000b) as 'the first subject for reduction, optional status or dis-application when more important initiatives need space'. Increased competition for curricular space from core subjects (English, Mathematics, Sciences), 'protected' subjects (Design and Technology, Information Technology and Modern Foreign Languages), non National Curriculum subjects, vocational courses and non core subjects since 1995 has had an unfortunate impact on geography at GCSE level and beyond. Option choices post age 14 have become wider, often placing geography in direct competition with a large number of possible educational paths. This period of 'pragmatic accommodation and negotiation' from 1993 to 1997, as Rawling (2000b) has called it, saw a decline in the influence of New Right ideology and the gradual inclusion of teachers and professional educators in the development of the geography curriculum. It is now clear that the Dearing Review was in effect a single focus act to save the National Curriculum.

The QCA Review (1998–2000) of the National Curriculum, the timing of which adhered to Dearing's advice that changes to the National Curriculum should not be made until five years after his own review to allow teachers a period of stability, saw further amendment and consolidation of the curriculum. Following the election of a New Labour government in 1997 the focus for review was spread more widely to incorporate the policy initiatives of the new administration. It has been argued by Rawling (2000b) that this Review was more concerned with developing Labour's 'New Agenda' for education and less concerned with restructuring individual subjects – hence the Geography National Curriculum has, following this latest review, become steadily more manageable, benefiting from greater professional dialogue and consultation with the subject community. There is now general agreement amongst geographers about the relevance of key aspects of the subject at school level following this recent period of 'less ideology, and more control' (Rawling, 2000b). However, the place of geography within the National Curriculum has again become less secure as a consequence of the QCA Review.

Rawling (2000c), in her assessment of the impact of the two reviews of the National Curriculum, draws upon the work of Lawton (1996) to consider the past, present and future opportunities for curriculum development by schools. She concludes that the GNC produced for 'Curriculum 2000' is a 'very different beast' from its predecessors (see Figure 2.1) and that it provides 'greater opportunities for the creative interpretation and development which are crucial if geography is to maintain its status and make a strong contribution to the school curriculum in the twenty-first century' (p. 99). The review has therefore taken forward significant structural changes to the GNC, despite statements by the QCA that the process would only involve minimal changes and content reduction. Indeed the current structure of the GNC probably owes more to the curriculum development projects of the 1970s and 1980s than it does to the original 1991 Geography Order (Rawling, 2000c).

The 1990s have also witnessed increasing support for curriculum development and delivery being provided by 'official' agencies. QCA, and its predecessor SCAA, both established a small Geography Team to inform subject teachers and to work with professional subject associations in an effort to consult more widely about curriculum developments. Evidence of this is seen in their publication of a termly 'Geography Update', the establishment of regular meetings with the subject community and the publication of a wide range of reasonably progressive curriculum guidance materials (see SCAA, 1996a, 1997b, SCAA 1996e).

Ultimately Rawling (2000c) concludes by identifying two remaining problems for geography education associated with 'Curriculum 2000'. First, the failure to integrate assessment more meaningfully into the curriculum system – particularly highlighting the minor revisions to the eight level descriptions in geography and the continuing lack of clarity among teachers about how to use formative assessment; second, neither of the two curriculum reviews in the 1990s have taken into consideration the changing nature of geography as a subject.

Practical activity 2.1

Consider the development of geography education in England and Wales over the past three decades.

1. What have been the most significant influences on the teaching and learning of geography during this period? Have these influences mainly come from within, or beyond, the geography education community?

2. Why is curriculum development in geography considered to be so important to the survival of the subject within the school curriculum?

3. The development and status of geography within schools in England and Wales has been determined by educational, economic, political, historical and cultural factors. Research into how these, and other, factors have influenced the current standing of geography education in either Australia, France or the United States.

1.4 Geography education at the start of the new millennium

Following the election of a New Labour government in 1997, the strongly centralized control of schools, so much a feature of the previous Conservative administrations, was largely maintained. Despite considerable rhetoric about the increasing freedom for teachers, students and schools to exercise choice within the curriculum, many aspects of education are still heavily regulated and largely prescriptive. Inspections, target setting, league tables and statutory requirements have

Criteria	1991 Geography Order	1995 Geography Order	2000 Geography Order
1. Aims/rationale	No rationale for National Curriculum and no aims provided for Geography Order – though Geography Working Group did provide aims in its final report (1990).	No rationale for whole curriculum and still no explicit aims for Geography Order, although para. I of Order gives flavour of each Key Stage (KS).	Values, aims and purposes are given for the school curriculum and the National Curriculum, and the Geography Order has an overall rationale ('the importance of geography') and aims/purposes for each KS ('during the KS . . .').
2. Key ideas/ aspects	Attainment targets and statements of attainment focus predominantly on content. Key ideas/ aspects not drawn out, though hinted at in some statements of attainment.	Places, themes, skills division of programmes of study give greater coherence to the content, and general ideas receive some recognition in level descriptions.	Four key aspects of geography are identified and the general ideas and areas of knowledge, understanding and skills to be developed are outlined in PoS.
3. Minimum content	Content entitlement for each age range overlaps confusingly because programmes of study (PoS) repeat content from statements of attainment.	Each PoS more clearly identifies the content for the KS, although specific topics and general ideas are still mixed up together.	Specific topics/ content to be studied (para. 6) are clearly distinguished in each PoS from the general ideas/ understandings, skills to be developed (paras 1–5).
4. Integrated approach to learning	Geographical enquiry is mentioned at beginning of each PoS, but not explained or integrated into statements of attainment of PoS.	Geographical enquiry process is included as para. 2 of each PoS and as a section in each level description but it is not named.	Geographical enquiry is clearly outlined as one of four key aspects of geography and explicitly described for each PoS. It is linked with skills and integrated with content.
5. Outcomes for pupil achievement	Statements of attainment are intended to be the basis for assessment but they are mainly factual content or specific skills, so broader outcomes	Eight-level scale introduced. Geography level descriptions set out broad outcomes for pupil achievement. SCAA guidance clarifies how four key	Eight-level scale retained and very minor changes made to level descriptions to emphasize sustainable development education and

(e.g. enquiry approach) or higher intellectual skills (e.g. analysis, evaluation) are marginalized. Testing requirements never fully developed.	aspects of geography are represented and explains 'best fit' process for summative assessment. Further implementation left to schools and LEAs.	enquiry. Confusions about the distinction between summative and formative assessment remain.

Figure 2.1 *Comparison of the 1991, 1995 and 2000 Geography Orders (Rawling, 2000c)*

all combined to sustain a narrow view of school performance, as opposed to any notion of increasing the autonomy of teachers or extending greater trust in their professionalism. LEAs now engage in less advisory and INSET activity in geography than ever before, with most authorities' efforts being directed towards the support of national directives, rather than initiating broader curriculum development. Indeed many LEAs have now dispensed with their geography advisors altogether, or have restructured their work into a general 'humanities' brief fulfilled by one person for all schools within the authority. The newly introduced Schemes of Work for geography at Key Stage 3 (DfEE/QCA, 2000), whose production was co-ordinated by the Standards and Effectiveness Unit (SEU) of the DfEE in tandem with QCA subject officers, reveal an interesting tension between the two official organizations. Whilst the QCA seeks to extend its role of supporting subject teachers and engaging them in curriculum development, the SEU views the Schemes more narrowly as 'government approved' interpretations of the GNC (see Rawling, 2000c). The former approach recognizes teacher professionalism, the latter something far less trusting.

In advocating a return to school-based curriculum development in geography Rawling (2000c) acknowledges that the GNC (see Figure 2.2) may now reflect positive influences more reminiscent of the curriculum development projects of the 1970s and 1980s. Amongst these are a focus on key ideas, the promotion of geographical enquiry and opportunities for the subject to contribute to the wider skills and cross curricularity agenda. She identifies the need for an expansionist view of the GNC to ensure that school-based curriculum development occurs so that (Rawling, 2000c, p. 110):

1. the signs of curriculum decline are reversed so that geography remains popular in schools and is seen as a relevant subject, meaningful to the lives of young people;

2. teachers are provided with the motivation and stimulus to enjoy their teaching and to raise the quality of teaching and learning they offer;

3. the subject is enabled to address wider curriculum concerns (e.g. citizenship, PSHE, literacy, numeracy);

4. geography in schools remains linked to and part of the wider geographical education community, which includes geographers in universities and teacher education, and geographers in business and the professions.

Knowledge, skills and understanding (paras 1–5 of the PoS)	Breadth of study (paras 6 and 7 of the PoS)	Level descriptions (levels 1–8 and exceptional performance)
Four aspects of geography provide the underlying structure and identify the important ideas and understandings to be developed: • geographical enquiry and skills; • knowledge and understanding of places; • knowledge and understanding of patterns and processes; • knowledge and understanding of environmental change and sustainable development	The specific content to be used as the context for developing the important general ideas and understandings (i.e. list of topics/places) The scales and contexts to address during the work (i.e. local–global range of environments) The need to include fieldwork and topical issues	Nine level descriptions (levels 1–8 and exceptional performance) present the expectations for pupil performance The level descriptions provide the basis for making judgements about pupils' performance at the end of Key Stages 1, 2 and 3

Figure 2.2 *The National Geography Curriculum 2000 (Kent, 2000)*

2 | AIMS OF GEOGRAPHY EDUCATION

Successive changes in the nature of geography education, following the establishment of the first National Curriculum in the early 1990s, have had a profound impact on the aims stated for the subject at school level. Each of the incarnations of the GNC, from the original reports of the GWG to the latest QCA produced version for 'Curriculum 2000', has grappled with the need to clarify the educational aims of the subject. At certain times these aims were clearly stated, at others they remained implicit within the form and content of the curriculum documents produced. Professional associations, such as the Geographical Association, have also had an influence on these aims, either through the production of a statement of aims or through pressure on the bodies which have been charged with the responsibility of producing the geography curriculum.

Marsden (1995, p. 2) provides a helpful context to any discussion of the aims of geography education when he states that general educational aims should:

• serve an orientation function providing, amongst other things, guidelines for the planning of curricula;

• involve making value judgements and, as such, will be influenced by external factors, cultural, social, political and economic, which operate differentially from place to place and time to time;

• represent, therefore, relative and not absolute statements;

• remain as statements of aspiration, at a stage removed from making detailed decisions.

Arguably one of the most helpful definitions of the aims of geography education was provided by the GWG in its Final Report for geography in the National Curriculum (DES, 1990). These were divided into two sections the first of which, outlined below, defined the broad aims of geography education whilst the second gave more specific guidance as to the knowledge, understanding and skills to be delivered through geography:

- stimulate pupils' interest in their surroundings and in the variety of physical and human conditions on the Earth's surface;

- foster their sense of wonder at the beauty of the world around them;

- help them to develop an informed concern about the quality of the environment and the future of the human habitat; and

- thereby enhance their sense of responsibility for the care of the Earth and its people.

The aims of geography education as stated by the QCA for the creation of 'Curriculum 2000' were explored within an introductory section titled 'the importance of geography':

> Geography provokes and asks questions about the natural and human worlds, using different scales of enquiry to view them from different perspectives. It develops knowledge of different places and environments throughout the world, an understanding of maps, and a range of investigative and problem-solving skills both inside and outside the classroom. As such it prepares pupils for adult life and employment. Geography is a focus within the curriculum for understanding and resolving issues about the environment and sustainable development. It is also an important link between the natural and social sciences. As pupils study geography, they encounter different societies and cultures. This helps them to realize how nations rely on each other. It can inspire them to think about their own place in the world, their values, and their rights and responsibilities to other people and environments.
>
> (DfEE QCA, 1999a)

At the same time the GA (GA, 1999) produced a position statement for geography in the curriculum, part of which specifically referred to the purpose of geography education where the subject's aims are:

- to develop in young people a knowledge and understanding of the place they live in, of other people and places, and of how people and places inter-relate and inter-connect; of the significance of location; of human and physical environments; of people-environment relationships; and of the causes and consequences of change;

- to develop the skills needed to carry out geographical study (e.g. geographical enquiry, mapwork and fieldwork);

- to stimulate an interest in, and encourage an appreciation of, the world around us; and

- to develop an informed concern for the world around us and an ability and willingness to take positive action, both locally and globally.

It is worthwhile also considering the aims for geography education implicit in the International Charter on Geographical Education produced by the International

Geographical Union (IGU) in 1992. The Charter represents the foundations on which all geography education worldwide should be based and states in its Preface that the Commission on Geographical Education is:

- convinced that geographical education is indispensable to the development of responsible and active citizens in the present and future world,

- conscious that geography can be an informing, enabling and stimulating subject at all levels in education, and contributes to a lifelong enjoyment and understanding of the world,

- aware that students require increasing international competence in order to ensure effective co-operation on a broad range of economic, political, cultural and environmental issues in a shrinking world,

- concerned that geographical education is neglected in some parts of the world and lacks structure and coherence in others,

- ready to assist colleagues in counteracting geographical illiteracy in all countries of the world,

- supporting principles set out in:

  - the Charter of the United Nations;

  - the Universal Declaration of Human Rights;

  - the Constitution of UNESCO;

  - the UNESCO Recommendation concerning Education for International Understanding, Co-Operation and Peace;

  - the Declaration on the Rights of the Child; and

  - many national curricula and statements on geographical education.

2.1 Aims of education

It is important to place the aims for geography education into the context of more general educational aims (or statements of educational intentions). Educational aims are usually classified as being either *intrinsic* or *instrumental*, that is those which involve children in worthwhile educational activities and which are desirable to develop in their own right for the good of the individual child (intrinsic), and those concerned with educating the child for the good of the state, society or religion (instrumental or extrinsic).

Educational aims are determined largely by the society in which the process of education is taking place and are therefore a reflection of the values, beliefs, economic and social development, and culture of that society at a given point in time (Butt, 2000a). They are defined by policy advisers and governments, particularly in states where there is a centralized education system, who also determine how the curriculum content is selected and taught. The existence of a National Curriculum, as well as its structure, contents and restrictions, is a potent statement about the aims of education defined by the society in which it exists. The first National Curriculum made explicit a series of broad aims to prepare children for adult life and to promote their spiritual, moral, cultural, mental and physical development – although these aims were not expanded upon within the specific subject orders. This perhaps reflected the intention of the government of the day to bed the curriculum on a series of subject-based objectives which it preferred to remain undebated.

The revised National Curriculum attempts to make its educational aims, as well as the values and purposes of the curriculum, more explicit. It claims as its focus the need

> to ensure that pupils develop from an early age the essential literacy and numeracy skills they need to learn; to provide them with a guaranteed, full and rounded entitlement to learning; to foster their creativity; and to give teachers direction to find the best ways to inspire in their pupils a joy and commitment to learning that will last a lifetime.
>
> (DfEE/QCA, 1999a, p. 3)

Practical activity 2.2

Why should geography be included within the secondary school curriculum in England and Wales? What do we expect students to gain from learning geography that they could not access from other areas of the school curriculum?

To what extent can the learning of geography from ages 5 to 16 be justified for all children?

CONCLUSION

Developments in geography and geography education have acknowledged the importance of the link between subject content and pedagogy. Without stimulating the interest, motivation and cooperation of young people geography educators will not be able to convey the relevance and importance of their subject. The variety of teaching approaches adopted by geography educators is the pedagogical key to maintaining interest in the subject, but there are also clear links to developments within the subject. School geography should therefore be seen as part of a larger interdependent system of 'geography in education', analogous to one of the four wheels on a cart – the other 'wheels' representing teacher education, academic geography and lifelong learning (Gersmehl, 1996; Rawling, 2000a). Geographers should be aware of the issues and concerns developing within all of these areas, such that they can ensure that they are cogniscent of the wider influences on their subject. At present the component parts of this system are largely funded and operate independently; they are also regulated, assessed and monitored differently.

As Walford (2000) points out geography incorporates the study of two of the key dimensions of life – space and place. Without an appreciation of the significance of these it is impossible to develop one's understanding of environments and societies – and without such an understanding a person cannot be considered to be truly educated. Thus Walford considers the gaining of world knowledge through geography as a kind of 'coat-hook' on which to hang other learning, where the combination of geographical knowledge and conceptual understanding can lead to an appreciation, explanation and analysis of the real world. From these foundations other aspects of education can either be enhanced, or uniquely provided, by geography and geographers – for example, the development of the skills necessary to understand, interpret and use maps. At a time when schools are being asked to focus upon the teaching of numeracy, literacy and (by implication) oracy, it may be pertinent to recognize that graphicacy provides the 'fourth ace in the pack'.

Many writers have pointed out the steady shift towards a rationalist, politically centralized educational system in England and Wales during the past 30 years, which has largely overridden any prospect of the development of a progressive geography education curriculum (see Slater, 1995; Naish, 1996a; Rawling, 2000a). However, the most recent reviews of the National Curriculum have seen a gradual relaxation of the implicit restrictions on curriculum development within subjects, offering the prospect of some advancement in the twenty-first century. It is towards this issue that we turn in the next chapter.

CHAPTER 3

Teaching and learning geography in the twenty-first century

> ... what – within the generally accepted canon of the school subject that we call geography – will be of interest, and relevance to the education of pupils in the twenty-first century? What could justify or will justify the continuation of school geography in the future?
>
> (Walford, 2000, p. 309)

> The function of geography in schools is to train future citizens to imagine accurately the conditions of the great world stage and so help them to think sanely about political and social problems in the world around them.
>
> (Fairgrieve, 1926)

INTRODUCTION

Following the review of the National Curriculum by the QCA from 1998 to 2000, in preparation for the introduction of a revised curriculum in September 2000, geography maintained its curriculum position as a non core subject which should be taught from ages 5 to 14 in state schools. The third version of the Statutory Orders for geography (DfEE/QCA, 1999a) which resulted from this review was less prescriptive than its predecessors, benefiting in its production from the professional involvement of members of the GA, COBRIG, and RGS-IBG.

The Geography National Curriculum (DfEE/QCA, 1999a) follows the general structure and design of each of the other twelve National Curriculum subjects, incorporating several innovative features not previously seen within such statutory documents. The 'breadth of study' requirements for Key Stage 3 state the students' minimum entitlement to study at least two countries and ten geographical themes – highlighting the necessity to incorporate a range of spatial scales, parts of the world in different states of economic development, fieldwork and issues of topical significance into their geographical education. The programme of study makes clear that 'teaching should ensure that geographical enquiry and skills are used when developing knowledge and understanding of places, patterns and processes, and environmental change and sustainable development' (DfEE/QCA, 1999a, p. 22). In addition an overview is provided which outlines what each child should learn during the Key Stages, whilst notes in the margin of the programmes of study indicate where links can be made between geography and other subjects. Definitions of key words or phrases are also offered and opportunities for the use of ICT highlighted. Key Stages 2 and 3 end with a section on locational knowledge, giving examples of 'significant places and environments' with reference to the British Isles, Europe and the World.

Beyond Key Stage 3, the geography curriculum tends to follow a 'standardized' structure similar to that created by the GNC. This has largely been dictated by the requirement that each awarding body for geography at GCSE and A/AS Level bases its specifications on sets of National Criteria.

Unfortunately, as stated in Chapter 2, geography does not yet occupy an unchallenged or secure place within the school curriculum. Rawling (2000a) notes that both the status and quality of geography education is currently at risk from the growth of vocational courses, so called 'basic skills' initiatives and from the introduction of Citizenship into the National Curriculum in 2002. Geography, compared to other subjects, also shows less evidence of regaining the creative flair and spirit of curriculum innovation than was often a feature of its development before the implementation of the National Curriculum. Each of these factors combine to create a somewhat worrying picture of geography's declining importance as a subject within schools in the twenty-first century. Since the creation of the first National Curriculum in the early 1990s – with its expansive entitlement to a breadth of educational experiences – we have witnessed the gradual erosion of the broad based, subject led, curriculum (Walford, 2000). Like other non core subjects geography has suffered greatly from these changes. In primary schools the introduction of National Literacy and Numeracy strategies, combined with the release of non core subjects from any statutory obligation for delivery from 1998–2000, led to the marginalization of geography at Key Stages 1 and 2. It appears doubtful that the subject will ever fully recover from this blow at the primary level. The prominence of the core subjects within this curriculum hierarchy, as well as the introduction of the 'New Agenda' since 1997, has also served to downgrade geography at Key Stage 3 and beyond. The focus at present is not upon the development of subjects, but upon wider curriculum initiatives – as such the future of geography may be determined by how it reacts and responds to these initiatives, rather than by how it is constituted as an academic discipline.

The first major blow to the status of geography in secondary schools (which was not entirely unexpected) was its removal from the compulsory Key Stage 4 curriculum following the Dearing Review (Dearing, 1994). In the immediate future the introduction of Citizenship and new PSHE requirements from September 2002 will place more pressures on curriculum space, where geography appears to be one of the first contenders for removal from school timetables. Geography has therefore suffered directly as a result of government policies designed to improve the whole curriculum. The impact of recent curricular change is readily witnessed within the candidate entry statistics for public examinations in geography. From 1998 to 2000 entries for Geography GCSE have declined by around 14 per cent, whilst those for A Level show an even greater reduction of over 18 per cent.

New Labour has championed a curious mix of its own initiatives alongside those which it inherited from the previous Conservative government. It has consulted widely on intended educational changes and, to its credit, has included professional educators in the process. Nonetheless, once intial decisions have been made ministers have single-mindedly forged ahead with strategies and initiatives, giving little pause for reflection on the impact these policies might be making. We therefore see a plethora of target setting, performance indicators, emphasis on 'excellence' and the introduction of Numeracy and Literacy initiatives – a continuation of New

Right policies – coupled with the 'New Agenda' to introduce Citizenship, Sustainable Development, creativity and culture, and PSHE (Rawling, 2001). Ideology has been downplayed, pragmatism has come to the fore. However, we must be aware that although initiatives from 'outside' geography education may impact on the curricular space available to teach geography, there are also disturbing tensions within the subject. Geography in higher education must maintain its unity, vigour and innovation if it is to be both attractive to undergraduates and capable of stimulating growth in the subject at school level.

Walford (2000) provides us with a characteristically thought provoking, even radical, view of the wider issues affecting geography education at the start of the twenty-first century. Whilst advocating a possible return to a 'deficit model' of geography curriculum construction, as adopted by the Geography Working Group in 1989, he questions the advantages of 'curriculum flexibility'. Walford concludes by calling upon geographers to rethink 'some long-cherished beliefs' (p. 298) with respect to the role that their subject might play in the delivery of new initiatives, fearing a further loss of curriculum ground.

1 | CRITIQUING THE GEOGRAPHY CURRICULUM

Morgan (2000a), in a thought-provoking piece of writing, has explored some of the tensions inherent within the current geography curriculum, considering different ways in which such a curriculum can be conceptualized. He argues that the school geography curriculum has traditionally sought to operate like a mirror, striving to reflect the real world 'as it is'; this is evident during both the 'capes and bays' period, when geographers attempted to accurately describe places and features, and through the positivistic phase when geographers attempted to create generalizations, explanations and laws for the phenomena they observed. A distinctive body of knowledge that constitutes geography is thus taught in schools, with due regard to continuity and progression within the curriculum, and learned by students who gradually attain more sophisticated and detailed knowledge, understanding and skills. Morgan describes this process as the teaching of 'curriculum-as-fact', where the educational outcome is essentially the same for all those taught, for the teacher simply acts as a guide through the geography curriculum. As witnessed with the GNC such an approach to the teaching and learning of geography requires an almost constant updating and revision of the curriculum to ensure its relevance.

Morgan directs us towards phenomenological critiques of the curriculum. These suggest that curricula are largely imposed on the learner and make little reference to the experience, knowledge and understanding which students can bring to the study of geography. Other constructions of the geography curriculum are possible, most notably those created by advocates of humanistic geography in the 1970s and early 1980s. These avoided the fixed and unyielding attempts to create a curriculum that conveyed an absolute reflection of reality. Because such humanistic approaches can lead to relativism, where each different perspective is equally valued, some geographers chose to adopt a more radical stance, recognizing that certain aspects of knowledge in the geography curriculum should be afforded greater status and value. For example, the geography curriculum frequently represents the interests of some groups (say, industrialists and men), whilst downplaying or marginalizing those of others (say, industrial workers and women). As Morgan (2000a) states, 'In this view, the geography curriculum operates as ideology, systematically representing the interests of capitalism' (p. 34).

During the 1980s and 1990s some geographers abandoned the search for representations of the fixed, real world and focused upon the ways in which we represent the world. The world was no longer viewed as something external to the observer, but something that is interpreted differently by people. Thus 'different people, with different outlooks and experiences, will produce different meanings' (p. 34) – a postmodern perspective on the world that can be translated into the ways in which the geography curriculum is constructed. Teachers and students can interpret this curriculum in various ways, finding new understandings in a curriculum which now possesses no fixed meaning. Morgan believes that geography teachers have 'forgotten the debates' about the curriculum, partly because of the necessity in recent years to deliver a prescribed National Curriculum, and should strive to orientate their teaching towards 'representations' of the world rather than trying to accurately convey aspects of the 'real' world. In this way the subject is seen as 'discourse', rather than 'fact'.

Practical activity 3.1

1. What are the best ways to maintain and develop a meaningful geography curriculum for schools in the twenty-first century? Who should be the main agents involved in curriculum development in geography and what roles should they adopt? (You might consider the roles of some of the following: geography teachers, ITT students, NQTs, academics, students, LEAs, HEIs, professional associations and government.)

2. Morgan (2000a) discusses the problems inherent in teaching 'the geography curriculum-as-fact', focusing on the issue of relevance to the learner. Are there other ways of structuring the geography curriculum to ensure its longer term relevance, vitality and flexibility?

3. What should be the key foundation upon which the geography curriculum for the future is based? Consider the importance of subject content, assessment, pedagogy, educational research and other factors.

2 | THE IMPORTANCE OF CURRICULUM DEVELOPMENT IN GEOGRAPHY

Not only is it important to have a clear conceptualization of geography, but also to contemplate the changes that might occur within world geography, and their potential impact on the subject at school and university level. As a consequence school-based curriculum development within geography is a key to the future of the subject. The development of a National Curriculum saw the implementation of a centrally devised framework into which teachers and students had to 'fit' – only recently have we seen how geographers have been able to loosen the bindings of such a framework and engage again in curriculum development in their subject. This has occurred due to a rise in confidence among teachers about the geography curriculum they have to deliver, through the steady liberalization of this curriculum since its inception in 1991, and through newly qualified teachers constantly bringing a fresh perspective to the teaching of geography. The professional guidance and support which emerged during the major Schools Council curriculum development projects in geography in the 1970s and 1980s will probably never again be repeated in quite the same way. However, the aim of curriculum development in geography in the twenty-first century should be similar: to bring together advances in educational theory and practice with those of the conceptual changes in the subject to provide an exciting, innovative and relevant school geography for the new millennium. Rawling (2000a) highlights that although the National Curriculum had a major impact on changing the content of geography, it had an even bigger impact on redefining and relocating curriculum control. By dictating the way in which the geography curriculum was structured, particularly in terms of its content, the GNC took the initiative away from geography teachers, who merely became the handmaidens of its delivery in the classroom. Combined with an initial lack of guidance about how this curriculum could be taught – which only began to be alleviated following the 1994 Dearing Review (see SCAA, 1996a, 1997b) – it was not surprising that OFSTED inspection evidence for the late 1990s revealed a need for geography teachers to receive further professional development in curriculum and assessment practices (OFSTED, 1997, 1998).

3 | 'FUTURES EDUCATION' AND THE GEOGRAPHY CURRICULUM

It is clear that to remain credible both in curriculum terms and in the eyes of young people the geography curriculum for the twenty-first century must be orientated towards the future. Many aspects of existing geography curricula already look to the future – by implication any study of sustainable development, or of the impact of technological change, must adopt such a perspective – but it is worthwhile considering whether this orientation is clear enough within contemporary specifications and schemes of work. It can be posited that all education is 'education for the future' and that if curricula do not reflect such a perspective they are, by definition, unacceptable. However, by far the majority of curricula are oriented towards the past. This is both a product of the necessity to select aspects of our previous scientific, artistic and cultural heritage to teach about, and of those educational traditions that have valued the 'passing on' of worthwhile ideals through education (such as classical humanism). Education has, to some degree, always been about helping to prepare children for their future as adults; as geographers we have a special responsibility in preparing young people for their lives in a rapidly changing world. Huckle (1997) argues that geography education can develop an understanding of one's identity by helping young people to find (and question) their place in the world – whilst also creating an appreciation of the importance of social justice, democracy and citizenship which can combine to create a better world.

Incorporating a futures dimension into the teaching of geography is not easy. It faces the dangers of appearing to be 'bolted on' to the existing curriculum, or may seem to exemplify an absurd 'guessing game' where children are allowed to speculate freely (and unrealistically) about the shape of their future world. Ensuring that such teaching is both credible and relevant to the future lives of young people is a major challenge. Futures education also encompasses political education and the development of political literacy, for any consideration of the future encompasses the possibility of pursuing different options – the resolution of choices, priorities and alternatives within the world involves political action. The work of Greig *et al.* (1987), Huckle and Sterling (1996), Morgan (2000b) and Hicks (1993, 1994, 1998) along with his various co-writers (Hicks and Steiner, 1989; Hicks and Holden, 1996), aid our understanding of the futures perspective within geography education.

4   GEOGRAPHY IN SCHOOLS, GEOGRAPHY IN UNIVERSITIES

Much has been written about the connections between school and university geography, with particular reference to the influence of the latter on the former. Many educationists have noted how the 'gap' between the two foci of geography education has grown wider over the years, leaving behind a period in the 1960s and 1970s when school teachers and university lecturers met periodically to discuss their subject (Goudie, 1993; Bradford, 1996; Haggett, 1996; Rawling, 1996; Unwin, 1996; Kent and Smith, 1997; Brown and Smith, 2000). Indeed this division has become so great that one geographer has been forced to conclude that 'from a position of considerable influence on the school curriculum in the 1960s, those in university departments of geography now have little effect on what is taught at the secondary or primary level' (Unwin, 1996, p. 23).

The days of conferences such as those held at Madingley in 1963, where geographers from higher education came to update geography teachers about the 'new geography', are largely gone – despite recent successful efforts by COBRIG to instigate such meetings on a bi-annual basis in the 1990s (see Rawling and Daugherty, 1996). However, on a positive note, the tenor of recent meetings between university academics and school teachers is perhaps not as 'top down' as in the past; now geographers from both sectors of education meet on a more equal footing, with a genuine concern for ensuring the well being of geography education at all levels. The implementation of the National Curriculum, amongst other changes within state schooling, has meant that university academics have needed to update themselves on school curriculum changes, just as teachers have required information about developments at the research frontiers of geography.

At the end of the 1970s secondary education was no longer being seen narrowly as a preparation for university entrance. Many of the students who 'stayed on' to complete sixth form studies were not focused on higher education at the end of their time in school (although the numbers who were moving into the tertiary sector were increasing annually). Thus post-16 geography courses, together with courses in other subjects, could no longer be designed just for the 'most academically able' – the curriculum development projects of the time incorporated into the geography curriculum changes in educational theory and practice; developments in curriculum structure, assessment, and pedagogy; and recognized the needs of the majority of students who would *not* go on to study geography within higher education. This explains, to an extent, the steady dislocation in the influence of university-based geographers on what was happening in primary and secondary schools (Unwin, 1996). It also goes some way towards understanding why the interface between the secondary and tertiary sectors of education increasingly displayed a worrying 'discontinuity in methods and content' (Bradford, 1996, p. 277). This was clearly witnessed by the surprising lack of involvement of university geographers in the debate which surrounded the creation and implementation of the first Geography National Curriculum (Butt, 1997a).

Walford (1996) remembers how professors and lecturers of geography in a previous era devoted many hours and covered many miles to speak to geographers at GA branches and sixth-form conferences, eager to propagate their geographical beliefs. One of the apparent reasons for this was a realization that disciples and adherents to the geographic vision were important to the long-term health of the subject. Walford also reminds us that 'Today, the insistent demands of publication and research make it more difficult to allocate time to such activity. But there may be no research to pursue if the supply of students dries up' (Walford, 1996, p. 141). A similar point is made by Bradford (1996) when he states that 'Research has become the prime criterion for promotion, and service to the discipline in other ways has counted for little ... there are relatively few academics actively involved in secondary education' (pp. 280–1).

Fears are also expressed about the fragmentation of the subject within higher education and the need to rediscover a 'core' for the discipline. As Rawling and Daugherty make clear:

> there are many research developments in particular areas of geography, but few people trying to develop an overarching picture of the subject. There would also appear to be fewer opportunities for specialists to talk to each other than there were in the mid-1970s. The pressures of research assessment ensure that the minds of most university geographers are focused on depth to ensure a strong position in research ratings and the associated funding decisions.
>
> (Rawling and Daugherty, 1996, p. 360)

This combines with a situation in schools where:

> the hard-pressed teacher is more likely to be concerned with managing statutory assessment requirements, contributing to the school's performance in league tables and meeting the demands of school inspections than with following up new ideas in geography.
>
> (Rawling and Daugherty, 1996, p. 360)

In conclusion it is clear that the growing divide between school and university geography has been accelerated by the implementation of the GNC, but is not simply the result of it. These changes have their origins some twenty-five years earlier. The confidence and growth of the positivistic 'new geography' in universities in the 1960s led to enthusiastic university lecturers offering their somewhat paternalistic advice and guidance to geography teachers in schools through courses, conferences and publications. In turn the schools produced the next generation of geography students to study geography in higher education, some of whom would go on to train as geography teachers, thus completing the circle. Academics were well represented on A level examination boards as examiners and syllabus designers, whilst also writing school textbooks and having an input into curriculum developments. However, this symbiotic relationship was already beginning to break down in the late 1960s. Bradford succinctly encapsulates the situation when he describes the growing diversity of university programmes in geography in the 1980s and 1990s where 'there has not been one major trend affecting as many areas of the subject as did either the scientific revolution in the 1950s and early 1960s, or the radical geography movement in the early 1970s. The absence of such major changes may partly account for the reduced impact of higher education on the geography taught in secondary education' (Bradford, 1996, p. 282). Comprehensivization meant that more and more geography teachers were faced with a wider range of abilities to teach – the advances made in geography in the recent past could not merely be replicated for *all* these students. Thus the focus for many secondary teachers was taken away from the academic progress being made within higher education, to the restructuring of the education system and what its aims should be. Where curriculum development in geography occurred, as it did most successfully within the Schools Councils Projects, some of the recent thinking at the research frontiers of the subject were incorporated. As a result certain radical, behaviourist and welfare themes can be still be seen in today's geography curriculum. However, the importance that geography should remain a successful and unified medium for education in schools, rather than being driven in different directions by research initiatives at university level, was realized by many.

5 THE NEED FOR STRONG UNIVERSITY–SCHOOL LINKS IN GEOGRAPHY

In the twenty-first century it is increasingly obvious why the gap between geography within schools and universities should be breached. The reasons are easily stated:

1. Schools provide university geography departments with their undergraduates; only with a strong subject at GCSE and A level, which attracts healthy numbers of candidates, will the geography departments in universities continue to flourish.

2. Universities provide schools (indirectly and following initial teacher education) with geography teachers; almost 95 per cent of trainee geography teachers for secondary teaching follow a university-based Post Graduate Certificate of Education (PGCE) course.

3. A smooth progression between school geography and university geography will only be maintained if university-based geographers have an input into what is taught at the secondary level; this may occur through a variety of avenues such as revision of examination syllabuses, involvement in curriculum developments, lectures and conferences, publications.

4. Both sectors need to understand the tensions and pressures that exist within the other; geography teachers in schools need to appreciate the changes occurring in the subject, the demands for research and publication, and the structural changes in higher education. Geography lecturers in higher education need to

appreciate the impact of the GNC, syllabus changes at GCSE and A level, league tables, class sizes, pedagogical changes, resources.

5. Recent innovative changes in courses, such as the growth of vocational education, affects both sectors and requires a united position with regard to the influence on geography education.

6. Demands to develop transferable skills at all levels of (geography) education are increasing. Educators in both sectors are increasingly expected to focus not only on the development of subject knowledge, but also on the personal, social and moral growth of their students.

7. Geography, as a discipline, needs a clarity, coherence and purpose that can be agreed upon and understood at all levels of education. Identifying and promoting these fundamentals must be key. With a changing content focus in geography in higher education (the re-emergence of place, regional geographies, cultural geography, environmental perspectives, political geography, global awareness) the school geography curriculum must be able to reflect significant shifts in the discipline.

Whilst by its very nature and purpose the geographical education of students at school and university level will be different there should be a clear 'core' of content, understanding, skills and pedagogy that both sectors engage with. This geographical core should be relevant to geography teaching at whatever level. For this to occur the relationship between these sectors needs to be strong, open and discursive. A partnership of like minded individuals needs to be established, which does not elevate nor denigrate either side of the partnership, but realizes that the common goal is high quality education through the medium of geography (Daugherty and Rawling, 1996). Here initial teacher education has taken something of a lead. Since the early 1990s all ITT courses have been encouraged by government circulars to establish strong and equal partnerships between HEIs and geographers in schools for the purpose of training new entrants to the teaching profession. Somewhat perversely the relationships between geographers in university geography departments and those in Schools of Education in the same institutions are often weaker than those established by the latter with their partner schools.

It is salutory to consider the developments in school geography since the 1970s from the perspective of a university-based geographer. Michael Bradford, as a professor of geography, ex-president of the GA and chief examiner of an A level geography awarding body, is in some ways uniquely placed to comment:

A view of secondary education since the mid-1970s suggests that it has been more concerned with pedagogy than with the content of the subject, at least until the national curriculum, which was initially highly content driven. The subject at the secondary level seemed still to be strongly affected by the scientific revolution of the late 1950s and early 1960s. In GCSE and A level courses, hypothesis testing abounded and still does, in many cases as the sole form of investigative work. Locational analysis and models prevailed in many syllabuses (and remarkably still do in some), which perhaps as a result are highly economic in their view of human geography. Yet physical geography, were positivist approaches are more appropriate, was, until the National Curriculum, poorly represented in many GCSEs and in some A level syllabuses. This was a focus of complaint for many in higher education, some of whom decided to mount remedial classes for those who had taken the highly innovative Geography 16–19 syllabus. This incorporated an enquiry approach to learning and was probably more innovative in terms of pedagogy than content, though it did lead the way in placing much emphasis on a people-environment approach. Until very recently this was the 'new syllabus' and yet it was devised in the late 1970s.

(Bradford, 1996, p. 282).

Practical activity 3.2

Discuss ways in which university–school links in geography education might be strengthened in the future. What structures would need to be established (i) to ensure that all geography teachers remain aware of the changes occurring in geography at degree level, and (ii) to enable geography teachers to implement relevant aspects of these changes within the school curriculum?

It is still largely true that the success of geography courses at degree level build upon the firm foundations, dynamism and innovation established at the primary and secondary levels. Perhaps there are warning signs for the future from the United States of America, where the progress of geographical education in schools and universities has traditionally taken a very different path than in Britain. Geography has, until recently, been poorly represented in schools in the States, often being taught as part of humanities-based social studies courses (see Clark and Stoltman, 2000). President Reagan's concern about the poor levels of geographical knowledge, understanding and skills of young people in the States led to the creation of a Geography Awareness Week back in 1988. Three years earlier the Geographic Education National Implementation Project (GENIP) was launched, supported by a consortium of major geographical associations committed to the improvement of the quality and status of geography education in schools and universities. Together with the National Council for Geographic Education (NCGE) this project eventually helped to produce five themes for geographical education which were the basis for the geography national standards for schools published a decade later. The current 're-birth' of geography within schools in many states, along with summer courses for teachers and state 'alliances' for geographical education, is encouraging; however one can see that in the preceding years the low status of geography in schools was a direct cause of the closure of geography departments in many universities, including Yale, Harvard and Northwestern (Walford and Haggett, 1995).

CONCLUSION

Rather than trying to make definitive statements about the future of geography education in the twenty-first century based on current trends, it may be more enlightening to consider possible responses to a variety of thought provoking questions. Helpfully Daugherty and Rawling (1996) encourage us to establish a dialogue about the future by posing a series of pertinent questions in their book *Geography into the Twenty-First Century*:

1. Which ideas from the research frontiers are relevant and appropriate for school geography?

2. What distinctive knowledge, understanding and skills can geography contribute to vocational education?

3. What are, or should be, the 'residuals' of a geographical education?

4. How can we better develop our students' ability to adopt appropriate modes of enquiry in their study of the subject?

5. How can we define and measure progression in geographical understanding?

6. How can we ensure that geography's contribution is recognized and understood by the general public and educational decision-makers?

Children who learn geography in the twenty-first century will face a variety of challenges in their adult lives. These challenges will not only confront their own communities and societies at the local and national scales, but will almost certainly threaten the future prospects of the planet's survival. Such challenges are readily apparent to geographers: the effects of global warming and the need to reduce harmful emissions of greenhouse gases; the use of finite resources and energy in more sustainable ways; the need to reduce pollution; the stabilization of a rapidly growing world population; the maintenance of social justice and removal of prejudice and inequality; and the protection of biodiversity (Carter, 2000). In addition the application of new technologies on the global scale is advancing at a staggering rate – their influence on all aspects of society, from education and business to arts and culture, are astounding. The so-called 'knowledge revolution' will have a more widespread and profound influence on the lives of young people worldwide than previous industrial revolutions which heralded the birth of modern societies. Associated with such changes are the dangers of youngsters becoming alienated, excluded or feeling unsupported by the very educational system that should be helping them to prepare for their rapidly changing worlds – with the inherent risks of their involvement in drug use and crime.

Rex Walford and Peter Haggett, two of the best known and respected geographers from the worlds of education and academia, used the occasion of the GA Centenary in 1993 to consider the future with respect to changes in world geography, in geography as a university discipline, and in geography in schools (Walford and Haggett, 1995). They identified seven possible changes in world geography (increases in world population, resource consumption, environmental pressures, collapse of long distance space, switch of resource development into offshore space, trends away from hierarchically organized structures and instability in major geopolitical hegemonies); and seven possible changes in university geography (in computerized mapping, climatic modelling, analytical regional geography, demographic history, integration of geographical thinking into the history of science, establishment of global benchmarks for measuring change and a 'coming of age' of spatial analyis). This list reminds teachers that they must keep abreast of changes within their discipline as well as within education – in essence that they are both learners as well as teachers of geography. With respect to geography education in schools Walford and Haggett identify three major variables – the effect of legal structures on the curriculum, the extent to which the subject continues to motivate students, and the future coherence and rationale for the subject. The potential future detachment of school geography from the subject in higher education is feared, as is the splitting of academic geographers into their various sub-disciplines rather than keeping an allegiance to the parent discipline. They conclude that we should not be pessimistic about geography's capacity to attract and interest students, and claim that 'it is difficult to be a dull geographer – or it ought to be, if only we let the subject-matter speak freely enough through us' (Walford and Haggett, 1995, p. 10).

CHAPTER 4

Resources for teaching and learning geography

INTRODUCTION

Teachers of geography have a considerable array of resources which they can utilize inside and outside the classroom to make the learning of their subject topical, relevant and exciting. Student motivation is obviously an important key to learning – it is therefore vital that in our selection and use of resources for teaching geography we consider how this motivation can be realized and sustained. Often the choice of resources for the trainee teacher is largely determined by what is already available within the geography department, combined with an assessment of whether particular groups of students will be able to engage purposefully with these materials. However, one should not forget that *the* major teaching resource is the teacher, whose inventiveness and flair should be tapped to create new resources and to use existing resources in novel ways.

Whilst it is acknowledged that how we teach is, in many respects, more important than the materials we choose to teach with (particularly from the learner's perspective) this chapter will predominantly focus on the major resources currently used for teaching and learning geography – namely textbooks and other forms of 'text', worksheets, role plays, games, simulations, decision-making exercises (DMEs), visual images, mapped images and fieldwork. Discussion of the use of ICT in teaching geography is found in Chapter 10.

1 TEXTBOOKS

Changes to the geography curriculum and examination specifications have tended to provide a stimulus for textbook production by the major publishing houses. This was particularly true of the curriculum changes resulting from the creation of the GNC, which saw schools receive money to purchase new resources to teach each of the Key Stages (Butt and Lambert, 1996). In geography this led to the initial domination of the resource market by one textbook series, partly because it was the first major series to be produced which promised teachers 'trouble free' coverage of the new curriculum (see Lambert, 1996). Often publishers confidently claim that their books will successfully meet all the requirements of a curriculum (or specification), almost regardless of the range of ability levels of the students who will use the texts, or of the issues of differentiation and progression that need to be addressed in their learning. This explains why some geography departments may build their schemes of work around one textbook series – although individual teachers often admit that they believe such an approach does not provide students with the best educational experiences in geography. Textbooks are like any other educational resource in that they are never capable of *replacing* the teacher – in other words, they are not 'teacher proof'. It must also be remembered that authors and publishers each have their own interpretations of geography and of the geography curriculum. These interpretations may not match the pedagogical approach selected by the geography teacher, who must carefully plan the most appropriate learning activities for each set of students.

Textbooks are one of the major teaching resources used in the geography classroom, but like any resource they can be used well or badly (see Lidstone, 1992). If textbooks are merely employed to occupy students in 'busy work' – typified by copying passages, completing low level comprehension exercises and engaging in repetitive tasks – they will not develop the range of learning skills we require of young geographers. By relying on a single set of textbooks, teachers may be forcing students to repeatedly undertake similar low order tasks which may not push their thinking towards (say) enquiry learning, problem solving or decision-making. However, the better texts encourage students to use language in various ways, to engage in a wide range of learning activities and to promote their development of thinking skills. These books often contain a diverse range of geographical source materials (images, maps, diagrams, etc.) as well as examples of texts of different kinds.

The production quality of geography textbooks has improved immeasurably in the last twenty-five years. Most textbooks are now more colourful, with better design qualities, fuller illustration, more legible fonts and clearer images than in previous years. Unfortunately, it is easy to be seduced by such impressive presentation – an analysis of the written text and of the activities that accompany it may not prove to be so appealing. Concern has recently been expressed about the lack of challenge, particularly for more able students, provided by many contemporary textbooks. Indeed some texts over simplify geographical concepts and processes, reproduce out dated or questionable models and theories, and are guilty of casually trivializing important issues. Reductions in the amount of text, and the common adoption of a formulaic double page spread format, may signal a lack of expectation about what students should strive to achieve in geography. When coupled with too many low order 'missing word' exercises, or simple tasks involving copying or transferring text to the students' exercise books, there is real cause for concern about the quality of learning that students are experiencing in geography. In recent years publishers have taken seriously the need to address any criticisms of bias concerning their texts, largely succeeding in eradicating such excesses from their works (see later in Chapter 11 section on Race and gender). Nonetheless, some examples of stereotyping and bias in geography textbooks still exist (see Winter, 1997).

Practical activity 4.1

Select three geography textbooks currently used at Key Stage 3.

Analyse their strengths and weaknesses with respect to geographical content, suitability of activities for students and overall presentation.

Consider two different groups of students you teach at Key Stage 3. Which textbook(s) would be most suitable to use with these groups?

1.1   Other 'texts' (newspapers, cartoons, literature, poems)

Geography teachers are in an almost unique position in that newspapers and magazines can provide them with topical case studies, data, views and opinions which can be readily adapted for use in the classroom. It is a mistake to think that textbooks are the only, or indeed the best, source of content for teaching a dynamic subject such as geography. 'Broadsheet' newspapers will often provide maps, interviews, statistics and analysis on a variety of world issues and events that can enliven and update existing geographical resources. The experience of using these different forms of text – written for distinct audiences and perhaps exhibiting aspects of bias – is extremely valuable for geography students. Many geography teachers will regularly cut out articles about particular events to create a portfolio of newspaper cuttings which can be used to update their teaching of geographical themes. Often this is done in a rather haphazard and unsystematic way, in effect creating an opportunity sample of what is currently available in the press – some geographers are very fortunate in that their school librarian may be persuaded to create topic files (with themes suggested by the geography department) in which relevant items can be collected from the daily papers. Whichever approach is taken the rewards of using up-to-date resources is apparent in the reaction of the students, who will increasingly see geography as a relevant subject, often addressing their concerns about the modern world. The texts may need some adaptation or editing before they can be used in the classroom – simplification, censoring, interpretation, removal of bias – although according to the ages and abilities of the students you may choose to direct them, as critical learners, to undertake these tasks for themselves.

Newspapers and magazines can also be useful sources of display materials for a 'Geography in the News' board within the classroom. This may be used to gather information about events at a variety of spatial scales – from a local controversial issue (say, the building of a bypass, a new shopping development, or pollution in a local river) to a global phenomena (say, global warming, population growth, or globalization). Natural hazards and disasters receive considerable coverage in many national newspapers, whose reports may be combined with maps and data to provide a teaching resource in the form of an interactive display. It is worthwhile regularly monitoring this display to ensure that an up-to-date, balanced, and 'positive' reflection of events is presented – it is very easy to convey a very gloomy and dated picture of life in developing countries if display materials of catastrophic events are not balanced by images that convey some of the more positive sides of everyday life! In this respect providing updates after national disasters to reveal how communities are coping is important.

The printed media are often a source of cartoons that express aspects of contemporary events, or illustrate a particular viewpoint on an issue. Cartoons are used extensively in many Key Stage 3 geography textbooks in the form of 'talking heads' to provide simple, concise statements on issues from typical respondents. Despite the attraction of using cartoon materials – namely that they are usually lively, engaging, amusing and invite students' attention – care must be taken. Many cartoons are highly sophisticated and convey very complex ideas, information and emotions which students may find difficult to interpret without considerable support; the 'I don't get it!' syndrome is frequently apparent. Cartoons may also contain considerable bias and be guilty of conveying over-simplified stereotypical views on complex issues, which may be reinforced if not explored with the students (see Marsden, 1992, 1995).

Literature, poetry, art, music and films can all provide stimulus material for the geography teacher. In conveying a 'sense of place' they may be used in imaginative ways to accompany other teaching materials and help to bring people, places and events to life. Such sources can be highly motivational – however, the true purpose of their use must be clear to both teacher and student so that these materials are not simply viewed as entertainment, rather than education. It is also important to note that students' tastes and preferences in the arts are rapidly changing and fashionable – a piece of music carefully selected by the geography teacher to convey some aspect of people or place may be roundly ridiculed by students because it is not what they recognize as being part of their popular culture.

Practical activity 4.2

Select either a poem, a piece of music, **or** a work of art that you believe has some geographical significance.

Plan a lesson for an A level geography group that could incorporate this item as a key resource. It is important that the resource is an *integral* part of the geographical learning, rather than merely being 'bolted on' to an existing lesson.

1.2   Worksheets

The advent of 'new technologies' in the classroom has made the production of high quality, teacher-produced worksheets a reality. There are now no excuses for the poorly reproduced, unclear, and badly designed worksheets that were a feature of much of the geography taught twenty or so years ago. Worksheets should be wordprocessed, clearly laid out, visually engaging and perhaps include images or data captured from the internet. Most importantly, the learning objectives which provide the foundations for the design of each worksheet should be clear to both teacher and students.

The main strength of worksheets as an educational resource is that they can provide, for a particular group of students, specific materials, data, case studies and activities not found in other resources (such as textbooks), differentiated to the needs of the class. They may also be designed by the teacher to 'dovetail' with an existing resource – for example as an additional stimulus or set of questions to be used alongside a picture in a book or a newspaper article. Often worksheets include specific language-based activities such as writing frames and DARTs (see Chapter

8), or may involve the completion of a partially drawn graph, map, systems diagram or table. One of the advantages of a worksheet is that it can be 'taken home' and used for homework, whereas a textbook is rarely allowed to leave the school premises.

Purpose
- What is the purpose of the worksheet?
- What are the learning objectives I want to cover?
- What specific geographical knowledge, understanding and skills will the worksheet address (in the GNC, GCSE or A/AS level)?

Planning
- What resources/materials do I need to construct the worksheet? Where are these available (textbooks, internet, CD-ROM, newspapers, photographs, cartoons, etc.)? Are these resources up-to-date and free from bias?
- Do I have the technical ability to construct and reproduce the worksheets?
- What activities should be included to meet the 'Purpose' outlined above? how will these activities be differentiated according to the abilities of the students?
- How will student learning be assessed?

Presentation
- What design do I want for the worksheet – portrait or landscape? font sizes and types? pictures? maps? cartoons? tables? diagrams? graphics?, etc. Will visual images reproduce clearly if the worksheet is to be photocopied?
- Amount of text? sequencing of text and activities?
- Is the text engaging and clearly sequenced for the students? Is the text readable and is the amount of technical vocabulary and use of jargon acceptable?
- What headings and labels do I need to include to identify where activities are, or where figures and tables can be found?
- Is there too much/not enough text?
- Should key words (and their definitions) be identified in bold type?
- Are maps correctly labelled with a scale, north arrow and key?

Use
- How does the worksheet fit into the lesson plan and its stated learning objectives?
- How will I introduce the worksheets to the students? Do I want them to complete it all in the lesson? Are any activities for homework? Are there different sheets and/or activities for different students?

Evaluation
- Did the worksheet help me achieve my learning objectives?
- Was the worksheet capable of providing differentiated learning for different abilities?
- Did the students find the worksheet interesting, motivating and stimulating to use?
- What might I change about the worksheet, or the way I used it, in future lessons?

Figure 4.1 *Some principles for designing a worksheet*

Textbook series are regularly accompanied by a teacher resource pack and a set of worksheets that link with the texts. The quality of such resources is variable and it is worthwhile considering whether they enhance the learning of your students, or not. The very best ideas conveyed by such commercially produced worksheets can always be incorporated into your own worksheet designs.

2	ROLE PLAYS, GAMES, SIMULATIONS AND DECISION-MAKING EXERCISES

2.1 Role plays

Role plays enable students to enact the particular role of a person in some form of simulated discussion, event, public enquiry or meeting from which a decision is eventually required. By carrying out such activities in geography lessons, students are able to better understand the values, attitudes and opinions of people in situations different from their own. This may enable students to appreciate why certain people act in ways that are initially difficult for them to comprehend, or contrary to the values currently held by the students. The advantage of employing role plays is that they can be designed to simulate a wide variety of very different events dealing with various social, environmental, political and economic issues – from global summits, to government meetings, public enquiries and village discussions.

Although role plays can be set up with minimal planning they usually require the students to posses a reasonable breadth and depth of knowledge and understanding for them to be able to adopt the roles of people they do not know, or to respond to situations or issues they have not previously encountered. Students' prior experience of using role plays, and their appreciation of the 'rules' that have to be followed for such exercises to succeed, also have a considerable influence on their outcome. It is therefore advisable that the preparation for a role play is extensive. This may include:

- supplying background information on the issue that will be debated in role (in the form of texts, video clips, photographs, 'testimony', maps, etc.);

- providing 'character cards' that describe the likely views and opinions of the players;

- providing stimulus questions or points to focus students appreciation of the issues;

- assigning roles to groups of students so they can compare ideas on what attitudes the player they represent may hold;

- supporting students in developing their communication and debating skills, such as itemizing the main points they wish to make, considering what arguments may be advanced by others, looking for support from like-minded players;

- establishing the rules for debate (order and duration of speech, procedures for asking and answering questions, behaviour during presentations, noting of significant points raised, obeying the directions given by the Chair);

- 'setting the scene' before the role play begins to remind students of the issues or question under consideration.

Although the outcomes of role plays are not predictable and students can sometimes fail to 'get into' a particular role, the benefits of establishing an appreciation of the values and attitudes of others are considerable (see Chapter 11). In addition, students often relish the element of 'performance' that is encouraged by playing a role. As with any activity of this type debriefing is very important – the main points which arise from the role play, a clarification of the issues, an exploration of why different views were held, the evidence used to support a position adopted, a further explanation of the geographical processes at work, and a 'free vote' for the players are all valuable ways of concluding the exercise.

Sometimes role plays can become heated. In these circumstances the teacher should intervene to clarify the 'rules' and, if necessary, refocus the issue being discussed and the likely opinions of the different players. If necessary it may be important to support players that are struggling, or to play 'Devil's Advocate' to break down an improbable consensus should one arise!

2.2 Games

Games used in geography education offer the teacher a student-centred approach that may work well with a range of different abilities. They are often employed to introduce aspects of human decision-making and chance factors into the learning process. Differentiation can be achieved through the sensible grouping of students before they play the games, through the nature of the tasks undertaken during the games and the debrief or follow-up activities devised for after the games have concluded. Games have been used to teach geography for a number of years. Walford, for example, wrote his influential text on their use in geography education back in 1969 (Walford, 1969). Indeed, gaming techniques had already been used in academic geography before this date (see Cole, 1966).

There are a number of different types of games, each with its own level of sophistication and educational demand. The most educationally significant games encourage students to empathize with the situation of those represented (for example their employment, lifestyle, environment, etc.), or expect students to make decisions either as themselves or in a role they are asked to adopt as a player. Games usually introduce an element of competition (compared to simulations which do not) and the teacher must be aware that some students in their eagerness to compete may not pay sufficient attention to the geographical significance of the game. Aspects of social and personal education may also be furthered from the playing of geographical games.

Games, like simulations and models, attempt to simplify reality to make it more easily understood by students. Importantly if the simplification becomes extreme, or represents a considerable distortion from reality, the game will not be effective in accurately conveying geographical knowledge, understanding and skills. Therefore the rules and structure of the game are important factors which determine the plausibility of the outcome of the game – some games also attempt to improve their validity by trying to simulate the occurrence of 'chance factors', usually by means of throwing a die or responding to a 'chance card'. The most realistic games usually involve students in some aspect of decision-making, which may alter their fate or the fate of others as the game unfolds. Teachers are important mediators – it is their responsibility in the debrief phase after a game to draw out the key geographical points, conceptual understanding, and values and attitudes that the game should have highlighted.

Walford (1987) notes a variety of advantages of using games in the geography classroom. They tend to:

- improve student motivation;

- improve students' understanding of geographical processes;

- provide opportunities to develop skills of analysis, synthesis, evaluation and decision-making (cognitive education);

- encourage discussion, negotiation, cooperation and collaboration (social education);

- develop empathy (affective education).

However, games are not a panacea for placating difficult groups. They may also serve to over simplify reality and can take a considerable amount of time to set up and use.

Educational games are currently available from a variety of commercial sources, within textbooks and from some charities (for example *The Trading Game*, (Christian Aid), the *Trading Trainers Game* (CAFOD), etc.).

2.3 Simulations

Simulations can take a variety of forms. Often they are designed as a model which can be used to represent, illustrate or imitate a process that occurs in the real world. The breadth of their coverage of geographical themes is considerable – simulations can be devised to show physical processes (such as the formation of a corrie, delta, or spit), human processes (such as innovation diffusions, migration, or population growth), or people–environment interactions (such as the impact of pollution, energy use, or agricultural practices).

Recently, interactive simulations, often using computers, have been devised in the form of newsroom or mountain rescue simulations. Here the computer is used to deliver information about an unfolding event such as a natural disaster, which students have to act upon within a given time frame. Every few minutes more information is delivered for the students to analyse. They consider what action they will take, feeding this decision into the computer – which then responds by revealing the outcome of their actions. Simulations of this type can be very realistic and engaging, giving students the impression that their decisions carry considerable consequences. Computer simulations have now become very advanced and can enable students to undertake geographical modelling where they can change different variables and witness the likely effects for people and environments. In this way the significance of various factors within geographical processes can be isolated and explored.

Physical simulations – such as the use of wave tanks, flumes, and models of coastal or river processes – have been popular in geography departments for a number of years, although they may be rather time consuming and messy to set up. Advanced simulators can sometimes be accessed in university geography departments and Schools of Education; these provide impressive representations of geographical patterns and processes for geography students of all ages. Simulations can be used to accelerate the time dimension and therefore they help students to understand the long-term effects of different physical processes. They can also be applied to reveal the difference between open and closed systems, and to explore the disparity between 'real life' and simulated processes.

Most geography departments will contain some form of physical geographical model – which is, in effect, a 'static simulation'. Relief models of landscape can be used in conjunction with map extracts (see Boardman, 1983; Norton *et al.*, 1999), whilst contour models will show how relief is depicted through contour patterns on a topographical map. A variety of models of features in human, physical and environmental geography exist depicting anything from glacial landscapes, to continental drift, or from tropical rainforests to squatter settlements. Students may often be encouraged to create their own models – for example some schools allow their geographers to build a squatter settlement in the classroom, at scales which vary from a 'desk top' model to a life-size shack!

2.4   Decision-making exercises (DMEs)

Decision-making exercises (DMEs) are used to assess students' abilities to undertake a structured sequence of enquiry about a geographical issue, question or problem. The decision(s) will often involve the student carrying out both factual and values enquiries about a real issue, represented by a geographical case study (Butt, 1998a).

The process of completing a DME may involve the student taking on a role. Here evidence and data provided within the case study have to be considered and a justifiable and defensible decision made from the perspective of the person whose role the student has had to adopt. In other DMEs students may simply be asked to express their own views.

All of the resources provided within a DME will be of some use in completing the task, although some resources are of greater use and relevance than others. In most DMEs resources come in the form of statistics, maps, data, personal statements, newspaper articles and photographs. It is important that DMEs enable students to use a wide range of geographical knowledge, understanding and skills – as such they are often employed as a 'synoptic' form of assessment, drawing together many elements within the students' geographical education.

Assessment of DMEs

The process by which a decision is reached by the student is perhaps of greater importance than the decision itself, although this should be reasonable and defensible. Four aspects of the DME are particularly considered for assessment (Butt, 1998a, p. 1):

1. The ability to follow a logical and well reasoned sequence of steps towards making a decision. This is referred to in some DMEs as a 'route to enquiry'.

2. Using appropriate methods and techniques in analysing data, resources and evidence.

3. Appreciating different values positions within the data. Clarifying one's own values position is often important.

4. Considering different decisions that might be made, justifying these and then making a logical reasoned decision that is defensible at the end of the enquiry.

DMEs are now common in external examinations at A and AS levels and have gradually been introduced into some geography GCSEs. They can be applied to a wide range of 'people–environment' issues but have only a limited application within physical geography. Making logical decisions is part of everyday life, but is a skill that needs to be taught. It is therefore important that students' experience of geography education prepares them for a decision-making role in later life, for becoming involved in decisions that are made within society at a variety of spatial scales is important.

An example of a DME used with A level students is provided in Figure 4.2.

3 | VISUAL IMAGES

Visual images provide a valuable aid to teaching and learning geography. The GNC is clear in its intention that students at Key Stage 3 should develop geographical skills in relation to the use of visual images, when it states that they should be taught:

> 2d. to select and use secondary sources of evidence, including photographs (including vertical and oblique aerial photographs), satellite images and evidence from ICT-based sources [for example, the internet].

> (DfEE/QCA, 1999a, p. 22)

The range of images that geography teachers can use is wide, including satellite images, aerial photographs, oblique photographs, slides and videos. CD-ROMs also provide visual images (see Chapter 10). Each of the different sources of visual imagery will be considered in turn.

3.1 Satellite images

Satellite images, like any images that are remotely sensed from above the earth's surface, convey information about the area they cover to a greater extent than any aerial photograph can ever achieve. An aerial photograph merely records what the eye can see using the spectrum of visible light from red to violet; a satellite image uses the wider electromagnetic spectrum from infrared to ultraviolet which is processed by computer to provide a greater expanse of detail about the surface it has been used to record. The resultant images are usually presented in 'false colour', as this is the most appropriate way of highlighting particular patterns or features that would not be recognized if they were presented in 'natural' colours – for example illustrating the degrees of wetness of soils, or the stages of growth of different vegetation.

Satellite images are readily available from the internet and from school data loggers that have satellite connections, or they can be purchased in commercially produced sets. The main sources of original images are weather satellites such as METEOSAT and land observation satellites such as LANDSAT (US) and SPOT (Satellite Probatoire pour l'Observation de la Terre, France).

3.2 Aerial photographs

Aerial photographs, taken from an oblique or vertical perspective, are valuable sources of geographic information, particularly so in the case of vertical photographs if used in conjunction with maps of a similar scale. Apart from conveying a 'real' image of the earth's surface (although this image is distorted with distance

DMEL: DEVELOPMENT AT A LOCAL SCALE: ASTON AND LONGBRIDGE

Development at local scale: Aston and Longbridge

Graham Butt

Introduction

You are to assume the role of a member of the Birmingham City Council Planning Department with responsibility for the continuing development of two contrasting enumeration districts (EDs) of Birmingham, namely Aston and Longbridge.

As part of your work you have to complete a report on the contemporary problems faced by residents within the ED. You are a new recruit to the Planning Department and as such your work is currently being evaluated on a marking scheme as part of the process of appraisal of new staff.

More information about Aston and Longbridge Wards is provided in *Birmingham – Decisions on Development*, pages 30, 31 and 42.

The tasks

1. Identify the major problems which you believe face the populations within the Aston and Longbridge EDs by comparing the two areas.

2. [i] Produce a management plan which addresses the problems you have identified above, using the data and information supplied to illustrate your answer. Suggest priorities for action.

   [ii] Justify your management plans and the priorities for action. Should each ED receive the same sort of management, or are there particular priorities in each ED?

3. Design an information leaflet for residents in each ED to explain the action that will be taken. You may have to consider certain aspects of design, layout, language and presentation of these leaflets.

Flats in Longbridge ED

Housing in Aston ED

DMEL: DEVELOPMENT AT A LOCAL SCALE: ASTON AND LONGBRIDGE   RESOURCE SHEET 1

You have received the following memorandum from your Director of Planning

MEMORANDUM

From: Sanjeeva Kirunaratnee   To: Ms Avril Marr
      Director of Planning   Planning Department
      Birmingham City Council

Date: 1 October 1995

Dear Avril,

Re: Aston and Longbridge EDs.

As you are aware the Aston and Longbridge EDs present a variety of challenges for the Planning Department which we would like you to become involved with as part of your first year of work with us. The results of your efforts will be part of this year's appraisal and I believe you have already received information on the 'marking scheme' that will be used to help us assess how effectively you have considered your tasks.

Enclosed with this memo are a variety of pieces of data and information that may help you to come to your decisions and prioritise the issues which you feel are important to pursue. You will see that the Aston ED has a range of typical 'inner city' challenges facing it and is different in many ways from the Longbridge ED. It may be worthwhile starting your work by clarifying the nature of these differences and suggesting possible reasons for them.

Also enclosed are some typical responses from residents which were recently collected by a door to door questionnaire survey. As you know the Council is very keen to be seen to be taking account of the views of residents and those comment should be treated as representative of the general feelings of the people living in each of the EDs.

I enclose with this memo, data and information for Aston and Longbridge EDs. [Resource Sheets 1 and 2].

Each includes:
1. Map of relevant ED.
2. Photo of a typical part of the ED.
3. Details on ethnic origin, age range, migration patterns and sex balance of the population.
4. Details of housing ownership or renting.
5. Two affluence indicators - rooms and car ownership.
6. Employment indices.

Resource Sheet 3 contains residents comments.

Resource Sheet 4 is a Birmingham map with both EDs marked.

The main concern of the residents can be gauged from the comments which accompany this memo. For your report I would like you to identify what you believe to be the main problems each ED faces, some of these problems may result from the previous management of the areas!

Please suggest ways of dealing with contemporary problems by creating a new management plan. Since it is financially very difficult to implement the whole of a plan all in one step please suggest parts of your plan which should be viewed by the planning department, and residents, as priorities. In order that residents are clearly informed about our plans it will be necessary to design information leaflets that can be posted to residents informing them of our actions. You may have to consider certain aspects of design, layout, language and presentation of these leaflets.

Yours,

Sanjeeva Kirunaratnee

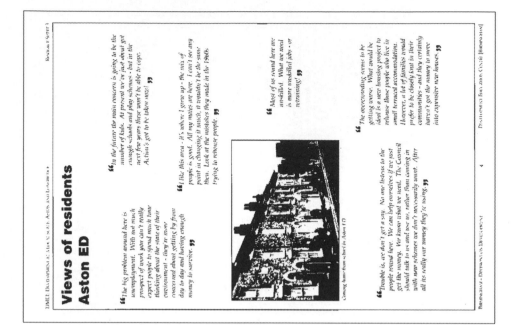

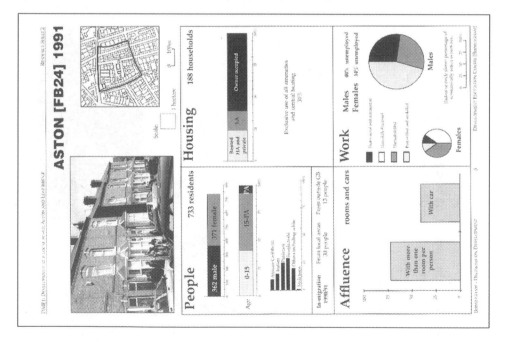

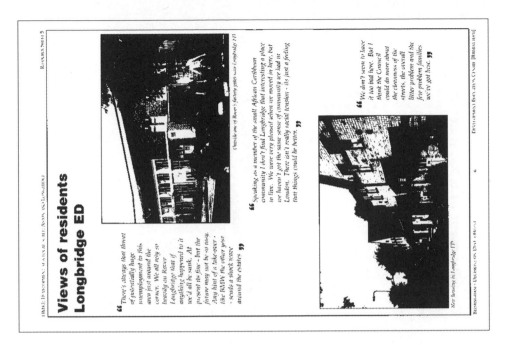

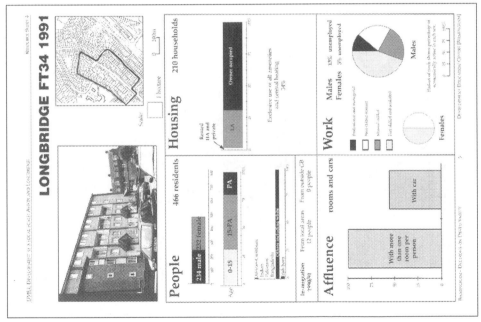

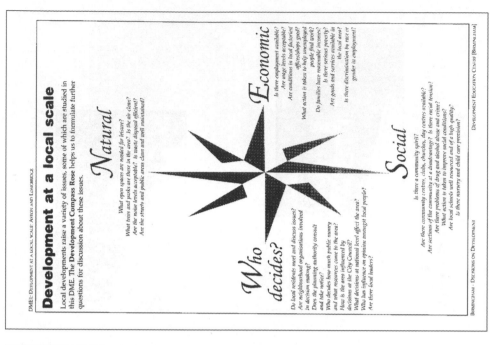

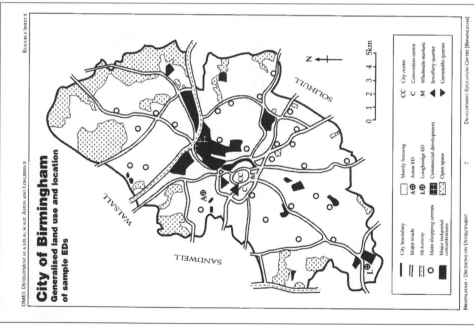

Figure 4.2 An Example of a Decision-making Exercise (DME)

Figure 4.3 *A satellite image*

from the camera lens and can be hard to interpret) they can serve to help students understand the simplification of reality represented by maps through their use of symbols and colour. The interpretation of aerial photographs, even with an accompanying map of the same scale, can be every bit as challenging as the interpretation of other geographic images. The basic orientation of a map and aerial photograph can prove problematic for many students, particularly if the image has few obvious significant features (such as a coastline or a river) which may help in the orientation process.

The skills associated with the interpretation and use of aerial photographs are essential for the compleat geographer. These may progress from handling a variety of ground, oblique and vertical photographs to appreciate the different scales and perspectives conveyed, to recognizing a series of human and physical features and patterns, to suggesting reasons for the existence of the patterns and relationships between features. Some geographers believe that using oblique photographs may provide a 'first step' towards students being able to confidently read and interpret vertical photographs alongside maps (Boardman, 1983). Given the issue of perspective, variation in scale from the foreground to the background of a photograph, and the problems of certain features obscuring others in the image this is obviously not always the case.

A particular strength of aerial photographs, which also exists for satellite images and to a lesser extent for comprehensively (rather than selectively) updated maps, is their ability to capture geographical patterns at a particular moment in time. By using images of an area taken at different times the changing geographical shapes, patterns and relationships within an area become clearer – also providing an insight into the geographical processes that have occurred.

Practical activity 4.3

Select an aerial photograph for which you also have a map at the same scale.

Devise an activity that would enable GCSE pupils to more clearly understand the geographical properties of both resources and how they compliment each as sources of geographical information. Remember that it is important for students to *recognize, identify* and *interpret* the information from both sources.

Which particular geographical skills would you wish to promote through your use of the aerial photograph and map?

3.3 Photographs, slides and videos

Photographs, slides and videos provide students with a range of visual images that initially may be more familiar than aerial photographs and satellite images, but which require just as careful interpretation and analysis. For the teacher of geography the world can be brought into the classroom by using visual images, which can be employed to create a 'sense of place' as well as conveying perceptions of different peoples and environments.

The visual literacy of many students is, by the time they reach secondary school age, quite advanced. We live in a highly visual age where we see and rapidly 'process' numerous images from different sources every day, although the sophistication with which these images are processed varies from person to person. Most images are provided for us by an 'editor' who wants us to see things from their standpoint, or to illustrate a particular point of view. The most extreme example of this process is in advertising, where the acceptance of an image and its associations may be enough to persuade us to buy a particular product. Students need, through geography, to be able to read, interpret and analyse for bias the myriad images that the world around them presents about people and places. They also need to understand their acceptance or rejection of images, and the empathetic or sympathetic reactions that such images may engender. Often this can involve some form of affective education where students' values and attitudes are clarified in response to a particular image (Robinson, 1987; Butt, 1991).

Photographs and slides can be analysed for both their physical content and the feelings they inspire in us. In the case of their content a structured approach may be adopted – recognizing and correctly labeling physical and human features contained in the photograph, identifying patterns within the landscape, commenting on possible processes at work, and clarifying relationships between physical and human features to explain people–environment links (see Hopkirk, 1998; Roberts, 1998a). In the case of the feelings that visual images inspire the application of the Development Education 'Compass Rose' to help students analyse and interpret photographic images is an active, enquiry-led, way of working with images (see Figure 4.4). Here the students not only consider the natural and economic evidence within the image but also the social and political (who decides?) elements that are contained. Students may alternatively place the image in the middle of a piece of sugar paper and 'ask questions' around it by writing down questions they would like answered about the image. The teacher or the students may then select which questions to pursue further.

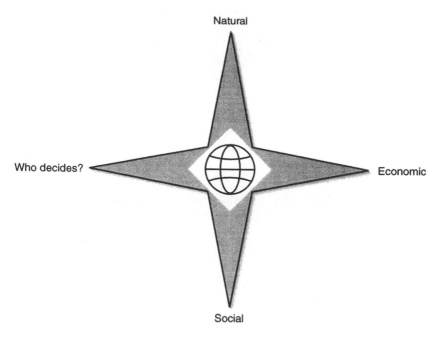

Figure 4.4 *The DEC Rose (Butt, 2000a)*

Developing the visual literacy of students through geography education is an important facet of both geographical and life skills education. It also helps students when they have to photograph geographical features, patterns and processes to illustrate fieldwork or coursework, for they can apply their understanding of the importance of the visual image to their framing and selection of images.

The value of being able to use moving images in the geography classroom, provided through video, television, CD-ROM or the internet, is immense. However, the standard caveats apply – we must remember that all images and sound-tracks are edited versions of a range of possible sights and sounds that might have been shown. An additional problem arises in that many students are used to passively watching televisual images and may need to engage in more active and enquiry-led ways of using them. The great strength of video is its ability to show moving images of geographical patterns and processes – this strength is entirely negated if students are merely told to 'take notes' when watching a video. Note taking often results in the students mostly *listening* and *recording* what is said in the commentary of the video, without noticing anything about the visual images.

Durbin (1995) suggests a number of things that televisual resources do well – for example they bring distant places into the classroom, enable people's (edited) views to be heard, can combine commentary, graphics and diagrams to explain difficult concepts, and can give a clear impression of spatial and temporal dimensions. However, many televisual resources do not convey complex geographical data well, lack breadth in the viewpoints they express, do not provide detailed maps or specific locational knowledge and move too rapidly between images. In addition, just as with any form of text, students should consider both visual images and commentary from the point of view of their possible bias, omission, values and impressions created.

A range of activities can be introduced when using televisual resources:

- 'freeze frame' where an image is paused and analysed, or a previously sketched picture of the image is annotated by the students

- watching a small clip of video (without sound) and students brainstorm where it is

- students note down their perceptions (positive, negative, neutral) of a place shown in a video (or alternatively provide the students with a set of adjectives to use)

- students provide their own commentary for a section of video

- students summarize the different viewpoints, values and attitudes of people in a video and look for supporting evidence

- provide a short transcript of certain sections of video commentary for deeper analysis.

Each of these techniques can be used by geography teachers on short clips they have recorded from news programmes (global, national and regional), current affairs programmes, documentaries and educational programmes or even 'soaps'.

4 | MAPPED IMAGES

4.1 Maps

Maps, as cartographic representations of phenomena on the Earth's surface (or below it in the case of geological maps), are a fundamental tool and resource for the geographer. They present spatial information in differing ways and can be produced in a variety of forms – their common feature is that a cartographer has encoded within the map a generalized conception of the world in the form of symbols, which the map reader then has to decode in order to interpret, analyse and understand the information conveyed. As teachers of geography we have an important role in helping students to develop the skills necessary to read, understand and use maps. We also have a role in enabling students to appreciate the unique form of communication associated with maps, the so called 'language of maps'. This is part of the development of graphicacy. Weeden reminds us that the 'investigation of spatial patterns and the development of locational knowledge form distinctive and central parts of the discipline, with the map in all its forms being a vital tool in this process' (Weeden, 1997, p. 168).

Students should encounter a wide variety of maps – including plans, cartograms, dynamic and interactive maps – which have each been constructed for different purposes and at different scales. In their use of maps, both inside and outside the classroom, students should learn the main functions of maps, namely to represent location, distance, direction, proportion and orientation; to display routes; to show relief; to store and display spatial information; and to help in problem-solving (Gerber and Wilson, 1984; Weeden, 1997). Both atlases and maps have their own language which may initially be difficult to understand. Interpretation problems arise with respect to the complexity of patterns and symbols, the density of information carried on certain maps, use of colours with ambiguous meanings (green may not mean 'grass', but an indication of height!), size and style of fonts, inclusion of choropleth or isolines, and spatial distortion because of the nature of the projection used (see Wiegand, 1996).

The Ordnance Survey is the main organization which surveys the UK for cartographic purposes producing a range of maps which can be used in geography education (see Figure 4.5). They also produce specialist maps such as historical maps, or Outdoor Leisure Maps (1:25,000) as well as some maps of overseas areas. It must be remembered that the Ordnance Survey is not the only source of maps and plans for the UK. A to Z maps and other cartographic representations produced for urban areas by companies such as Goad Plans (1:1056) are educationally important. For Europe other national mapping organizations produce maps, as do companies such as Michelin.

Weather maps and synoptic charts, either produced by the Meteorological Office or reproduced in various forms in national and local newspapers, should also be considered as maps which students should have access to at secondary level. These may be combined with satellite images using the Meteorological Office's weather information service MetFAX (fax 09003 400 480, e-mail metfax@meto.gov.uk, www.met-office.gov.uk) which provides weather data for locations at given times. The interpretation of weather patterns from synoptic charts is not straightforward as it requires a reasonably advanced understanding of meteorological processes. The information represented on such charts (air pressure, wind direction and strength, temperature, cloud cover, precipitation, fronts) need careful interpretation before the complexities of changing weather systems become clear.

The GNC requires students to be able to read, use, make and interpret maps at a variety of scales at Key Stage 3:

> 2. In developing geographical skills, pupils should be taught:
>
> c. to use atlases and globes, and maps and plans at a range of scales, including Ordnance Survey 1:25,000 and 1:50,000 maps.
>
> d. to draw maps and plans at a range of scales, using symbols, keys and scales [for example, annotated sketch maps] and to select and use appropriate graphical techniques to present evidence on maps and diagrams [for example, pie charts, choropleth maps], including ICT [for example, using mapping software to plot the distribution of shops and services in a town centre].
>
> (DfEE/QCA, 1999a, p. 22)

Although Gerber and Wilson (1984) have described a sequential programme for learning map skills there is conflicting evidence to suggest that certain skills should be learnt first, apart from obvious points that students need to understand what features such as (say) valleys are before they can appreciate the contour patterns which represent valleys. Boardman (1983) reveals that students do not learn map skills in a straightforward way. There are also no particularly conventional methods for *reading* a map (compared to, say, reading a book – from left to right

Scale	Area covered	General points
1:1,250	Superplan series. Available for large urban areas. 500 m × 500 m covered on each map extract.	Black and white. Useful for locality studies.
1:2,500	Superplan series. Available for areas beyond towns and cities (but not some upland areas). 1 km × 1 km covered on each map extract.	Black and white. Useful for locality studies.
1:10,000	Superplan series. Available for all areas. 5 km × 5 km covered on each map extract.	Black and white with brown contours (5 m vertical interval, or 10 m in mountain and moorland). Useful for locality studies; features such as roads, street names and major buildings clearly shown.
1:25,000	Pathfinder series. Available for all areas. 10 km × 10 km covered on each map extract.	Limited use of colour. Contours at 5 m vertical interval. Useful for place studies. Detailed to the level of showing field boundaries.
1:50,000	Landranger series. Available for all areas. 40 km × 40 km covered on each map extract	Coloured. Contours at 10 m vertical interval. Useful for regional studies. Less detailed than larger scale maps described above, but capable of providing a reasonably comprehensive overview of features within a region.
1:250,000 or 1:625,000	Travelmaster series.	Coloured. Contours and hill shading.

Figure 4.5 *Range of Ordnance Survey maps*

and from top to bottom) with most map readers scanning the map for recognizable features and names and then concentrating on the area of specific interest for known patterns.

Lambert and Balderstone (2000) suggest a variety of ways in which geography teachers can introduce mapwork skills into their classrooms (see Figure 4.6).

Map property	Activities to develop mapwork skills*
Location	• use of grid references to locate points • use of co-ordinates, alphanumeric, four figure and six figure grid references • understanding of eastings and northings
Direction	• use of compass points • cardinal points
Scale	• use of maps of same area at different scales • measurement of distance (or area) on maps and calculation of real distance (or area)
Routes	• use skills of location, direction and scale to follow routes • planning of journeys
Contours	• use contours to identify height, slope and relief • interpret physical landscape on topographical maps to identify features • understand contour patterns (valleys, cliffs, floodplains, hills, spurs, etc.) • understand particular landscapes (glaciated, chalk – dry valleys, etc.)
Cross sections	• use of appropriate horizontal and vertical scales (maximum of 5:1 for vertical exaggeration) • recording of contour patterns • drawing sections
Orienteering	• active learning of map reading skills (map interpretation, scale, direction, etc.)

* Many of these skills can be developed using computer software packages, GISs and CD-ROMs designed specifically to enhance their learning.

Figure 4.6 *Ways in which geography teachers can introduce mapwork skills into their classrooms (Lambert and Balderstone, 2000)*

4.2 Atlases

An atlas is a collection of maps or charts bound into a single volume. Particular atlases are produced for specific purposes but most include topographic, political and thematic maps at a range of scales from regional to continental. Some will also provide limited satellite images, information on geographical patterns and processes, phenomena and data of various kinds. In recent years electronic and interactive atlases have grown in popularity and have particular value within geography education, as many of them can be manipulated and questioned by students. Atlases complement globes, but even the most detailed globe can only carry a fraction of the information contained in an atlas.

Because of the larger areas covered by atlas maps they are ideal to use in explanations of projections. The inevitable distortions that occur to both shape and area when the features on a spherical surface are represented on a flat page should be understood by students, as well as the principles for selecting a particular projection for a particular purpose (see Sibert, 1998; Wright, 2000). A good starting point to illustrate the significant difference between an atlas map and a globe is to compare the shortest distance between two places on a globe (the Great Circle route) with the apparent shortest distance on an atlas map (the straight line route).

Students should be taught about the 'mechanics' of the atlas and globe, that is they should develop an understanding of longitude (meridians) and latitude (parallels); the significance of the equator, tropics and polar circles; the poles; the prime meridian; and the numbering of lines of longitude and latitude in degrees.

The teaching resources we use in the geography classroom should, as far as possible, be relevant, topical and stimulating. It is also important that we evaluate these resources for any forms of bias and either reject them, or use them to indicate the partiality of the information or images they convey. Geography has a major responsibility in ensuring that students receive a balanced and equivocal view of people and places – the range of resources we can use to do so is a particular strength of the subject.

Practical activity 4.4

Obtain copies of four atlases commonly used by geography departments for teaching the 11–18 age range.

Analyse the differences in the content, presentation, 'additional' information and layout of the atlases. Which atlas appears to suit the majority of the geography teacher's needs for this age range? What variations would you expect in the qualities of atlases designed for differing abilities and ages?

5 | FIELDWORK

Although not strictly a 'resource' in the sense that textbooks, worksheets, games and atlases can be considered resources, it is perhaps important to include fieldwork within any list of approaches to geography teaching. Geography education is fortunate in that fieldwork is still considered integral to the development of one's knowledge, understanding and skills within the subject. It enables the 'theory' of the classroom to engage with the 'practice' of the real world, bringing both together in a unique and fulfilling way. Some would also stress the importance of adopting a skills approach to fieldwork, emphasizing the need to allow students to utilize a range of practical, intellectual and organizational skills in their pursuit of answers to 'real world' questions and issues (Foskett, 1997, 2000; Lambert and Balderstone, 2000). Fieldwork, along with other forms of outdoor education (see Gair, 1997) is often the most memorable and distinctive aspect of learning that students recall from their curriculum experiences in geography. It involves aspects of personal and social education, the development of personal geographies, as well as often balancing both the cognitive and affective dimensions of learning.

The GNC makes explicit reference to the development of geographical skills in relation to fieldwork when it states that pupils should be taught:

2b. to select and use appropriate fieldwork techniques [for example land use survey, datalogging] and instruments [for example, cameras].

(DfEE/QCA, 1999a, p. 22)

Job (1996) provides a useful diagram which places various approaches to fieldwork into context (see Figure 4.7).

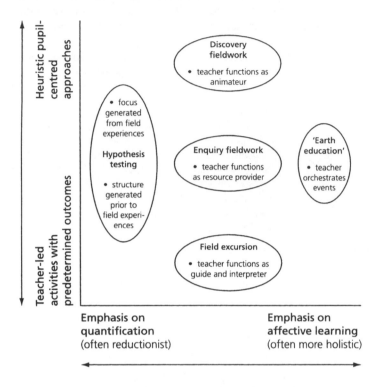

Figure 4.7 *Some fieldwork approaches (Job, 1996)*

The attractiveness of undertaking fieldwork, to both teacher and learner, is perhaps obvious. Whether residentially based for a number of days, within the local community for a day, or within the school grounds for a single lesson the experience of learning outside the classroom is welcomed by the majority of students. Fieldwork activities should be engaging and motivational, often involving group work and self direction. With respect to the GNC and examination specifications at GCSE and A/AS level much of the fieldwork will be 'enquiry-led', whereby the students have to devise their own questions to investigate within the framework of a structured set of key questions.

Unfortunately fieldwork, particularly that which is residentially based, is under threat in school geography. Field experience tends to be expensive and time consuming, with some schools in disadvantaged catchment areas finding that parents and guardians are unwilling (or unable) to make financial contributions to residential work. In addition, certain cultural and religious groups are nervous about their children being away from home for a number of days and are therefore reluctant to give consent to their attendance. The Senior Management Teams within schools may also view fieldwork as an unnecessary disruption to the teaching of other subjects; they are therefore wary of allowing residential experience that appears to be an unnecessary 'holiday' for geography staff and students. The cost of supply teachers to cover the classes of geography teachers who are conducting residential work is also not welcomed. The centrality of fieldwork to the GNC, external examination specifications and the development of geographical understanding is perhaps misunderstood or ignored in these circumstances.

Organizing fieldwork draws upon geography teachers' planning skills, their depth of subject knowledge and understanding, pedagogical expertise and reali-

Planning stage	Planning activity	Approximate timing ahead for day visits residential work
Obtaining permission	1. Preliminary discussion with head of department/ headteacher. 2. Consult school/LEA policy documents. 3. Consult professional association guidelines. 4. Seek formal approval from head/governors/LEA.	As early as possible probably in previous academic year, but at least 1 term/1 year
Pre-visit/background reading	5. Planning and site visit.	1 term/6 mths
Costing	6. Calculate budget and check charging policies.	1 term/6 mths
Insurance	7. Check insuracnce arragements.	1 term/6 mths
Transport	8. Arrange transport.	6 wks/3 mths
Pre-visit documentation	9. Provide information to parents/obtain parental permission/medical information.	6 wks/3 mths
Praparation for activity	10. Prepare resources, pupils and colleagues.	1 wk/3 wks
	11. Make safety arrangements (e.g. first aid kit, emergency contact lists).	1 wk/2 wks
Managing the activity	12. On the day – monitor weather, pupils, safety, assess for contingency plan.	Continuously during fieldwork
Follow-up	13. Pupil follow-up and product.	Immediately
	14. Evaluation of activity and planning.	No more than 3 wks after

Figure 4.8 *Outline planning checklist for fieldwork organization (Foskett, 1997)*

zation of health and safety issues. The planning aspects can be daunting and are easily misjudged by the inexperienced teacher (see Figure 4.8). There are always dangers that geography teachers, as experienced users of field study techniques and with a developed 'geographer's eye' for landscape and environment, assume too much regarding students' abilities to 'read' and interpret what is around them. Simply telling students your expert interpretation of the landscape, or getting them to engage in rather narrow teacher-led hypothesis testing, is not enough – they must engage actively with this new learning, either through an enquiry approach or some aspect of data collection in the search to answer specific questions about people, environments, patterns and processes (Job, 1996; Rynne, 1998). Often this will include an element of decision-making, or at least a consideration of the possible range of solutions to an environmental issue or problem.

In this respect planning fieldwork is an extension of planning any classroom-based lesson. Principles of establishing aims, learning objectives, methods, considerations of resources and equipment, and differentiation all apply – along with additional considerations such as transport, health and safety and integration within a scheme of work.

Foskett (1997) suggests a possible progression in fieldwork, in part reproduced below, involving:

- an increase in distance from school for field activities;

- an increase in duration of field activities (from single lessons to residential);

- an increase in complexity of fieldwork (from simple descriptive to issues-based enquiries)

- an increase in the demands of fieldwork skills (from description to analytical techniques, statistical techniques and ICT use)

- an increase in student autonomy in the design and practice of fieldwork (from directed to individual fieldstudy).

Various approaches to fieldwork have been suggested. Hart and Thomas (1986) describe a 'framework fieldwork' approach which identifies the consideration of elements of people–environment interaction, procedures and techniques for field enquiries, and ideas and concepts from geography when deciding upon what data needs to be collected in the field to answer a specific question. This eventually leads to the formulation of answers and the possibility of taking appropriate action to resolve issues. Bland *et al.* (1996) refer to 'observational', 'investigative' and 'enquiry-based' approaches to fieldwork, whilst others focus on fieldwork 'about', 'from' or 'for' the environment.

5.1 The legal dimensions of fieldwork

Currently under DES Circular 2/89 no charge can be made for fieldwork activities wholly in school time, although voluntary contributions from parents can be requested. This can create problems for certain schools whose catchment area may be deprived, for they will have little prospect of gaining additional financial support from parents for either day or residential activities. In these circumstances schools may only undertake local fieldwork, or no fieldwork at all.

Schools and LEAs also have clear policies on the necessary experience of field leaders, on staff student ratios for different types of fieldwork, on the suitability of different locations for fieldwork, and on levels of insurance. The legal aspects of any fieldwork undertaken beyond the boundaries of the school should be taken very seriously. It is vital that avoidance of risk, issues of child and teacher safety, overall 'duty of care' and sensible decision-making are paramount within the planning of all field activities.

CONCLUSION

Geography teachers must seek to develop in their students' subject-related knowledge, understanding and skills – highlighting the study of places, patterns and processes in the pursuit of a range of geographical themes. However, they must also encourage the students to engage with specific geographical techniques and enquiry methods. The link between subject content, teaching resources and pedagogy is extremely important. Without the stimulation, interest, motivation and cooperation of young people geography educators will not be able to convey the relevance and importance of their subject. The application of a variety of teaching approaches and the skillful use of an array of geographical resources is the key to effective learning.

CHAPTER 5

Continuity and progression in geography education

Continuity and progression are widely recognised as desirable qualities within a curriculum.
(Opening line of Trevor Bennetts' article on the subject in Teaching Geography, *1995)*

INTRODUCTION

The principles of continuity and progression within education are important to curriculum design, planning, teaching and assessment, for, as students mature intellectually, the geography curriculum they study should take account of their development. The National Curriculum was intended to strengthen both continuity and progression within subjects, although subsequent revisions to Subject Orders may have had an impact on both in recent years. The terms 'continuity' and 'progression' are complementary, but providing a definition of each is helpful to our understanding of the concepts:

- *Continuity* – the maintenance and development of different aspects of geography education within the geography curriculum over a period of study (for example in the GNC over three Key Stages). Continuity can relate to aspects such as the aims for geography education, sections of geographical content, types of teaching and learning activities or assessment procedures. Students should be ensured continuity within their studies so that they can build upon their previous skills, knowledge and understanding in a structured fashion as they pass from GNC, to GCSE, to A level, and to degree.

- *Progression* – the measurable advances in knowledge, understanding and skills made by students within geography. Progression should occur at a pace appropriate to the individual's learning potential and abilities. The term can also be applied to the design of a curriculum where the sequence of learning activities is planned to promote learning in a structured fashion over time. Assessment is used to monitor student progression.

Given the nature of continuity and progression it is readily apparent that both concepts are closely linked to curriculum structure and schemes of work, which represent (among other things) plans for student learning over a particular time period. If the curriculum has a strong sense of continuity it should ensure that particular aspects of students' previous learning in geography are built upon during the next course of study. However, without progression there may not be advances in learning, as students may merely continue to learn the same things. As such the GNC seeks to build up students' experiences in geography from Key Stage 1, to 2 and to 3, the latter of which should provide a now 'complete' statutory experience of geography education for those students who choose to end their studies at this point. There should also be apparent continuity from GNC to GCSE courses, and from GCSE to AS and A level.

Bennetts (1996) identifies some general ideas about progression that should be used to guide planning. With reference to geography these ideas stress that ideally teaching should build on students' previous knowledge and experiences in geography; that learning tasks should relate closely to students' capabilities; that the overall scheme of work should take account of how students mature intellectually, socially and physically; and that attention should be given to those aspects of geography that are likely to be important for students' future learning both within and beyond the parameters of the subject.

From a report by HMI (HMI, 1986), progression in geographical education should therefore, in general terms, gradually:

- extend the geographical content to include different places, processes, patterns, activities, etc. (e.g. increasing the **breadth** of study);

- increase the complexity, demands and abstraction within the geographical information provided in line with the students' growing intellectual maturity (e.g. increasing the **depth** of study);

- introduce geographical studies of larger areas, moving more from the local to the global (e.g. increasing the **spatial scale** of study);

- introduce a wider range of geographical techniques and enquiry strategies (e.g. increasing the **development of skills** within study);

- increase the opportunities for affective education (own and others' beliefs, values and attitudes) and the study of social, economic, political and environmental issues (e.g. increasing the **affective dimensions** of study).

Practical activity 5.1

Consider the aspects of continuity and progression between Key Stages 2 and 3 of the Geography National Curriculum. How far does this curriculum reflect the principles espoused by HMI in 1986 (see above).

Bruner's (1960) idea of a spiral curriculum directly involved notions of progression as students revisited aspects of previous learning which were then reinforced and refined. In terms of geographical learning this progression has been marked by the following 'rules' for achieving understanding (Marsden, 1995):

- from the familiar to the unfamiliar;

- from the near to the more distant;

- from the concrete to the more abstract;

- from the smaller to the larger scale;
- from the simple to the more complex (in terms of breadth and depth of coverage);
- from limited to expansive range of skills.

Embedded within these ideas, which are not uncontroversial, is the notion that in geography one moves from 'core concepts' through a process of differentiation to either enrich the experiences of the 'more able' to stretch their knowledge, understanding and skills, or reinforcement for the 'less able'. One of the problems in geography is that the 'core concepts' do not suggest a particularly clear sequence or progression – they may overlap and be of equal importance but often do not naturally follow on from each other.

1 | CONTINUITY, PROGRESSION AND ASSESSMENT

Planning for continuity and progression, and planning for assessment, are clearly related. Measurement of the advances made in students' learning are integral to concepts of progression, as are aspects of curriculum design and structure. Progression also indicates the expected knowledge, understanding, skills and competencies one expects to be attained by students at different stages of their passage through the geography curriculum. The plans for assessment of progression are different for the short, medium and long term (see Hopkin, 2000). It is evident that within the key stage structure of the National Curriculum, assessment has to take into account progression from ages 5–14 in geography *across* the key stages (long term), progression *within* each of the three key stages (medium term), and progression on a *day-to-day* basis (short term). Thus the long term assessment of progression may revisit certain key aspects of the geography curriculum, such as themes, skills, and concepts, whilst short term progression may be assessed specifically within a particular unit of work.

As Hopkin (2000) explains, planning for progression links two aspects of students' learning:

1. progression in learning objectives (linked to the programmes of study in geography);

2. progression in attainment (linked to the level descriptions in geography).

Both need to be considered when planning in the short, medium and long term as illustrated in Figure 5.1.

2 | PROGRESSION IN THE PROGRAMMES OF STUDY AND LEVEL DESCRIPTIONS

As stated, the GNC is designed to show progression across the Key Stages within its programme of study, as well as maintaining continuity of major geographical concepts, content and skills. The transition between key stages should therefore be

Planning for progression: learning objectives	Planning for progression: attainment and target setting
Long term	• Learning objectives for the Key Stage are general and closely related to the programme of study of GCSE syllabus, i.e. knowledge, understanding and skills. • The level descriptions in geography are designed as benchmarks against which to assess students' attainment over Key Stage 3 as a whole. • To promote progression over the Key Stage, decisions focus on how the programme of study/syllabus can be divided into topics or study units, and when these are planned. For example, a spiral approach to the Key Stage plan helps students revisit, develop and extend their knowledge, concepts and skills. • Level descriptions are useful as a focus for long-term evaluation of how successful the curriculum has been in promoting learning and providing opportunities for students to show their attainments. • This helps to set departmental targets and to make decisions about where to focus next to raise achievement and 'standards'.
Medium term	• Here progression is concerned with the development of knowledge, understanding and skills within a topic or unit. • Key decisions focus on identifying assessment opportunities to match the learning objectives. These should be developmental, to match progression over the unit as a whole. • The focus is on planning sequences of learning objectives that will help support students' progress, e.g. by broadening and deepening their knowledge and understanding, and relating these objectives to assessment. • Here the level descriptions are less useful, although they may help in deciding the level of demand of activities and the pitch of assessment. • Evaluation at the end of the unit helps focus on the progress students have made. • Student self-assessment and target setting help support their progress towards the next stages in their learning.
Short term	• Progression in individual lessons is concerned with the (often small) steps students make in the development of knowledge, understanding and skills. • Assessment within lessons can be based on a range of informal and more formal strategies, such as observing and talking to students and marking their work. • Planning is focused on deciding on specific objectives, activities and opportunities for assessment, and on differentiation. • The focus is on using information gained from these

Continued

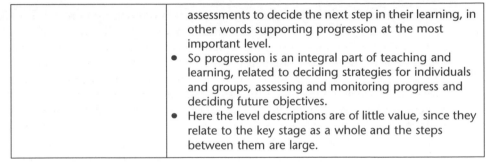

assessments to decide the next step in their learning, in other words supporting progression at the most important level.

- So progression is an integral part of teaching and learning, related to deciding strategies for individuals and groups, assessing and monitoring progress and deciding future objectives.
- Here the level descriptions are of little value, since they relate to the key stage as a whole and the steps between them are large.

Figure 5.1 *Progression in objectives and attainment*

seamless, however the step from Key Stage 2 to 3 which involves a change from primary to secondary schooling for most students often shows dislocation in progression (Marsden, 1997; Williams, 1997; Chapman, 2001). Surveys have revealed that both continuity and progression regularly break down in Year 7, where principles such as liaison between primary and secondary schools and the establishment of transition arrangements are often ignored (Fry and Schofield, 1993). In extreme cases students may actually regress at the start of Key Stage 3 (see Jones, 1999).

Within the Key Stages the programmes of study give little guidance about what to progress 'from' and 'to' – one is merely presented with a statement of what should be covered, without any impression of where to start from or what to move on to. This judgement is left to the professional expertise of the individual teacher who, hopefully, has an understanding of which are the more intellectually demanding skills, content and concepts. In a way there is nothing new in this – although progression is an important element within any curriculum it tends to be implicit and less tangible than components such as units of study, learning activities, assessment methods and content. There is therefore no straightforward principle to help us to determine what sequence specific items of knowledge should be presented in – this will be contingent on the context that learning, the activities devised and the use to which the knowledge will be put. This is a cumulative progress, with new learning being 'built' upon whatever geographical knowledge, understanding and skills have been previously learnt. What *is* clear is that there is a statutory responsibility for teachers to address the need to teach the GNC in all three Key Stages and for this to take account of the teaching and learning that has already taken place. As Bennetts warned:

> It is no longer acceptable for geography teachers in secondary schools to ignore what pupils have learnt in primary schools, nor for secondary schools to design humanities courses in which geography is only a weak component.
>
> (Bennetts, 1995, p. 75).

Greater guidance on progression can be gleaned from the level descriptions. These are broadly progressive from the lowest level up to the highest description for 'exceptional performance', moving from knowledge acquisition to comprehension, interpretation, analysis, synthesis and evaluation. The ability of students to describe and explain geographical patterns and processes is often linked to their abilities to develop their understanding of basic geographical concepts, generalizations and models as they progress. Although the progression within the programmes of study and level descriptions for geography is not based upon research evidence, the movement from knowledge to evaluation does parallel the work of Bloom (1964). Bloom's taxonomy of educational objectives forms a hierarchy, where the later categories subsume those that have gone before. The theoretical underpinning of the concept of continuity also owes something to Bruner's (1960) ideas of a spiral curriculum, where students returned to particular elements of their education on a systematic basis over time. Instead of repeating the particular theme, concept or skill the student would revisit it but take their understanding a stage further, appropriate to the level of intellectual maturity they had now reached.

The use of level descriptions (and the very concept of 'levels of attainment') is not wholly consistent with the notion of progression of intellectual capabilities and achievement. The concept of having distinct levels suggests progression up a series of steps, rather than along a gently sloping incline (see Bennetts, 1995). The reason for this is that the levels were primarily devised for assessment and reporting purposes at the end of a Key Stage where such 'stepping' provides a useful differentiation between students' abilities and attainment. However, in terms of planning for progression, the model would be more appropriate as a gently sloping incline of achievement. In reality, intellectual progression is much more complicated than either a stepped or incline model can convey – it approximates more closely to a mix of the two where individual students will advance more rapidly in their learning of some aspects of the subject than others, where progress is not always continuous and where, at times, regression may occur. Assessment of such progression is also fraught with difficulties as student performance may be affected by the particular geographical content, activities or skills being measured.

3 | PLANNING FOR PROGRESSION

As Bennetts states 'planning for progression should (therefore) take account of the past, present and future: what pupils have already experienced and achieved; what they can reasonably be expected to do at the time; and what will best serve their future needs. Although some pupils will not continue with the subject beyond Key Stage 3, all must be given the foundation from which to advance should they decide to take the subject further' (Bennetts, 1995, p. 76). Lambert and Balderstone (2000) helpfully adapt some of Bennetts (1996) work to illustrate some of the principles to be considered when planning for progression (see Figure 5.2).

CONCLUSION

As Bennetts commented on an earlier version of the GNC (DFE, 1995b):

> Progression is not a simple sequence of activities which, for example, proceed from identifying a feature to describing it and then explaining its characteristics. The nature and distinctiveness of the feature, and the quality of description and explanation are all relevant. A curriculum should be designed to give pupils opportunities to improve the quality of their descriptions and explanations, and to apply their understanding in increasingly sophisticated ways. Their explanations can reveal their understanding, and both will reflect their knowledge and their styles of reasoning.
>
> (Bennetts, 1995, p. 78)

Breadth of geographical knowledge	Depth of geographical understanding	Use of geographical skills	Attitudes and values
Strongly influenced by the content of the curriculum, including the requirements of the National Curriculum or examination syllabuses. To plan for breadth of knowledge: • identify the degree of choice that is available (topics and case studies); • identify previous learning (i.e. case studies, topics, places, themes, issues studied in previous Key Stage/level); • identify previously acquired knowledge which is relevant to new learning; • consider which information is to be used primarily as part of the learning process, and which information needs to be memorized for future recall.	To plan for progression in understanding within a current theme: • identify the ideas to be introduced; • analyse these ideas to clarify the meaning of each, the links between them, and the scope of their application; • consider the level of understanding appropriate for the age, ability and experience of the pupils; • explore pupils' pre-conceptions which inhibit their acceptance and development of new ideas; • take account of the various dimensions which can create barriers or difficulties for learning e.g. remoteness from experience; levels of complexity and abstraction; the degree of precision required; and the extent to which values are embedded in an idea relevant to a particular situation;	Distinguish between 1 *Specific techniques* – such as mapwork, fieldwork, statistical techniques, use of diagrams, IT and remote sensing. 2 *General categories of cognitive activity* – such as describing, analysing, explaining, evaluating. 3 *Enquiry strategies* – ways of carrying out investigations in order to arrive at valid and substantiated conclusions. Repeated use improves quality. Plan sequences of learning activities which enable pupils to improve the quality of what they do. Progression in skills involves: • building on previous learning; • matching tasks to pupils' responsibilities; • increasing complexity; • increasing the level of precision required in their use.	Values and attitudes usually appear in relation to issues arising from people's interactions with the environment. You should provide opportunities for pupils to: • explore their own attitudes and values on a wide range of issues and themes; • recognize those attitudes and values held by other people and how they influence their decisions and behaviour; • explore the impacts of these decisions and behaviour; • explore how decisions are made. Progression is determined by the extent to which pupils can demonstrate an increasingly detailed and reasoned response to particular issues and situations.

Continued

	• prepare learning materials and design learning tasks that are suitably matched to pupils' capabilities (differentiation); • devise an overall structure for the theme, which enables pupils to progressively develop their understanding.		
Key principles • breadth of knowledge is fostered by ensuring that pupils study a variety of places at a range of environmental and social conditions and processes; • the sequence in which knowledge should be acquired depends on context and use; • there should be a balance between breadth and continuity.		Do not divorce the application of skills from context. The link with knowledge and understanding is imporant in the development and use of the higher order skills of analysis, synthesis and evaluation, and in the carrying out of investigations.	Strategies that can help pupils to develop their understanding of different attitudes and values held by different individuals and groups include role play, simulation and decision-making exercises.

Figure 5.2 *Planning for progression in geography (Lambert and Balderstone, 2000)*

CHAPTER 6

Managing and organizing the geography classroom

INTRODUCTION

The key to good management and organization within the geography classroom lies in effective planning. It is rare, although not unknown, for a 'good lesson' to result from the teacher entering the classroom unprepared, without any procedure for the lesson clearly planned out beforehand. However, there is substantial evidence to suggest that poor teaching is often linked to inadequate planning. Experienced teachers who know their students well, who have built a rapport with them over time and who have a good understanding of the resources within their geography department may give the impression that they can successfully teach lessons that have barely been planned at all. Nonetheless these teachers bring to the classroom pedagogic and subject-related experience which the trainee has little knowledge of and certainly will not yet possess at the start of their initial teacher training. Lesson planning takes time and a range of skills that all trainee teachers need to master quickly within their period of training.

1 WHAT FACTORS NEED TO BE TAKEN INTO ACCOUNT IN EFFECTIVE PLANNING?

A number of things need to be considered in the planning process. Some of these are obvious and straightforward, others are more complex or may only apply within the first few lessons that you teach each group. Let us consider a preliminary list of the questions that might need to be taken into account:

- What is the scheme of work that the children are following?

- What has been taught and learnt in the previous lesson(s)?

- What do you want the students to learn in the lesson you are planning (and in future lessons)?

- How will your lesson plan facilitate learning?

- What resources will you need? What activities will the students undertake?

- How will you know what the students have learnt (assessment)?

- How will you know how effective the lesson has been from your perspective as the teacher and the students' perspective as learners (evaluation)?

- What action will you need to take in future lessons to ensure that effective learning is taking place?

In essence, these questions break down into considerations of the *purpose* of the lesson (the aims, objectives and expected learning outcomes), the *substance* of the lesson (the geographical knowledge, understanding and skills), the *methods* of the lesson (the strategies employed to ensure learning) and the *evaluation* of the lesson (of student learning and teacher teaching).

This list of questions is also underpinned by an even broader range of considerations that may be phrased as questions: how do students learn in geography? what are the best ways to match one's teaching to the different 'abilities' of student? what are the most appropriate forms of assessment in the classroom? Although these questions may not be directly 'answerable' for each specific learning event in every lesson you will need to appreciate why such generic questions are important.

1.1 Lesson planning

As a beginning teacher you will be given fairly clear guidelines as to the geographical content you are expected to teach. This content, and to an extent the teaching methods and assessment of learning, will have been outlined for you in a variety of ways. In general the geography curriculum taught within schools is determined externally – for example at Key Stage 3 all students must follow a programme of study in geography related to the Geography National Curriculum. Those students who later opt for geography will follow a GCSE syllabus designed by an examination board/awarding body and then a specification for A/AS level after the age of 16. However, the interpretation of these curriculum documents and specifications is a matter of professional judgement within the geography department and by individual teachers. Some schools interpret the content of the curriculum 'closely' and have detailed schemes of work that all geography teachers must follow; others interpret it 'loosely' and leave the interpretation of the curriculum to the individual teacher, having established its broad parameters. Schemes of work usually cover the entire programme of geography teaching and are often broken down into half-term units.

The methods by which teachers actually teach their lessons are not usually closely defined either by the curriculum, specification or departmental diktat. It is therefore the professional responsibility of each teacher to apply the methods which both personally suit their teaching style and also take account of the ways in which students learn. We know that students have different preferred learning styles – this implies that teachers should adopt a variety of teaching methods. An essential part of the process of learning how to teach involves experimenting and evaluating a range of teaching strategies and approaches from the perspective of the learner.

A lesson plan is a relatively concise document which outlines the teaching and learning that will be conducted within a single lesson. It is a practical working document which should be used within the lesson as an aide memoire and which can follow a standard format, often reproduced within departments as a pro forma.

The lesson plan should 'fit' within the broader scheme of work and be written in such a way that it is clear to another teacher (or observer) what is intended within the lesson – the plan should be 'teachable' by another teacher; also it should be possible for another teacher to watch your lesson and then construct a similar plan simply by observing what happened at different times in the lesson! A lesson plan is not a script to be read out (although it may contain appended notes on the geographical content of the lesson) and should not be followed slavishly if events within the classroom mean that a change in direction for teacher and learners is advisable and justifiable on educational grounds. Moving from one learning activity to the next before the first activity is finished properly, and just because the lesson you have planned states that after ten minutes a change of activity is due, is not good teaching. (Although grossly misjudging the amount of time an activity takes is similarly not good planning!)

A variety of suggestions for lesson plan formats are given below (Figure 6.1). The exact form of the lesson plan you adopt is very much a personal choice, however note that all lesson plans contain similar common elements – such as aims, learning objectives, teaching and learning activities, timings, assessment and evaluation. It is most important that you are clear about what the students should know, understand and be able to do as a result of your planned lesson being taught. Considering which activities students will engage in to achieve this learning is obviously a key to the planning process. In many lessons it will be possible to share the learning objectives, expected outcomes and criteria for success with the students. In this way students will be able to take some responsibility for their learning and will not be entirely reliant on you for guidance and success.

Each of the lesson plans has a range of 'features' that can be briefly explained as follows:

- *Aims* – the overall purpose of the lesson, a broad statement of educational intentions (in geography) usually more general than the learning objectives.

- *Learning objectives* – specific goals or purposes to be achieved, targets for students' learning in this lesson. Objectives help to narrow down the aims of the scheme of work or syllabus/specifications into a more workable form.

- *Subject content* – determined by the GNC, GCSE or A/AS level followed, but mediated through departmental schemes and units of work. Importantly, the *mode* of delivery of this content is a professional choice for the teacher.

- *Learning activities* – a sequence of 'phases for learning' in the lesson, from beginning to end. Statements of learning activities imply making a choice of the most effective ways in which you think the group will learn – such activities should be designed to deliver the previously stated learning objectives.

  Learning activities can be either 'student-centred' or 'teacher-centred', but should be designed to engage and motivate the students, and to have challenge and pace. A variety of supporting strategies can be employed related to these activities: to introduce the lesson, 'hook' students, encourage a sound working atmosphere, conclude activities, and problem solve. The activities must be differentiated according to the needs of the students in the group (see O'Brien and Guiney, 2001). It should be remembered that for any learning activity the teacher will need to introduce the task, ensure that all students understand the task and can cope with it, clarify and explain the resources to

LESSON PLAN 'A'

Lesson Plan

Day/period   Year group

Aim of lesson

Objectives

Unit of work

Resources

Methods/procedures
(timings)

Homework

Evaluation

Continued

LESSON PLAN 'B'

Lesson Plan	
Day/period	Year group
Aim of lesson	
Objectives	
Unit of work	
Resources	
Methods/procedures (timings)	
Teacher activities	*Pupil activities*
Homework	
Evaluation	

Continued

81

LESSON PLAN 'C'

Lesson Plan

Day/period   Year group

Aim of lesson

Objectives   (1) Geographical ideas
                    (2) Geographical skills
                    (3) Values and attitudes

Geographical content

Unit of work

Equipment and resources

Methods/procedures
(timings)

Teacher activities   *Pupil activities*

Homework

Evaluation

Continued

LESSON PLAN 'D'

Date_____Lesson_____Time_____Class_____Room_____

Title of Lesson

Lessons aims

Learning objectives and enquiry questions

Subject content: National Curriculum/ syllabus links	Cross-curricular links/themes/ competences

Resources	Advance preparation (room and equipment)

Differentiation	Action points

Learning activities/tasks	Time	Teaching strategies/actions

Learning activities/tasks	Time	Teaching strategies/actions

Continued

Assessment opportunities, objectives and evidence	
Evaluation of learning	Evaluation of teaching
Action points	

Figure 6.1 *Examples of different lesson plan formats ((a), (b), (c) Butt, 2000a; (d) Lambert and Balderstone, 2000)*

be used, and introduce any new vocabulary. At the end of the activity/lesson there should be a review of what has been learnt, target setting, and a clarification of links forward to the next lesson(s) and future learning.

- *Assessment* – consideration of the assessment of students' learning is integral to the planning of effective lessons. Assessment may be both formal (through set work, exercises, outcomes of activities, oral questions and answers, testing) and informal (general monitoring of students' progress, working atmosphere in the lesson, discussion with students).

- *Evaluation* (see Figure 6.2) – a critical reflection on both your teaching and your students' learning. Evaluation is an essential tool in the process of learning to teach and helps to solve problems faced within the classroom. A lesson evaluation is not merely a *descriptive* account of class management or events that happened in the lesson, rather a means of *analysing/problem solving* the ways forward for future teaching and learning. All aspects of the lesson planned and taught should be evaluated (including the geographical content of the lesson) and improvements sought through the establishment of a set of constructive targets. Lesson evaluations are central to any teachers' professional development.

On some lesson plans you may wish to detail wider aspects of the students' education that you seek to promote *through* geography. For example this might include a particular aspect of literacy or numeracy, PSHE, citizenship or a cross-curricular theme. Additionally you may have appended some notes on geographical

1. Aims	• Were the aims of your lesson wholly or partly achieved? • Did you manage to cover the content of the lesson? • Could pupils understand and use the geographical knowledge/skills you introduced? • What do you think they have actually learnt? • What did any assessment show?
2. Methods	Did you have success with the various methods you used? • question and answer technique • visuals and OHP • pair work, group work • games, role plays, simulations • differentiation • teacher-led sessions.
3. Management	• Was the start and finish of the lesson orderly? • Was the change of activities orderly? • Were pupils organized into effective learning (groups)? • Were your instructions clear? • Did you cope with interruptions? • Did you create a good learning atmosphere? • Was prior preparation of resources sufficient?
4. Control discipline	• Type and use of reward/praise (smile, look, encouragement). • Type and use of censure (look, talk, action). • Tone and approach adopted towards class and individuals.
5. Resources	• Use of board, textbooks, worksheets, maps, atlases, OHP, ICT, etc. • Were these resources used effectively?
6. Follow up	• What should be planned next? • Should the content be covered again in a different way, or should you teach something new? • Marking of books and feedback? • Specific targets for next lesson?

Figure 6.2   *Some ideas for themes for lesson evaluation*

content; indications about groupings; ability ranges; and differentiation of activities. These will be of use to you, or to a support teacher or an observer if they are present.

It is worthwhile remembering that a lesson plan which, when taught, produces a 'buzzing' classroom of intense student activity may not actually represent an *effective* plan – for it may have resulted in a lesson in which the students were not actually learning anything. For example, if the students are told to colour in maps of South America for 70 minutes the result will probably be industrious and focused activity; but very little geography will have been taught or learnt during this lesson! One would have to question the aims and learning objectives planned for such a lesson.

Not all the learning outcomes that result from your lessons will be planned. At times unplanned outcomes of discussion work, or a phase of oral 'question and answer', will show that valuable learning can be unpredictable – particularly if it is heavily student-centred, has an enquiry route where the end-point is not fixed in advance, or has a strong element of open decision making. Such guided, rather than planned, learning has a major role in geography education which links back to the geography curriculum development projects in the 1970s and 1980s such as GYSL, Bristol Project and Geography 16–19. Here lesson plans may focus more heavily on key questions as opposed to learning objectives, recognizing that a fixed 'end-point' may not be predictable but that a guided sequence of enquiry (or 'route to enquiry') can be planned, along with teaching and learning strategies and resources.

Practical activity 6.1

Plan a series of lessons for different ages and abilities of students. Use the geography department's scheme of work as a guide to geographical content and activities.

Discuss these lesson plans with your mentor or tutor before you teach the lessons. If possible ensure that these lessons are observed.

Evaluate the lessons when you have taught them.

2 | CLASSROOM MANAGEMENT

It is not the purpose of this book to exhaustively detail aspects of classroom management for the teacher of geography as many excellent references already exist which take this as one of their major themes (Kyriacou, 1986, 1995; Cohen *et al.*, 1996; Capel *et al.*, 1999). Most of the techniques of class management are generic in that they apply equally to teachers of all subjects, although certain teaching situations in geography are in some ways unique and require particular management techniques to be applied. An example of this would be fieldwork and the management of residential fieldstudy courses.

Nonetheless it is worth stating some of the basic aspects of class management that most beginning teachers need to consider.

2.1 Lesson beginnings

The start of a lesson is most important. It is the period when students decide whether they are being offered a valuable educational experience that they will engage with, or whether they will reluctantly endure the next 70 minutes! A variety of things convey an impression of whether the lesson will be useful (from the students' perspective) and how far you have the confidence and authority necessary to teach the lesson:

- If possible, arrive in the classroom before the start of the lesson. Put the aim of the lesson on the board, organize whatever teaching resources or technology you will use, check the classroom layout and make sure you have everything you need 'to hand'.

- Greet the students at the door, either line them up and organize an orderly entrance to the classroom or supervise their entry with reminders to sit down quickly, get coats off, take out exercise books, etc.

- When the majority of students are in the classroom settle them down, get them to look to the front (try to get eye contact and scan the classroom) and to put down any pens, pencils or books they may be distracted by. Try to ensure complete silence before you 'start' the lesson – expect it, ask for it, wait for it. Students must not be talking and should be listening. A register is often taken at this point which also helps to establish control.

- Be clear about the aims of the lesson. Students perform best when they understand both the purpose of the lesson and your expectations of how they should behave and perform (academically and behaviourally) within your classroom. Problems often occur if students are unclear about what they have to do, how they should do it and what will happen if they don't! Lessons should be given a context – what did you do last lesson? What you are going to do this lesson? What will this lead onto and why is this important in geography?

- Try to learn and refer to pupils by name (a seating plan will help). Some names you will learn very quickly (perhaps for obvious reasons!) – class management is much easier once you can directly refer to an individual student by name rather than offering vague comments to a group of students.

- Be clear and concise when giving instructions about activities you want the students to undertake.

2.2 Transitions within lessons

- Once the lesson is underway and the students are [say] engaged in an activity, move around the classroom and support individuals/groups in their learning activities. The pace of the lesson should be brisk and purposeful, but not at the expense of less able students' learning. Scan the classroom the whole time to spot potential problems. Act confidently if problems occur – you do not have a lot of thinking time in many situations but will soon develop an ability to 'think on your feet' and predict where problems might arise (and how to cope with them).

- When you wish to change an activity be clear about how students should carry out the new activity and how long it will take. Stop students working and get them to look towards you, with pens down and listening. Establish silence before you explain what you want the students to do. Do not be in too much of a hurry to move on – it is essential that students understand what they should do for the next x minutes and how they should do it. It is often best to run through an 'example' with the whole class to check that they all understand what they have to do. You do not want to spend ages going around to individual students dealing with the same problems time and again because you failed to explain the task clearly enough to the whole class.

- Reinforce your classroom 'rules'. Be clear and consistent about procedures for giving out and taking back equipment, about when students are allowed to talk, about the levels of noise you will accept during discussion work, about moving around the classroom, etc. If you are sensibly consistent and reasonable students will also learn these rules and adhere to them, although some groups will require more reminders than others!

- Use you voice to help maintain control and management. Don't shout. Always aim to have silence when you talk. Remind students of this. When teaching use the full range of your voice to make what you say interesting and stimulating to listen to – vary the tone, loudness, pitch, inflection and pace of speech to give it interest.

- While students are working move around the class. Offer help if you see problems occurring, monitor what is going on, move towards trouble spots, catch students doing the 'right thing' as well as the 'wrong thing' and praise them for it! Aim to be as positive as possible in your class management.

- When you think that the time you have given pupils to complete an activity has come to an end scan the classroom. Consider whether a little more time is still needed to get the whole class (or a very substantial number of students) to the end of what they are doing. Be flexible, but consider whether your timings need to be altered for similar activities in future lessons. Do not let activities 'drag on', keep the pace of the lesson brisk.

2.3 Lesson endings

- Be aware of the amount of time you will need to gather resources back in from the students. This is a particular issue if large numbers of resources are being used, if students are in groups, if furniture needs rearranging before the next lesson or if the students have been engaged in role plays. The end of the lesson should be slick and orderly.

- The lesson must have a complete and tangible ending, just as it has a definite beginning. The end of a lesson will probably encapsulate the students' views of their learning experience with you in geography – ensure that they go away with a positive impression of what they have achieved and how they have worked. Yours is just one of a range of curricular experiences students have each day, you want them to think it is something special.

- Recap on the students' achievements, set homework and ensure students have recorded this. Inform the students of what they are leading on to in the next lesson.

- Dismiss the students in an orderly manner – there should be no rushing, no fighting to get to the door first, no noisy disruption.

3 | ESTABLISHING A MANAGEMENT ROUTINE

It is important to quickly establish a set management routine for the classroom which is understood and adhered to by all the students. This will take longer with certain groups than others! However, the students you teach will be used to other teachers' standards for classroom behaviour and will be sophisticated in their understanding of what will be allowed in each teacher's classroom. It is important that students have clear ideas about what will happen if they behave in certain ways – consistency and fairness of teacher response in given situations is essential to establishing a routine. Students expect you to have rules – about how they should work, when they are allowed to talk (and about what!), whether free movement is allowed around the classroom, about how they enter and leave the classroom, about oral question and answer sessions. It is wise to observe how other teachers approach these routines and to make some decisions about what rules you wish to establish before you teach each group of children.

3.1 'Prevention is better than cure'

Experienced teachers become well practiced in judging when teaching situations may become difficult to manage and when preventative action may be needed. Often they will act on an almost subconscious 'impulse' which has resulted from a particular behaviour exhibited by certain students, or an impression about the ways in which the whole group of students is working. This is, of course, difficult to quantify and hard to convey to the beginning teacher! Anticipating problems and acting quickly and effectively to defuse them is a skill that develops with time.

Practical activity 6.2

With the permission of the member of staff involved, observe a series of geography lessons taught by an experienced teacher.

Consider the ways in which he or she deals with aspects of classroom management, beginning and ending of lessons, and transitions between different activities. What rules, routines and standards have been established for the class? Are there any set expectations about behaviour and working practices that are clearly apparent?

4 | COMMON PROBLEMS

Good teachers get used to 'expecting the unexpected' and then being able to deal with situations calmly and in a confident manner. Various incidents will affect the delivery of your lesson as planned, however many of these incidents will be predictable. The teacher is therefore able to consider what his or her response will be *before* the event. Dealing with such problems in such a way that the learning of the whole class is not affected more than is absolutely necessary is a sign of effective class management. For all other unexpected or bizarre occurrences you will have to think on your feet!

Below are a number of common problems that occur within geography classes and suggested responses for the beginning teacher:

4.1 Talking out of turn

This is the main problem that teachers face on a daily basis as identified by the Elton Report (DES, 1989). It is generally not the occasional 'big confrontations' with students that provide most stress for teachers, but the continual low order disruption that some students create by constantly talking out of turn.

What forms can this disruption take?

This can vary from virtually all the students talking at some time when you are trying to address the whole class or individuals; students taking any 'gap' in the lesson as a cue to talk; students talking about things other than the activities they have been set to discuss; students shouting out answers rather than putting their hands up; or interruptions to your exposition to the class.

How can this be addressed?

Repeat your class rules for communication: no talking when I'm talking; wait to be asked before you answer a question and always put your hand up; reminders of the task to be completed; a 'quiet word' with main offenders; waiting for silence and reinforcing when that silence is achieved the standards of classroom behaviour you expect; praising students when they get it right! In extreme circumstances it may be best to start chatty groups on low order work which they can easily do without too much fuss and then use the resultant quiet to establish your platform for teaching. Non verbal communication is also very important in stopping students talking out of turn – for example gaining eye contact with students who are talking when you are; pointing or clicking fingers in their direction; moving over to the area where talking is occurring as you continue to teach. The main aim is not to break the 'flow' of your lesson – to stop the talking with the minimum disruption to the lesson and the learning of others.

If only one or two students are the main problem get the rest of the class working and then deal with them directly. A quietly assertive word – rather than an aggressive shout which disrupts all the students and may show that you have lost your temper and control – is the best way to deal with this. Don't be put off by distracting comments from students about the work being 'boring'; show students that they are capable of doing the work and that you fully expect them to complete it to a high standard under your support and guidance. If there are persistent offenders talk to other staff who teach them for advice.

4.2 Movement around the classroom

What forms can this disruption take?

Usually student movement around the class may have a 'legitimate' reason to justify it – a student needs to borrow an eraser, or to get a book from another student, or to get a set of colouring pencils, and so on – but may also be used as an opportunity for students to meet and chat. Movement can actually hinder other students' performance (as well as the performance of the person moving) and can create extreme management problems.

How can this be addressed?

The best way to regulate, or stop, unwarranted movement is to establish a rule that no-one should be out of their seat without your permission. The reason for movement should always be sanctioned by you. On the first occasion that a student gets up to move they should be asked why they want to move, be reminded of your rules and have whatever item they need taken to them (by you). It is a little more laborious for you to pass materials to students, but actually this is a better way of managing out of seat occurrences which may escalate (think of what would happen if all 32 students got up to move in your class at the same time!).

4.3 Swearing

What forms can this disruption take?

It is now unfortunately a fact of life that swearing is reasonably commonplace in many schools. In point of fact it probably always has been and certain students will regularly punctuate their discussions with swear words. Most students are very aware that it is considered unacceptable to swear in front of teachers and will be 'skilled' in moderating their language whilst in the classroom. However, beyond the teacher's hearing a considerable amount of swearing goes on in most schools!

How can this be addressed?

The major issue is whether the swearing is 'accidental' – an oath which has just slipped out and which the teacher might gently rebuke and correct – or whether it has been aggressively targeted at an individual such as yourself, or another pupil. If it is obvious to others that you have heard the swearing you must take action. It must be assertively pointed out that you will not tolerate swearing in your classroom. If you are sworn at by a student this is a major incident for which a sincere apology should be sought and further action taken by yourself, the regular class teacher, the students' tutor or a member of the senior management team in the school.

A problem can occur as to the definition of what actually constitutes a swearword – for example the words 'crap' and 'bloody' now appear to have gained the status of acceptable terms to be used in the public domain, whereas a decade ago these would have been deemed offensive in many situations. You will have to gather advice from other teachers about what is acceptable in the context of your school and enforce your standards on the groups you teach.

4.4 Calculated idleness

What forms can this disruption take?

Calculated idleness can take numerous forms. Often students claim that they do not have a pen or pencil to write with, have forgotten their exercise book or file, do not have work from a previous lesson that is to be completed in this lesson, or simply do not settle into work.

How can this be addressed?

Always have a supply of basic equipment to loan to students, *but ensure that you know who the equipment has been loaned to and that you get it back at the end of the lesson.* Persistent calculated idleness such as lack of equipment or forgetting exercise books should be punished, having warned the student beforehand of future sanctions if the idleness continues. In some cases it is advisable for you to keep the students' exercise book (if they have no homework) so they cannot lose it from this lesson to the next.

4.5 Personal questions

What forms can this disruption take?

Teachers often get asked personal questions about their background, partner, age, dress, where they live, their views on controversial topics, on incidents in school, on another teacher's sanctions, or methods of teaching. Be extremely careful how you answer these questions as they have a habit of escalating into a series of further questions! It is very easy to get drawn into situations you would never have thought you would find yourself in and any information given in innocence may be turned against you in another situation. Some enquiries from students are genuine, inquisitive and offered in a spirit of 'getting to know you' as their new teacher; others may have been asked through rather darker motives. Often such questions are an attempt to get you 'off track' and are a form of time wasting.

How can this be addressed?

Seek to deflect the questions, or merely refuse to answer saying 'I would never ask you something like that!' following up with a comment that the question asked has nothing to do with the geography the students are studying. Often a jokey response will be enough to dissuade further questioning. Some teachers say they will answer students' questions at the end of the lesson and then either conveniently forget to do so, or have other more pressing things to do when the bell goes! An explanation of why a particular question is an unreasonable thing to ask of a teacher may also be useful.

4.6 Rapid completion of work

What forms can this disruption take?

Although not specifically a student-initiated disruption, as the examples above are, the rapid completion of set work – leaving the teacher with a vacuum to fill in the second half of the lesson – can present problems. The issue is largely one of planning of timing for the lesson and its activities, although there may also be considerations as to whether the work that has been completed quickly has been finished to the standards you would wish.

How can this be addressed?

Reflect on your lesson plan and re-orientate your timings for similar groups who will attempt these activities. Also think about the instructions you give to students about how they should complete their work and the standards you expect. Is the work too easy? Should it be differentiated for certain students? Is the work the students have completed acceptable? Are the tasks 'pitched' at the right level for this group of students?

If a 'gap' appears in your lesson that you had not expected there are some short-term methods by which it might be filled:

- Ask extension questions on the theme of the lesson to be answered orally and/or in written form.

- Revise the main theme of the lesson to check understandings; rely on the students to tell *you* rather than you repeating the lesson's content.

- Set the scene for the next lesson; reveal the continuity and progression in the theme for the students.

- Set up small discussion groups among the students on one or two key questions or concepts you have taught.

- Have a 'generic' worksheet [or extension questions] available for the particular unit of work that might be used in any lesson.

- Ask students to devise questions on the theme. Use this as a way of finding out areas that the students are not yet fully confident about and start the next lesson from where the students 'are at'.

- Discuss the homework they have been set for the lesson.

4.7   Too much work planned

What forms can this disruption take?

Often if students feel that they have to complete tasks that are too challenging, either in terms of the amount of work they are asked to do in a given time or the intellectual demands of the work, they will lose motivation and disrupt. This is a problem that is easily exacerbated by simply having too much work planned for a lesson and attempting to get through it all too quickly.

How can this be addressed?

Essentially it is within the teacher's professional judgement as to whether the work that has been planned for a lesson is either too great, or too demanding. It is wrong to 'undersell' a lesson – that is, by making the activities too simple or unchallenging to ensure that both the teacher and students have a relatively easy time of the teaching and learning process. However, it should not be the case that every minute of the lesson should be spent in exhausting intellectual struggle and a race against the clock! Getting the balance right is important.

Sometimes the solution to the problem of planning too much work is very straightforward – simply plan less work and have a more realistic, but honest, appraisal of what students are capable of doing within each lesson. It is a natural reaction to 'overplan' lessons at the start of one's career, through fear of running out of material.

4.8   Requests to leave the classroom

What forms can this disruption take?

Some students will regularly attempt to leave your classroom for whatever reasons (requests to go to the toilet, claims that items of personal equipment have been left in a previous lesson, statement that another member of staff wishes to see them urgently, etc.). Such requests may be made at any point within the lesson.

How can this be addressed?

Most schools have set procedures to deal with such requests, as absence from the classroom during lesson times is unsupervised and therefore outside the direct control of the teacher. Often students must take with them an 'absence slip' that has been signed and dated/time recorded by the teacher such that if they are stopped outside the lesson they have verifiable evidence for their absence.

Students 'know the rules' about requesting to leave the classroom and often try to push these parameters with new staff. It is worthwhile, at the time of the first request from a student in a particular group to be released, making clear to the *whole* class what your/the school's rules are. Be firm – if a student must leave the classroom give them a reasonable time limit for their absence and make sure they know you have registered what time they have returned and whether this is acceptable or not.

5 | AVOIDING, OR DEALING WITH, CONFRONTATIONS

Confrontations between yourself and students will occur. Nonetheless, if possible, avoid confrontations as they only serve to sour relationships between you and your students. Achieving an acceptable 'balance' is important – do not allow yourself to be gradually pushed into a weaker and weaker position by not 'standing your ground' when particular situations warrant a firm response, but don't overreact. The aim is to manage the classroom positively, not through confrontation but through praise and gentle assertion.

It is important to be clear about your rules and standards for the classroom. Do not compromise on these, as it is only possible for you to be 'firm yet fair' if these rules are conveyed to students and are consistently observed. Needless to say, your rules should be reasonable and realistic. Think about class management scenarios before they happen – consider a number of 'what ifs?' and plan how you will react to these in given situations. It is very easy, when under pressure and trying to cope, to over react to a relatively minor offence and thereby generate an unhelpful confrontation. Always try to stay calm and in control.

If a major confrontation occurs in the classroom you will need to think rapidly about how you can resolve the problem swiftly, without losing 'face' and with the least disruption to the learning of the rest of the class. Often the student at the centre of the confrontation will be looking to play to an audience – deny them this audience either by not reacting, by talking to them quietly 'one to one', or by removing them from the classroom before you talk to them. Be clear and firm about your reasons for disagreeing with the student – be assertive, not aggressive. Try not to lose your temper as this invariably means a loss of control and dignity. The message this sends to the rest of the class is not positive.

In very extreme confrontations (a student becoming verbally abusive, aggressive, violent, threatening) ask the student to leave the classroom, or if they attempt to leave do not stand in their way! Seek help from another member of staff – you could send another student to request this – do not leave your class unsupervised. Once you have an opportunity, talk to the disruptive student. Remain quiet and calm, let the student do most of the talking. If the reaction from the student has originally been extreme there must be a strong reason for this – it is usually not productive to simply 'lay down the law' in these situations, you have to be more subtle in getting to the heart of the problem.

During a confrontation always look for acceptable 'ways out' – to bring the confrontation to a swift conclusion, but without losing respect. Often you will need to be skilled in also giving the student a possible 'way out' from the confrontational situation they have found themselves in, such that they do not lose respect from the rest of the class, or you. To be aggressive and overly dominant within a confrontation, which you subsequently 'win', will ultimately be damaging to your long-term relationships with the student. Once the confrontation is over think carefully about how and why it occurred – and how you can avoid a similar situation occurring again in the future!

CONCLUSION

Managing and organizing geography classrooms is rarely straightforward. It is the one activity that most trainee teachers are nervous of when they begin teaching – 'will I be able to control the class?' In by far the majority of cases trainees *do* achieve the necessary skills and techniques to manage classes within their period of initial training. This is not to say that once learnt these skills merely have to be applied in the same way to every class to be successful; many experienced teachers still face challenges and new demands within the classroom on a daily basis.

Good management is clearly achieved through sound preparation. In essence, the teacher is always attempting to reduce the number of 'unknown variables' that might occur within his or her geography lesson – if the lesson is well planned and organizationally 'tight' these variables are greatly reduced. Therefore if something untoward occurs, such as an unexpected confrontation with a student, the teacher can give this incident their full attention safe in the knowledge that other aspects of the lesson (the learning activities, resources, timing, assessment) are all carefully planned and running smoothly.

CHAPTER 7

Geographical enquiry: *the* route to learning?

> Learning is not simply a matter of somehow absorbing discrete facts and principles. Most of what we learn is learned through the framework of what we already know.
>
> (Leat, 2000, p. 139)

> Many lessons in geography and other subjects are parodies of what learning should look like: they are more concerned with teaching than learning.
>
> (Leat and Kinninment, 2000, p. 152)

INTRODUCTION

Consideration of the processes by which students learn geography should be fundamental to any exploration of pedagogy within the subject. This chapter therefore seeks to address the ways in which we think such learning takes place, the differentiation of learning activities to take account of the variation in students' learning abilities and their preferred learning styles, and the use of enquiry learning techniques in geography education. Space is also given to describe activities in geography education which may develop 'thinking skills' within students.

The title of the chapter – 'Geographical enquiry: *the* route to learning?' – has not been chosen casually, and the question mark is significant. There are a wide variety of ways in which we learn, or in which we *prefer* to learn. Some of these 'ways of learning' have recently attracted considerable attention in geography education and have heavily influenced current pedagogical approaches, whilst others have gradually become discarded or discredited. Undoubtedly the 'route to enquiry' approach, introduced in the late 1970s with the Geography 16–19 Project, provides a stimulating, student-centred way of teaching and learning geography highlighting the importance of adopting structured ways of understanding issues. By focusing on questioning, decision-making and challenging students' values and attitudes the enquiry approach has been a significant influence on curriculum development in geography over the past 25 years. However, it does not represent the only way in which geography can be learnt and geography teachers have very different ideas about the types of pedagogy associated with enquiry (see Roberts, 1998b; Davidson and Catling, 2000). The enquiry approach does not always constitute the best way for *all* students to learn geography, particularly if applied in an uncritical or unsystematic manner. •

1 | HOW DO STUDENTS LEARN GEOGRAPHY?

Considerable research has attempted to answer the question 'how do children learn?'. Whether we will ever discover the answer(s) to this question for each of the students we teach is a moot point given the range of preferred learning styles that exist, nonetheless we do have some theories about the main ways in which children learn (see Figure 7.1). Students' abilities to think and learn develop as they mature and gain experience of different environments, stimuli and learning situations. Most learning theories visualize students passing through a series of developmental stages towards intellectual maturity. Significantly if one attempts to teach students to perform tasks that are beyond their current stage of intellectual development – such as trying to get them to grasp an abstract concept or theory, when what they actually require is a concrete example to aid their understanding – the teaching and learning process will fail. The various theories of learning have been explored within the context of geography education (see Gerber, 1984), but it is not possible to consider each of these theories in depth within the space available here.

What these theories of learning also demonstrate is that one's ability to learn geography is determined not only by intelligence, but also by motivation, interest and the teaching experience we have been exposed to. None of these variables is fixed – they can be changed to stimulate and accelerate the learning process, or vice versa. What is clear is that teacher planning, and the learning objectives outlined for different abilities of students within the geography classroom, are fundamental to the learning that will occur. The role of assessment of learning in this process is also significant (see Chapter 9).

Learning can be classified, or rather described, in different ways. As geography teachers we will be concerned with planning learning objectives for each lesson – but these objectives might be expressed in the form of a particular learning *outcome*, or as a learning *process*. At times it may be difficult to differentiate between the outcome, and the process of learning (to borrow an aphorism the 'medium is the message' in some learning situations) and it may be easier to characterize the learning event by posing a series of key questions.

Figure 7.2 below attempts to bring together a variety of teacher and learner characteristics and show how they may influence both the process and outcome of learning for students. When applied to different teachers and students, within a variety of contexts, we can see that the prediction of educational results is neither simple nor straightforward.

1.1 Learning styles

An individual's learning style is the preference he or she has for a particular way of learning, usually resulting from their previous learning experiences, personality and the environment in which they learn best. Because of their personal nature, and the fact that one's preferred learning style may alter over time or with respect to the subject matter being learnt, defining such styles is sometimes problematic. The study of geography is often assumed to accommodate a variety of learning styles due to the diverse nature of its subject content and the range of skills required of the learner. The most effective learners appear to be able to understand and apply a range of different learning styles, or strategies, to different situations.

Cognitive Developmental Theory (CD)	Social Constructivist Theory (SC)	Information-Processing Theory (IP)
All children pass through a series of stages before they construct the ability to perceive, reason and understand in mature, rational terms.	Share some important areas of agreement with Piagetian theory, particularly activity as the basis for learning and for the development of thinking.	Develops elements of CD (sequences, activity) and SC theory (experience) but emphasizes cognitive strategies rather than structures.

Central Aspects

Cognitive Developmental Theory (CD)	Social Constructivist Theory (SC)	Information-Processing Theory (IP)
1. Children's thinking is different in kind from that of more mature individuals.	1. Relationships between talking and thinking.	1. Fundamental processes and strategies underlie all cognitive activity.
2. All children develop through the same sequence of stages before achieving mature rational thought.	2. Role of communication, social interaction and instruction in scaffolding thinking and cognitive development is crucial.	2. Brain's systematic processes of perception, memory and problem-solving process information in the short-term memory and store it as abstractions in the long-term memory.
3. Structures of children's thinking at each stage are distinctive, i.e. the same for all children at the same stage and differ from the children and adults at other stages.	3. Learning involves search for patterns, regularities and predictability (Bruner).	3. Processes are the same for all individuals but speed and efficiency vary from learner to learner.
4. Development is not a continuous accumulation of things learnt step by step but 'intellectual' revolutions are marked by a change in structure of intelligence.	4. 'Zone of proximal development' (Vygotsky) is the gap that exists for an individual between what she can do on her own and what she can achieve with help from a more knowledgeable or skilled person.	4. Cognitive development is the process of learning more and more helpful strategies of analysing, remembering and problem solving.
5. Active, experimental learning encouraged.	5. 'Guided discovery' learning is encouraged.	5. Concrete examples and experiences are important in developing abstractions. Instruction important in strategy development.

Figure 7.1 *Three of the major theories of learning (Butt, 2000a)*

A variety of definitions of learning styles exist. It is doubtful that we could ever accurately categorize learners into watertight classifications using such definitions, as most people will be able to apply some aspect of each style to different learning situations. However these definitions do represent an interesting attempt to outline

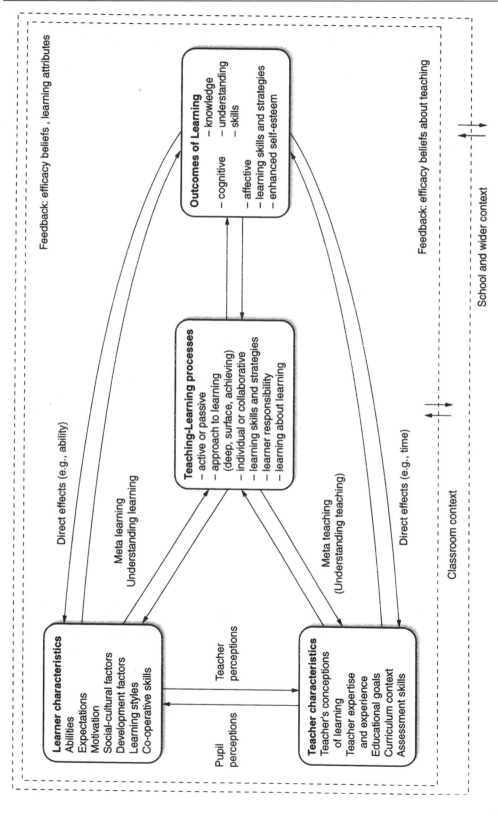

Figure 7.2 *A model of learning in school (Lambert and Balderstone, 2000)*

Accommodators (dynamic learners)	**Divergers** (imaginative learners)
• independent and creative • likes taking risks and change • enjoys and adapts well to new situations • curious and investigative • inventive, experiments • shows initiative • problem solvers • involves other people • gets others' opinions, feelings • can be impulsive, 'rushes in' • uses 'trial and error' and gut reaction • relies on support network	• imaginative and creative • flexible, sees lots of alternatives • colourful (uses fantasy) • uses insight • good at imagining oneself in new/ different situations • unhurried, casual and friendly • avoids conflict • listens to others and shares ideas with a small number of people • uses all senses to interpret • listens, observes, asks questions • sensitive and emotional, deep feelings • cannot be rushed until ready
Convergers (common-sense learners)	**Assimilators** (analytic learners)
• organized, ordered and structured • practical, 'hands-on' • detailed and accurate • applies ideas to solving problems • learns by testing out new situations and assessing the result • makes theories useful • uses reasoning to meet goals • has good detective skills, 'search and solve' • likes to be in control of the situation • acts independently then gets feedback • uses factual data and theories	• logical and structured • intellectual, academic • enjoys reading and researching • evaluative, good synthesizer • thinker and debater • precise, thorough, careful • organized, likes to follow a plan • likes to place experience in a theoretical context • looks for past experiences from which to extract learning • reacts slowly and wants facts • calculates probabilities • avoids becoming over-emotional • often analyses experience by writing it down

Figure 7.3 *Descriptions of learning styles (Lambert and Balderstone, 2000)*

one's predominant thinking and learning skills. The learning styles adopted by students each have advantages and disadvantages; however they do not form a hierarchy and no single style is 'better' than another. Definitions exist for activist, theorist, reflective and pragmatist styles of learning. Figure 7.3 shows a variation on these divisions – into dynamic, imaginative, analytic and common sense learners.

Geography teachers will need to adopt different teaching strategies to address the variations in preferred learning styles of their students, or may choose to plan their learning activities to promote a range of styles of learning in order to develop the students 'all round' learning abilities.

1.2 Aspects of learning

It is possible to identify particular aspects of learning within geography education which link to intellectual development and the eventual creation of the autonomous learner. A knowledge and understanding of these terms aid lesson and curriculum planning.

- *Abilities* – a wide range of intellectual skills which encompass the learning of principles, concepts and exemplars (see below). The intellectual skills include those of *recall* (or remembering), *comprehension* (or understanding), *problem solving* (which may include application, analysis, synthesis and evaluation), and *creativity* (which involves the use of imagination).

- *Principles* (or *key ideas*) – principles may be formulated by linking together two or more concepts. They form the 'higher level assumptions' (Peters, 1977) that give each subject its structure by bringing together its constituent concepts.

- *Concepts* – a concept is a way of categorizing thoughts into such a form that they are commonly understood, usually by concentrating on the essential attributes of certain experiences. This requires some degree of abstraction from reality. Concepts can be further explained through a series of exemplars. The major concepts of geography have been variously classified as: spatial location, spatial distribution and spatial relations (Catling, 1978); distribution, integration, distance, scale, region and spatial change (Naish, 1982); and planning, development, inequality, systems, classification, location (Leat, 1998). Some believe that concepts can be ordered into hierachies with more 'abstract' concepts at the top and more 'concrete' at the bottom.

- *Exemplars* – examples of something, which can be used to explain particular concepts.

The hierarchical structure of principles, concepts and exemplars has been utilized in the construction of examination specifications and curricula in geography, to which geographical content is then added.

1.3 Spatial cognition and spatial concept development

For geographers a particular type of learning, unique to the discipline of geography, relates to spatial cognition and spatial concept development. This is linked not only to the ways in which we develop our abilities to perceive and understand space, but also to the manner in which we store and relate that information ('mental mapping'). These abilities are often subsumed within the term graphicacy, which is sometimes referred to as one of the four foundations of communication (along with numeracy, literacy and oracy) (see Balchin and Coleman, 1973; Boardman, 1983). Graphicacy covers 'not only the development of map reading skills, but also the interpretation of photographs and other forms of graphic communication' (Marsden, 1995, p. 79).

As children grow they develop their ability to understand the space around them, first through personal physical interaction with that space and then, increasingly, through intellectual perception and conception of space. Spatial concept development can be broken down into a variety of component parts – concerning distance, direction, and the relationship between objects in space – all of which have implications for teaching and learning geography, either through mapwork or fieldwork. By the time students reach secondary schools it is assumed that they have gone through a basic developmental sequence of spatial cognition, enabling them to conceptualize space and distance without the need for concrete examples (see Rhys, 1972). However, the extent to which students appreciate spatial factors – particularly those removed from their personal experience – is extremely variable.

Enabling students to engage in mental mapping exercises is a valuable way of assessing their level of spatial concept development and their basic mapping abilities. By asking students to map from memory an area known to them (their neighbourhood, school, or journey to school) the sophistication of their spatial cognition may be revealed, although as Boardman (1987, 1989) reminds us such maps do not always show the true extent of the students' spatial knowledge and may be restricted by their drawing skills. When compared to 'objective' maps of these areas or routes, either by the students themselves or by the teacher, the extent and accuracy of spatial perception is revealed. Detailed analysis of the ways in which students perceive space, what they perceive, how they chose to represent it, and what is included or left out of the mental maps is possible (see Matthews, 1984; Blades and Spencer, 1988; Boardman, 1986b).

Practical activity 7.1

Ask students of differing abilities at Key Stage 3, GCSE and A/AS level to draw mental maps of their home neighbourhood.

Use a large-scale map to compare these mental maps to a more objective spatial image of the area.

What does this exercise show? What aspects of their neighbourhood space do students consider significant, recognize and record? Where does bias, distortion and subjectivity occur? What does this tell us about variations in students' spatial concept development?

1.4   Concept acquisition and concept mapping

The acquisition of geographical concepts is fundamentally important in the process of learning geography. As Lambert and Balderstone explain:

> If we are aware of the level of difficulty of particular concepts for children's under-standing, and how they come to acquire understanding of these concepts, we might be able to identify and prepare appropriate learning experiences for pupils of different ages and abilities more effectively.
>
> (Lambert and Balderstone, 2000, p. 205)

Leat (1998) believes that enabling students to map out their concepts, or ideas, on any given subject is a very effective way of helping them to learn. Students might be asked to write down, either individually or in groups, a number of points in response to a question or problem (for example 'What issues arise from the increasing use of cars in cities?' or 'What are the effects of attempting to protect the coastline at Barton-on Sea?'). They can be encouraged to link the main points they note down with arrows, either to explain their thoughts more fully or to provide a clearer picture of the geographical processes they believe to be at work. This provides students with a helpful visual record of their current thoughts, with the links acting as organizing connectors which often have the effect of spurring new, or more detailed, ideas. For the student this process makes their knowledge more concrete and opens up deeper understandings, for the teacher the visual record of their thoughts provides a key to the level at which the students are working and an indication of any major misconceptions. As such concept maps may provide helpful differentiated assessments of student knowledge and understanding, as exemplified by the quality of the connections and explanations added. Good concept maps may even push the teacher into making connections between concepts and ideas that he or she may not have previously considered.

1.5   Teaching thinking

The White Paper 'Excellence in Schools' (DfEE, 1997b) acknowledged the increasing importance of teachers being able to 'teach thinking'. It encouraged teachers to embrace:

- accelerated learning, based on the latest understanding of how people learn, which has enabled groups of pupils to progress at greater speed and with deeper understanding;
- the systematic teaching of thinking skills, which research has shown to be strongly associated with positive learning outcomes.

   David Leat has been a prime mover in the promotion of 'thinking skills' in the teaching and learning of geography. Together with a group of geography teachers he has trialled a number of innovative teaching materials designed to accelerate the conceptual learning of students based upon constructivist learning theories. This 'Thinking Through Geography' group, drawing upon previous cognitive acceleration projects (see Adey and Shayer, 1994), has produced a variety of influential publications which seek to share their methods, ideas and research findings (see Leat, 1998; Leat and Nichols, 1999; Nichols, 2001). Central to the process of creating such teaching materials is a focus on how students *learn* (rather than on how teachers *teach*), with geography being seen as a vehicle for learning. The simple acquisition of geographical content is not seen as a particularly worthwhile educational end in itself (see Leat, 2000).

   The overall aim of 'teaching thinking' is to enable students to realize their learning potential and accelerate their intellectual development as they progress towards becoming autonomous learners. In essence this means that teachers must acknowledge that the intelligence of their students can always be developed further and that it is not a fixed, immutable 'given'. Leat's approach is based upon the contention that once teachers believe they can develop their students' intelligences, they begin to concentrate on changing the students' facility to cope with challenging tasks and difficult concepts – rather than simplifying and ameliorating the existing geography curriculum to accord with their perceived limitations.

   A variety of teaching materials and resources devised by the Thinking Through Geography group to accelerate cognitive development are described below.

103

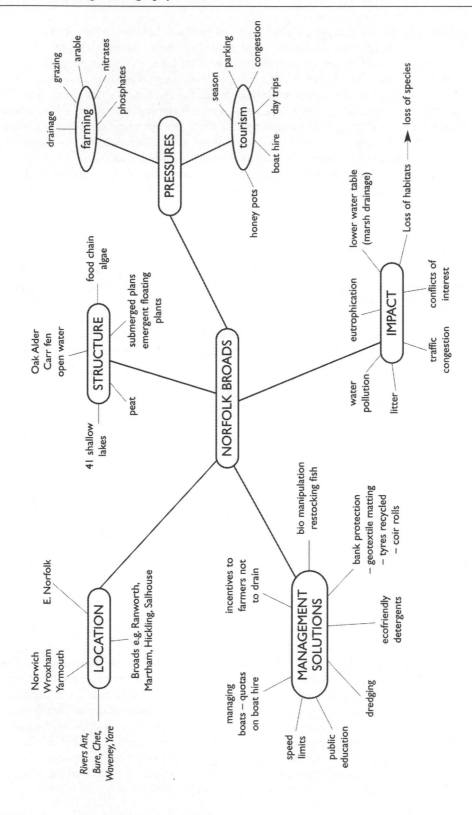

Figure 7.4 *Example of a concept map (taken from a geography department which uses Avery Hill material in a Cardiff school)*

Mysteries'

A mystery is a student-centred task where students 'solve' an open question by working with a number of pieces of data (usually between twelve and 30 cards, each containing information). The information provided on the cards varies – they may contain statistical data, descriptions of an event, pieces of social or economic information, something directly 'geographical', or a distractor of some kind (a 'red herring'). Often the data forms a narrative, which usually helps students to piece together aspects of the mystery to be solved (see McPartland, 2001). Leat and Nichols (1999) have produced research evidence of students' thought processes based upon the ways in which they arrange such cards when attempting to solve a mystery. The patterns of cards produced as students attempt to order, sequence, web, re-work or reject data indicate aspects of thinking which Leat and Nichols (1999) believe teachers can interpret to support students' learning. Giving students the opportunities to talk about their thinking (metacognition) is also believed to be important within the wider learning process.

Leat (2000) identifies a number of 'trigger' and 'background' factors which students use to help them make sense of the data and arrange it into a logical and convincing story. He has also witnessed the ways in which many students will 'go back' to the evidence on the cards to check the reliability of the solution they are proposing. This, with the most capable students, eventually leads to a 'cognitive autonomy' whereby they can deal with complex information, see patterns and connections between data, and choose between a variety of mental models to solve problems. Importantly students are not taught different ways of applying particular reasoning methods and techniques, rather they are allowed to work things out for themselves and share their findings with their peers and the teacher (see Leat and Kinninment, 2000). An example of a mystery is given in Figure 7.5.

Students are asked to respond to the question 'Why did Vicki get clamped?' and to provide a reasoned justification for their answers. They are instructed to lay out the cards in such a way as to help them explain the structure of their answers. Once this activity is completed and debriefed they may be asked supplementary questions such as 'What are the effects of increases in traffic in urban areas?', 'What can be done to reduce traffic in urban areas?' and 'Why are some of the solutions difficult to put into operation?'.

Living Graphs

Living Graphs utilize graphs in ways which help students to understand what they show. Usually the exercises involve students being given a graph and a set of statements (often descriptions of events, or things people have said, or ways in which people are affected by circumstances) which they then have to match to the most appropriate point on the graph. By so doing the students are not being asked merely to 'describe what the graph shows' or carry out a simple data response exercise, but to convey a more detailed understanding of the graph. One of the main points expressed by Leat (1998) is that Living Graphs enable students 'to make connections between the abstraction of the graph on the page and the people and events that lie behind it' (p. 23).

The example of a Living Graph shown here (Figure 7.6) is that of a stage model of tourism. It was used with middle band Year 8 students who had already carried out some work on factors which determine choices of holiday destinations.

1. On Saturday 2 July 1998 Vicki Adams returned to her car to find it being clamped.

2. Raymond voted Labour in the last election but won't next time if he is not going to be allowed to drive his Volvo to work.

3. The government is considering charging supermarkets £100 a year for each parking place they provide.

4. Vicki has a Nissan Micra which costs her less in petrol to use than taking the bus.

5. 'Buzy Buses' have just had their buses painted yellow and black.

6. Vicki parked in a solicitors firm's parking space.

7. Vicki's brother, Mark, was knocked off his bike on his way to work last year.

8. Dennis Wade, the clamper, replied that he was just doing his job, there was no need to be personal.

9. Climate experts are worried that low-lying countries such as Bangladesh will be affeced by the melting of the polar ice caps.

10. Between 1974 and 1996 rail and bus fares have gone up by 50%. The costs of motoring have gone down by 3%.

11. Raymond takes his two daughters to their private school on the way to work.

12. About 10% of school children suffer from asthma.

13. Many people prefer to go to the Metro Centre rather than use their local shops.

14. London requires Heavy Goods Vehicles to have a special licence to use its roads.

15. The value of shares in Stagecoach, the biggest bus company has gone up a lot in recent years.

16. The government is worried about inflation.

17. Vicki had to pay £100 to have the clamp removed.

18. The Minister of Transport is very keen to reduce car use. He is considering letting Councils charge drivers for bringing cars into town.

19. Sheffield's 'Supertrams' have lost the council a lot of money.

20. Vicki does not feel safe walking home or getting public transport late at night.

21. Many parents are worried about letting their children walk to school.

22. Between a quarter and a third of children are overweight.

23. Vicki had been to pick up her wedding dress with Mark. All the car parks were full in town.

24. Raymond Storey, the solicitor, is fed up with people using his parking space. He employs people to clamp illegal parkers.

25. Some experts say that unless new roads are built, traffic jams will soon be blocking some roads all day long.

26. The government plans to introduce 'super' bus lanes.

27. Vicki called the clamper a 'b*****d' and burst into tears.

28. Raymond always plays golf on Saturday.

29. Since bus services were 'de-regulated' by the Conservatives in the 1980s, city centre roads have become even more congested with almost empty buses.

30. Mark held Vicki up by 10 minutes by going to look for a new CD.

Figure 7.5 *Data slips used in the 'Vicki gets clamped' mystery (Leat and Nichols, 1999)*

Statements—Changes in tourism
Task
Put the following statements on the graph:

1.	Carlos, a fisherman, gets up early in order to take his boat out.
2.	Neil gets drunk one night and on the way back is mugged, losing all his money, credit card and his passport.
3.	Durta, a German tourist will not let her son go to get an ice cream because of the extremely busy roads.
4.	Miguel goes out to look for work. Only two years ago he had regular employment for the summer period that allowed him the luxury of not working for the rest of the year.
5.	Mercedes relaxes on an empty beach, after doing her chores, enjoying the afternoon summer sun.
6.	José is an ornithologist who now has to travel miles down the coast to see the birds that used to nest here.
7.	Linda and Andy decide not to go back to Torremolinos next year. Linda thought it was 'naff'.
8.	Juan gets a well paid job in the construction industry. Many of his friends also get jobs.
9.	Angela has difficulty finding somewhere to get her travellers' cheques changed into pesetas.
10.	Carlos gets a job picking up litter off the beach every evening.
11.	The local farmers get better prices for their vegetables.
12.	The local council decides to build a new and bigger sewage treatment plant.

Continued

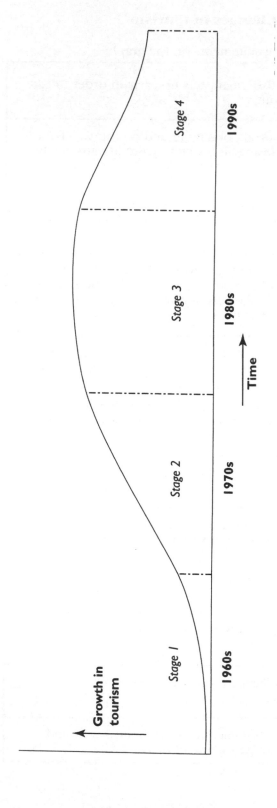

Figure 7.6 *The example of a Living Graph shown here is that of a stage model of tourism.*

Students worked in groups to locate the statements at different points on the graph within the four stage model of tourism. Debriefing involved a discussion of how they had chosen where to place the statements, which often elicits responses about previous classroom-based learning, personal experiences from holidays, films and videos seen, tour operators' brochures, and stories. Extension activities may involve students isolating causes and effects, as well as considering whether these effects might be positive or negative.

Mind Movies

Mind Movies are a way of accessing what children know, but they require students to trust the teacher and be confident about sharing their knowledge. They are about quick, motivating, response activities which give an insight into students' thinking – they challenge students to reveal their visual memories, rather than relying on what is written down.

The nuclear disaster script, used initially with an able Year 9 group, was part of a unit on human disasters and followed on from some work on Chernobyl. The passage was read to the students who were asked to note down their first thoughts and then to consider what possessions they, and their parents, would want to salvage from the disaster. After five minutes discussion the students wrote down what was similar between the two bags, what was different, what they found surprising about the contents of the other bag and what would be different for the adults' bag. Students then wrote down which six things they would take and why, and were asked to think about their own, their family's and their neighbour's future lives. They were also asked to consider what the authorities might need to do to take care of them. The debrief involved focusing on the students' answers to the last question.

Odd One Out

Odd One Out enables students to think about the characteristics of things as an aid to classification. As the name of the activity implies it involves students picking the 'odd one out' from a list of words (although variations of this strategy exist) and is perhaps used most effectively at, or near, the end of a unit of work. The advantages of this technique are that students become more familiar with the meanings of words and they recognize the similarities and differences between key terms. The activity is quick (10–15 minutes) and can be done with a variety of student groupings.

The example shown here concerns traffic management and was originally used with a Year 10 group that had previously studied issues of commuting and solving urban traffic problems. Some of the sets provided are deliberately ambiguous to get students thinking and making connections. Students worked in pairs, some clarification of terms was required. The debrief focused on task four where students had to think about traffic management – several common headings were suggested (materials, movements, problems, solutions, effects, cars, parking, rush hour, causes).

The nuclear disaster script

Imagine that you are sitting on your bed at home, listening to the local radio station. Look around the room and see what's there. Relax.

An urgent voice on the radio says:

This programme is interrupted for an important news bulletin.... At 4:00 p.m. a sequence of events at Hartlepool Power Station [insert the name of your nearest nuclear station] *led to the meltdown and explosion of the main reactor. Dangerous levels of radiation have been released into the atmosphere.*

The Department of the Environment and the Department of Health have declared a 30-kilometre evacuation zone. This includes the towns of Hartlepool, Middlesborough and Sunderland. Gateshead and South Shields will also be evacuated. Coaches will be at the end of each street starting in one hour. The police will begin clearing houses in 45 minutes. Please be ready to leave your homes. Each person will be allowed one small bag— and no more.

I repeat: a nuclear alert at Hartlepool means that your homes will have to be evacuated. Coaches will have to leave in one hour. This ends the news bulletin, programmes have been suspended until further notice.

Figure 7.7 *A Mind Movie for a nuclear power station disaster*

Wordsheet—Traffic management

1. Cycle track	18. Speed cameras
2. Wheel clamp	19. Bus passes
3. Exhaust fumes	20. Bypass
4. Park and ride	21. Intersection/junction
5. Inner-urban motorway	22. Bus lanes
6. Vibration damage	23. Road rage
7. One-way street	24. Sleeping policemen
8. Journey to work	25. Multi-storey car parks
9. Tailbacks	26. Double yellow lines
10. Rush hour	27. Pedestrianised streets
11. Rapid transit system	28. Photochemical smog
12. Pedestrian crossing	29. Accidents
13. Tidal flow	30. Dust particles
14. Noise	31. School runs
15. Roundabouts	32. Taxis
16. Petrol consumption	33. Ring road
17. Shopping trips	34. Congestion

Continued

Instructions

Task 1

Each of the numbers in the sets of four below relates to a word to do with traffic in urban areas. Can you work out with your partner which one is the *Odd One Out* and what connects the other three?

Set A	8	15	17	31
Set B	4	17	19	33
Set C	5	11	22	32
Set D	10	12	26	29
Set E	2	9	18	24
Set F	14	28	30	31
Set G	1	13	16	34

Task 2

Still with your partner, can you find *one more* from the wordsheet to add to *each* of the sets above so that all *four* items have something in common, but the *Odd One Out* remains the same? Think about why you have chosen each one.

Task 3

Now it's your turn to design some sets to try out on your partner! Choose three numbers that you think have something in common with each other and one that you think has nothing to do with the other three. Get your partner to find the *Odd One Out*, then do one of theirs. Try a few each, but remember to be reasonable.

Task 4

Can you organise all the words into groups. You are allowed to create between 3 and 6 groups and each group must be given a descriptive heading that unites the words in the group. Try not to have any left over. Be prepared to rethink as you go along.

Figure 7.8 *An 'Odd One Out' exercise on traffic management*

Story telling

Story telling (and the use of narrative) is a powerful and effective way of conveying geographical information (see McPartland, 2001). Leat (1998) lists some of the advantages of story telling as an educational device, including its ability to put geography into a real life context with actual people, its topicality and relevance, the exposure of students to extended pieces of text, the developing of sequencing skills ('storyboarding') and the promotion of listening skills. The activity below was used with a middle band Year 9 and a mixed ability Year 10 in a module on population and migration; the intention was to develop the students' ability to remember information in a variety of ways, to develop notions of cause and effect and to practice writing explanations. The story below was re-written from a newspaper article.

Students were numbered 1, 2 and 3 in groups and told that they would hear a story which would help them to remember a particular aspect of geography. Numbers 2 and 3 were briefly removed from the class whilst 1s had the story read to them. Number 1s were told they would have to pass this information to 2s, who would retell it to 3s. No note taking was permitted at this point, although paper could be used by 1s once 2s have returned to the classroom. 1s retell to 2s, then 2s retell to 3s with 1s listening to see if they deviate or miss-tell the story. Lastly 3s attempt to retell what they have heard to 1s, with 2s listening. The teacher finally asks 'What did you remember?' and 'How did you remember?' (students often say they remember by storing information as visual images). In the debrief the teacher instructs students about points they can use to help them remember information, such as: don't try to remember too much small (irrelevant?) detail, try to remember the story as a sequence or chain of events, some stories with geographical elements can be remembered better as 'mental maps', link parts of the story to images you have from elsewhere (films, news reports), certain aspects of stories can be remembered by looking for moral points. Some teachers also highlight the use of storyboards where students add eight to ten words per frame and have to make decisions on what information to include, the sequence of events, and the importance of the information shown. Storyboards are claimed to have a similar impact on student learning as writing frames.

Fact or opinion?

Fact or opinion? can be used to highlight the belief that in geography we are often faced with different viewpoints and have to make a judgement as to their veracity. These exercises help students to develop their own opinions and to understand the views of others. In some ways they are very advanced as they require students to differentiate between fact and opinion, and to test the very nature of knowledge. The example below (Figure 7.10) was taught in a unit on North America to a middle band Year 8 group.

The unit touched upon migration, urban geography and the 1993 Los Angeles riots. The newspaper article, which was slightly edited, raised significant questions about values and was read by students in groups of three. Students could ask questions about anything they did not understand in the text, they were then instructed to look at the underlined sections and to decide whether they thought these conveyed 'fact' or 'opinion'. Debriefing after the event is very important to

*Kingsley's story—based on an article by Julian
Nundy from The Guardian, 11 December 1995*

Kingsley Osufu, aged 24, was a casual dockworker at
Takoradi, one of the ports in Ghana. Often Kingsley went
home to his wife Agnes with nothing after a day spent
waiting for work that never came. He won some money in
the lottery and saw his chance. In October 1992, Kingsley
(along with seven others, one of them his brother, Albert)
stowed away aboard the Ukrainian ship *MC Ruby* which
was carrying a cargo of timber and cocoa to Europe.
Kingsley left his wife who was expecting their first child in
Ghana. He wished to go to Europe to receive training so
that he could return to Ghana as an engineer.

The eight of them hid in a hold full of expectation.
However, they eventually ran out of supplies and two of
them went to look for water after a day or so when they
had plucked up the courage to leave their safe hideaway.
The two people who went to find water found four other
stowaways who had got on board at Cameroon. They also
were trying to go to Europe. They shared out the food that
they had brought and exchanged stories of what they
would do when they got to Europe. However, they did not
realise that when they had gone to get the water they had
left footprints on the deck.

The next morning six sailors appeared armed with knives
and revolvers. 'Who are you? Where are you from?' they
asked in English. Kingsley quickly became the group's
spokesperson and told the sailors where they had
embarked. The sailors then asked if they had money and
Kingsley replied that they did. 'Get it ready and we will
come back to put you up somewhere else', one said.

That evening the sailors returned and, taking the money
led the stowaways to the bow of the ship where they
pushed them through a hatch into a space like a storage
tank. One morning a sailor opened the hatch to throw
down three bottles of water. Otherwise they were given
nothing and were left to live in their own filth for three
days.

In the early hours of 3rd November, after ten days at sea,
the hatch opened and two sailors ordered the men out 'in
groups of two or three'. Finally only Kingsley and Albert

Continued...

remained. When the two sailors came for them they noticed the other four standing in the shadows. Some had blood on their clothes.

Kingsley asked where the other stowaways had gone. A sailor responded by hitting him across the head with an iron bar. He broke free and ran along the deck; he turned in time to see two men throw Albert into the sea. Some of the sailors opened fire on him but missed. He managed to reach number three hold and hid amongst sacks of cocoa.

For the next three days he hid while every morning and evening the sailors searched the hold.

One evening, the *MC Ruby* docked. As the engines stopped Kingsley left his hideaway. Filling his pocket with cocoa beans and hiding his Ghanaian dockers work-card under a sack, he climbed up a ventilation shaft and forced open the rusty grill at its mouth.

Early on the morning of 6th November he jumped to the quay side and ran towards a street-cleaning vehicle. The two operators spoke no English but pointed him in the direction of the harbour police. He eventually found the police station. At 4am he began his story. Looking at the wall he saw a map, on it was the word France. Until then he had not known where he was.

After daybreak the Le Havre police searched the *MC Ruby*. They found Mr Osufu's work-card. Still terrified he was allowed to watch an identity parade on the deck hidden behind a porthole to identify his six tormentors.

The investigators concluded that five members of the crew and Captain Vladimir Ilnitsky were responsible. They were charged with offences ranging from complicity to murder to extortion, kidnapping and acts of piracy. Four admitted the crime immediately, two denied it, those who admitted their role said they were worried because of the heavy fines imposed on the shipping companies whose vessels bring stowaways into European ports.

Story-board

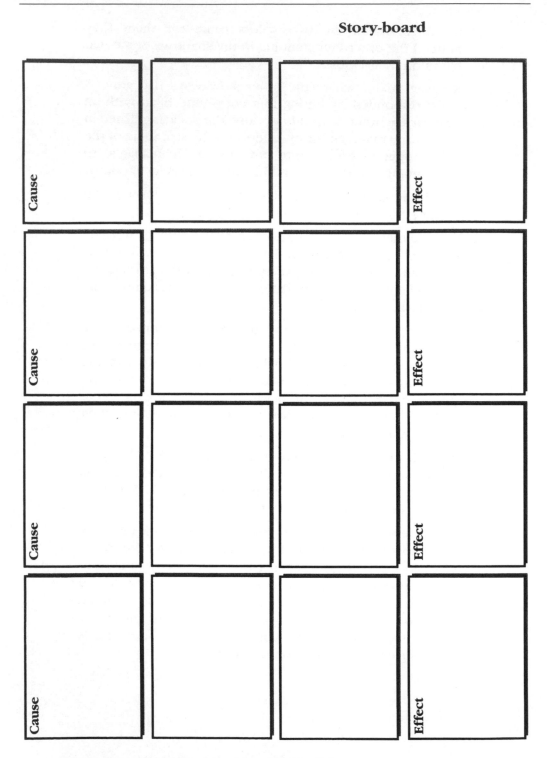

Figure 7.9 *Materials used in a 'story telling' activity*

| Fact or Opinion? |
| Exemplar 2: |
| The Los Angeles riots |

Extract one: inspired by an article 'Fear and loathing in Hollywood' by Cynthia Heimel in the Independent on Sunday.

On the first day of the LA riots when thousands of fires raged and most of Los Angeles resembled Beirut, a bunch of women gathered for a baby shower given by one of the most famous movie stars at her most fabulous home. Everyone was in peach, mint or white. Everyone wore the palest ivory stockings. They sat under umbrellas while little tea sandwiches and scones were served deferentially by Mexican women.

Then the housekeeper appeared. 'Ma'am,' she said, 'The city is burning. People are getting killed. There's gonna be a curfew.'

South Central Los Angeles takes up about one-quarter of the city. Nobody who doesn't live there would ever be caught dead going there. Nobody who does live there ever leaves except to go to wait on rich people. Before Wednesday affluent Los Angeles denied the existence of South Central Los Angeles. The gulf between the haves and the have-nots is terrifying; the haves enjoy the inflated salaries of the entertainment industry; the have-nots subsist on minimum wage or welfare.

During the curfew we watched (on TV) the looting and fires spread to middle-class neighbourhoods. That's when people got scared.

'Oh my God, Sammy's camera repair!' said a screenwriter. 'They've got my Nikon there. Shi....'

'What if the tailor shop that's redoing my dress for the wedding burns down?', asked an actress.

During the curfew I discovered ugly things about people I thought I knew.

'It's black people's own fault they're in the trouble they're in. Look how well the Koreans do', said an animator.

'I feel like I should go up and apologise to black people,' said Paula, a musician. 'This has been coming on for so long. Our government is so unresponsive. The Rodney King ruling just lit a match. This country isn't working.'

'We should just find Reagan and give him to the rioters,' said Harriet, a journalist. 'Isn't it all his fault? His whole message to poor people was "Screw you, we're all getting rich as we can, and some money might trickle down if you're lucky. If not, tough".'

During the curfew, we had nothing to do but watch TV and see our city burn. And think.

Continued

117

Extract two

Fact or Opinion?
Exemplar 2:
The Los Angeles riots

US blacks: the facts

Fifty-three per cent of blacks believe African Americans are less intelligent than whites; 51 per cent believe they are less patriotic; 56 per cent believe they are more violence-prone; 62 per cent believe they are 'more likely to live off welfare' and less likely to 'prefer to be self-supporting'.

From a 1990 survey by the University of Chicago's National Opinion Research Center.

- **Black males have the lowest life-expectancy of any group in the United States.** Their unemployment rate is more than twice that of white males; even black men with college degrees are three times more likely to be unemployed than their white counterparts.

  About one in four black men between the ages of 20 and 29 is behind bars. Blacks receive longer prison sentences than whites who have committed the same crimes.

- **Suicide is the third leading cause of death for young black males.** Since 1960, suicide rates for young blacks have nearly tripled, and doubled for black females. While suicide among whites increases with age, it is a peculiarly youthful phenomenon among blacks. Many black males die prematurely from 12 major preventable diseases.

- **Nearly one-third of all black families in America live below the poverty line.** Half of all black children are born in poverty and will spend all their youth growing up in poor families.

From a 1991 report of the 21st Century Commission on African-American Males.

Figure 7.10 *An exercise designed to enable students to differentiate between 'facts' and 'opinions'*

avoid confused, biased or stereotypical images remaining. The exercise was used as a focus on the difficulties surrounding what constitutes facts in geography.

Classification

The act of classifying is an important cognitive ability in geography which enables processing of data and the construction of concepts about the world around us. Students need to learn that different characteristics can be recognized which help us classify things into groups or events. The act of classifying helps to make students into better information processors.

Reading photographs

Photograph-based exercises help students to 'read' photographs, rather than seeing them merely as decoration or a means of 'breaking up' text in books and worksheets. The aim is to develop students' visual literacy – often through the use of photopacks. Geography examination papers and DMEs regularly include photographs which need to be interpreted. Geography teachers must help students to look more closely at photographs, to link what is in the photograph to what they already know, and then to use the evidence in the photograph to answer questions.

1.6 A note about debriefing activities

Debriefing is important. It is used to enable students to explore what they have learnt and the ways in which they have learnt it, so that this knowledge and understanding might be transferred to other learning situations (sometimes referred to as 'bridging'). Debriefing can take a variety of forms and employ different levels of teacher involvement – from collating ideas, providing feedback and managing discussions to bolstering the self esteem of students, encouraging responses, indicating connections and clarifying thinking. The debrief usually involves allowing students to give their solutions to a question and the reasons why they have chosen these solutions. It should also give students the opportunity to explain how they have carried out the task and the individual and/or group processes involved in so doing – students can then be helped to recognize how these processes and techniques might be used in other contexts. Sharing a common language for problem solving and talking about thinking is an important consideration.

Effective debriefing, which some would claim is rarely seen in geography classrooms, relies on trust and openness in discussion and may display the following features (Leat and Kinninment, 2000, p. 169):

- maintaining a high proportion of open questions which require the articulation of reasoning by pupils;
- encouraging pupils to extend and justify their answers, if necessary giving thinking time;
- encouraging pupils to evaluate each other's contributions to discussion;
- providing evaluative feedback to pupils, not necessarily in the form of 'that was good/not so good', but in terms of criteria that pupils can apply;

- using analogies, stories and everyday contexts to help pupils to understand the wider significance of their learning and encourage them to transfer it;

- drawing attention to the cognitive and social skills that the pupils have used and encouraging distillation of good practice in relation to these skills;

- relating thinking and learning described by pupils to the important concepts or reasoning patterns in subjects;

- drawing on what one has heard or seen during small group work preceding the debriefing.

2 SPECIAL EDUCATIONAL NEEDS (SEN)

Since the 1944 Education Act the special educational needs of children have gradually been redefined in terms of their educational and physical development, rather than narrowly on medical criteria. The Warnock Report in 1978, which resulted in the 1981 Education Act, sought to redefine such needs and introduced the requirement for LEAs to make particular provision for students according to their specific learning difficulties. The Report encouraged schools to take a broader view of their responsibilities to meet the special needs of children and not to expect them to be educated separately. Subsequent Education Acts, in 1993 and 1996, saw the introduction of a Code of Practice (DFE, 1994) and made statutory the need to include in any assessment of need an educational, psychological and medical component. The Code also required all schools to appoint a Special Needs Coordinator (SENCO), introduced a five-stage programme of identification and assessment of special needs, and directed schools to produce Individual Education Plans (IEPs) to outline the particular learning needs of students with special educational needs.

A child is said to have a special educational need if he or she has a learning difficulty which requires special teaching, or the provision of special equipment to aid their access to learning. Up to 20 per cent of children may need help relating to a special need at some stage of their schooling, often on a temporary basis. The term therefore covers a number of learning, emotional and behavioural difficulties including exceptionally severe learning difficulties (such as multi-sensory impairment), moderate or specific learning difficulties (such as dyslexia or dyspraxia), physical or sensory impairment (such as visual impairment), and, in some definitions, exceptionally able or gifted children.

In geography education certain special educational needs may require particular attention and the use of a specific pedagogy – for example supporting a child who is colour-blind in their use of an OS map, or a physically-impaired child during fieldwork. However, it is more common for geography teachers to be faced with dealing with general learning difficulties, such as reading problems (see Corney and Rawling, 1985; Dilkes and Nicholls, 1988). According to the severity of a child's special educational needs the geography teacher could expect the assistance of a specialist support teacher in the classroom (see Benton and O'Brien, 2000). It is not possible for geography teachers to single-handedly respond to each of the often very specialist needs of such children. As Lambert and Balderstone state:

What is important is that you know the specific nature of the difficulties experienced by particular pupils, how these difficulties manifest themselves and affect those pupils' learning of geography, and what strategies might help them to limit the impacts of these difficulties on their work in geography.

(Lambert and Balderstore, 2000, p. 186)

Practical activity 7.1

Produce a report on a student (who should not be identified by name) who has a special educational need.

Describe the nature of the special need and give examples of changes made to the curriculum, resources, learning activities and environment to help him or her gain access to the geographical curriculum.

3 | DIFFERENTIATION

Differentiation is fundamental to effective teaching and learning (O'Brien and Guiney, 2001). In essence the term refers to the targeting of teaching and learning activities to different abilities of students such that their learning potential is realized. This can be considered in a variety of ways, namely through the planning of the curriculum, educational goals, subject content, pedagogy, learning activities, and assessment methods. There are also very close associations between differentiation and the extent to which students experience continuity and progression within their geographical education. Differentiation can be used to 'separate out' students of different 'abilities', via assessment, so they can be taught a particular version of the curriculum – however in most schools differentiation is now applied such that students receive their optimum learning conditions and support without major changes to their grouping or to the aims of the curriculum.

The concept of effective differentiation may be easy to grasp, but the ways in which this concept becomes reality reveals many tensions. The geography curriculum may be based upon broad aims which are appropriate for all the students who study it, however these students each differ in their aptitude and abilities and may find accessing this curriculum problematic. Trainee teachers often feel this conflict most acutely. They experience problems in trying to help all students to 'follow' a common curriculum and find that on a day-to-day basis some students competently complete all the tasks put before them, whilst others in the same classroom struggle. In addition some students work well on their own, and prefer to do so, whilst others perform better within a group; some are better readers, or writers; some like practical tasks, others show abilities to work conceptually or theoretically. The prospect of an ever widening gap opening up between the 'achievers' and the 'laggards' gets worse from lesson to lesson. OFSTED reports regularly comment upon the lack of appropriate differentiation of tasks and activities according to students' abilities in all subjects (OFSTED, 1995, 1997). Such reports also mention the lack of appropriate challenge, insufficient motivation and inappropriate pace that has been a feature of many of the lessons observed.

◦ Achieving successful differentiation in the classroom is not straightforward; it ∕ does not just happen and must be planned for. Professional judgement is required to ascertain what is both manageable and achievable within the context in which you are teaching. It is possible to state a series of considerations for planning for differentiation, including (Battersby, 1995, p. 26):

- establishing clear learning objectives and outcomes with respect to students' knowledge, understanding and skills;

- devising a variety of teaching and learning strategies, tasks and activities to differentiate the students' learning experiences;

- using a variety of teaching and learning resources;

- opportunities to vary the pace and depth of learning; and

- different strategies to assess, feedback and target set for students.

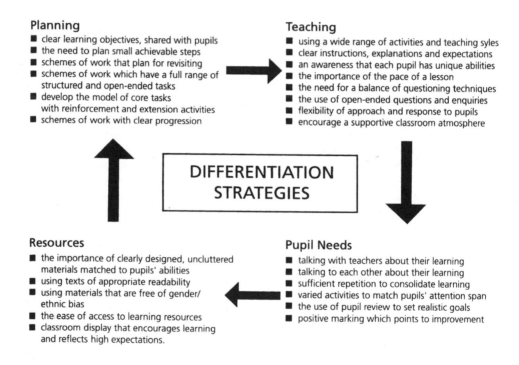

Planning
- clear learning objectives, shared with pupils
- the need to plan small achievable steps
- schemes of work that plan for revisiting
- schemes of work which have a full range of structured and open-ended tasks
- develop the model of core tasks with reinforcement and extension activities
- schemes of work with clear progression

Teaching
- using a wide range of activities and teaching syles
- clear instructions, explanations and expectations
- an awareness that each pupil has unique abilities
- the importance of the pace of a lesson
- the need for a balance of questioning techniques
- the use of open-ended questions and enquiries
- flexibility of approach and response to pupils
- encourage a supportive classroom atmosphere

DIFFERENTIATION STRATEGIES

Resources
- the importance of clearly designed, uncluttered materials matched to pupils' abilities
- using texts of appropriate readability
- using materials that are free of gender/ ethnic bias
- the ease of access to learning resources
- classroom display that encourages learning and reflects high expectations.

Pupil Needs
- talking with teachers about their learning
- talking to each other about their learning
- sufficient repetition to consolidate learning
- varied activities to match pupils' attention span
- the use of pupil review to set realistic goals
- positive marking which points to improvement

Figure 7.11 *Differentiation strategies (Lambert and Balderstone, 2000)*

Waters (1995) expresses these points to some effect in a diagram reproduced in Lambert and Balderstone (2000) (see Figure 7.11).

Battersby (1997) suggests a variety of approaches that might be adopted to achieve differentiation. These include the use of common tasks and materials whereby the students' various levels of achievement show 'differentiation by outcome'; or the use of a range of differentiated resources, and/or tasks, where a range of outcomes are achieved by students. A variety of permutations and combinations of tasks, materials and outcomes can be achieved such that student entitlement to a common curriculum does not suffer.

Many of the problems witnessed with poorly differentiated lessons are easily identifiable. These may relate to the very structure of the lessons taught – which can follow a predictable and far from stimulating pattern from one week to the next, only engaging students in passive and repetitive learning tasks. This has a clear impact on students' motivation and interest in the lessons. They soon learn 'what comes next' and how long it will take, they lose concentration and fail to respond to more innovative tasks which may occasionally be introduced by the teacher in an attempt to liven up proceedings. Variety, pace, direction and clarity of purpose are the keys to effective teaching. Equally important is creating what Lambert and Balderstone (2000) refer to as a 'culture of success' in the classroom, based on high expectations of what students can achieve in their learning of geography. We should be wary of colleagues who tell us that a particular teaching technique 'won't work with these students!' – an attitude which can stifle inventiveness, challenge and variety in one's teaching with consequent effects on student motivation.

The National Curriculum is founded on the principles of an education system that is 'broad, balanced, relevant and differentiated' with an entitlement for all students to be able to experience the curriculum whatever their learning needs. The ideal of making the curriculum accessible for all implies that it is not the curriculum that needs to change, but the teaching. This is not achieved by treating all children the same. External examinations such as GCSEs are based on the principles of differentiation in that they should enable students across the ability range to have opportunities to show what they know, understand and can do. As such in geography there are tiers of papers (higher and foundation) as well as differentiated questions.

As Battersby concludes:

> Differentiation is best thought of as an ongoing process that needs to be planned for and is characterised by flexibility. It is the means of maximising learning for all children by taking account of individual differences in learning style, interest, motivation and aptitude, and reflecting these variations in the classroom.
>
> (Battersby, 2000, p. 72)

4	ENQUIRY LEARNING

Many of the approaches to learning described in this chapter engage students in active responses to tasks. Some of these approaches can be described as involving aspects of enquiry learning, particularly if they involve students in developing 'an investigative, critical approach to knowledge ... in the classroom and in their lives outside school' (Roberts, 1998b, p. 167).

The term 'enquiry learning' has been variously defined and described. Recent research has shown that what geography teachers understand by the term varies significantly, concluding that 'teachers had different views of what geographical enquiry was and they interpreted it in different ways' (QCA, 1998a,b). Roberts (1998b) conducted small scale case study research into the nature of geographical enquiry at Key Stage 3, exploring teachers' thinking about their overall classroom practice. In response to two key questions – 'What do you understand by geographical enquiry?' and 'Can you give examples of geographical enquiry in your

Key Stage 3 course?' – she discovered that many teachers linked enquiry to field-work, or stated that it involved students working independently within a sequential process of learning. Teachers also placed different emphasis on the collection of quantitative and qualitative data, either from primary or secondary sources, during the enquiry process. Even though each of the geography teachers interviewed followed the same GNC their interpretations of what enquiry meant varied markedly – perhaps emphasizing the need for exemplification materials on enquiry to be published. Davidson and Catling (2000) similarly believe that many geography teachers are unclear about the role and nature of enquiry in geographical learning and are unsure about how enquiry skills can be integrated within the study of places and themes. Some teachers think 'enquiry' refers to any kind of active learning, others see it as a task ('an enquiry') typically completed during a sequence of lessons, or believe that enquiry learning involves students responding to open questions rather than receiving information passively from the teacher. A degree of difference in interpretation is also seen amongst geography educationists, although almost all agree that an enquiry approach is often central to effective geography education. In its original form – taken here as the approach adopted by the Geography 16–19 Project team – enquiry learning implies the use of a logical sequence of key questions which direct students along a 'route to enquiry' enabling them to discover for themselves the answers to a particular problem, question or issue within geography (see Figure 7.12). This 'route' could be described in terms of both factual and values led enquiry, investigating questions that address issues of both cognitive and affective learning.

In more recent geography education materials this has been expressed as follows:

Use a route for enquiry	To pose key questions
Observation/perception	What do I observe/perceive? How do others view it?
Definition/description	What is the key question which emerges? What is the issue to be studied?
Analysis/explanation	What processes are involved?
Evaluation/prediction	What might have happened? What are alternative viewpoints/solutions?
Decision-making	What decisions might be/should be made?
Personal response	What is my personal response? How might I justify my views? What action, if any, should I take?

The route for geographical enquiry mirrors the hierarchical stages of intellectual development, starting with 'low order' processes of observation and progressing through analysis and evaluation to the 'higher order' ability to make reasoned decisions and judgements. The route was also devised with the 'people-environment' dimensions of the 16–19 Project syllabus in mind.

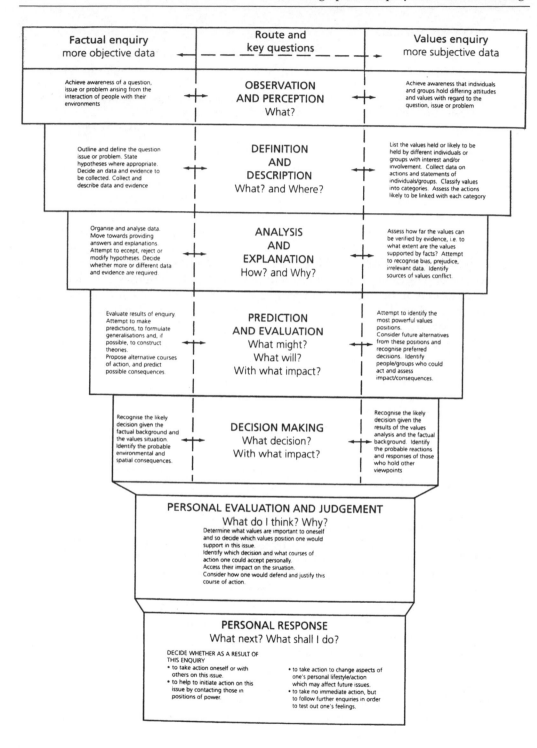

Factual enquiry more objective data	Route and key questions	Values enquiry more subjective data
Achieve awareness of a question, issue or problem arising from the interaction of people with their environments	**OBSERVATION AND PERCEPTION** What?	Achieve awareness that individuals and groups hold differing attitudes and values with regard to the question, issue or problem
Outline and define the question issue or problem. State hypotheses where appropriate. Decide an data and evidence to be collected. Collect and describe data and evidence	**DEFINITION AND DESCRIPTION** What? and Where?	List the values held or likely to be held by different individuals or groups with interest and/or involvement. Collect data on actions and statements of individuals/groups. Classify values into categories. Assess the actions likely to be linked with each category
Organise and analyse data. Move towards providing answers and explanations. Attempt to eccept, reject or modify hypotheses. Decide whether more or different data and evidence are required.	**ANALYSIS AND EXPLANATION** How? and Why?	Assess how far the values can be verified by evidence, i.e. to what extent are the values supported by facts? Attempt to recognise bias, prejudice, irrelevant data. Identify sources of values conflict.
Evaluate results of enquiry. Attempt to make predictions, to formulate generalisations and, if possible, to construct theories. Propose alternative courses of action, and predict possible consequences.	**PREDICTION AND EVALUATION** What might? What will? With what impact?	Attempt to identify the most powerful values positions. Consider future alternatives from these positions and recognise preferred decisions. Identify people/groups who could act and assess impact/consequences.
Recognise the likely decision given the factual background and the values situation. Identify the probable environmental and spatial consequences.	**DECISION MAKING** What decision? With what impact?	Recognise the likely decision given the results of the values analysis and the factual background. Identify the probable reactions and responses of those who hold other viewpoints

PERSONAL EVALUATION AND JUDGEMENT
What do I think? Why?
Determine what values are important to oneself and so decide which values position one would support in this issue.
Identify which decision and what courses of action one could accept personally.
Access their impact on the situation.
Consider how one would defend and justify this course of action.

PERSONAL RESPONSE
What next? What shall I do?
DECIDE WHETHER AS A RESULT OF THIS ENQUIRY
• to take action oneself or with others on this issue.
• to help to initiate action on this issue by contacting those in positions of power.
• to take action to change aspects of one's personal lifestyle/action which may affect future issues.
• to take no immediate action, but to follow further enquiries in order to test out one's feelings.

Figure 7.12 *The route for geographical enquiry (Lambert and Balderstone, 2000)*

As the QCA state:

> Geographical enquiry is an integral part of the geography national curriculum requiring students at key stages 1, 2 and 3 to be given opportunities to ask geographical questions and investigate places and themes. The programmes of study at all three key stages refer to opportunities to develop the skills of geographical enquiry and these also form an integral part of the level descriptions.
>
> (QCA, 1998a, p. 4)

At present, partly because of confusion about what enquiry learning is and how it can be achieved, the enquiry approach is not fully integrated into the planning of geography lessons (see SCAA, 1996c; OFSTED, 1999a). Even where teachers believe they are following the 'route to enquiry' by structuring their planning around a series of key questions, these may not be applied to achieve enquiry learning but rather as a means of delivering content (see Davidson and Catling, 2000). In assessment terms the scales of enquiry learning are interpreted differently by different educationists, adding to the variety of interpretations of what enquiries consist of. For example in Hopkin *et al.* (2000) student enquiries are referred to as more formal, in depth, 'medium term assessments' – special assessment occasions which supplement the regular day-to-day formative assessment conducted within the classroom.

In conclusion the importance of adopting an enquiry approach within geography education is firmly supported by Davidson and Catling when they state:

> Enquiry promotes a view that knowledge should always be examined, questioned, re-examined and never be taken as absolute and it encourages children to develop their own ideas and to articulate them.
>
> (Davidson and Catling, 2000, p. 279)

CONCLUSION

It is clear that students learn most effectively when they are motivated, interested and actively engaged in tasks. The geography curriculum must reflect this understanding of how students learn and offer them opportunities to engage in a variety of learning opportunities which concentrate upon both cognitive and affective learning, possibly within an enquiry framework. Recently, geography education has taken more seriously the need to research into the ways in which students learn and to apply these findings within practical approaches to teaching and learning in the classroom. In particular the work of David Leat and the 'Thinking Through Geography' group has combined an understanding of constructivist ideas about student learning to a range of activities designed to promote high order thinking skills and a realization that students need to engage in metacognitive analysis of their thinking. Some advocate the application of a clearly 'question-led' curriculum which views enquiry and investigation as fundamental to learning geography (Davidson and Catling, 2000), whereas others acknowledge the importance of adopting an enquiry approach but believe that it cannot be applied to all teaching and learning (Walford, 1995; Storm, 1995).

CHAPTER 8

Language and communication in the teaching of geography[1]

INTRODUCTION

Establishing effective communication in the classroom is fundamental to teaching and learning geography. However, the importance of helping students to spell, punctuate and communicate with grammatical accuracy in geography should not dominate our classroom teaching. The realization that talking, reading and writing in geography are all central to the *process* of learning, and as such should be carefully planned for, is of far greater educational significance (see Slater, 1989; Roberts, 1986; Butt, 1997b). Additionally it should be remembered that geography has it own subject specific vocabulary and that certain forms of communication are uniquely geographic – for example the use of maps, satellite images, and air photographs.

A considerable literature exists concerning the relationship between language, thought development and learning, some of which has been interpreted specifically for teachers of geography (see, for example, Williams, 1981; Slater, 1989; Carter, 1991; Butt, 1997b). There are also several general texts that help teachers promote the broader use of language in their classrooms (Andrews, 1989; Sheeran and Barnes, 1991; Wray and Lewis, 1994, 1997; McCarthy and Carter, 1994; SCAA, 1997c, 1997d). This literature has recently been supplemented by a variety of QCA booklets which seek to promote the improvement of young people's literacy in line with government initiatives (QCA, 1999a, 1999b). The drive to improve the literacy of all children through the National Literacy Programme in primary schools, and through various initiatives at secondary level, builds upon the requirements of all subject specifications at GCSE, A and AS level and GNVQs to assess students' spelling, punctuation and grammar.

1   COMMUNICATION IN THE GEOGRAPHY CLASSROOM

It is a truism that teacher talk tends to dominate the communication that occurs within the classroom. Geography teachers are like all other subject teachers in that they create fixed sets of rules for the ways in which they want students to

[1] This chapter draws significantly on a previously published monograph by the author, *Theory into Practice: Extending Writing Skills*, published by the Geographical Association in 2001. This work is duly acknowledged.

communicate with them (such as 'hands up', 'don't shout out'), they establish periods of each lesson when students are expected to restrict the communication they engage in ('When I'm talking you must listen to me', 'Too much noise – you should all be writing now'), and they encourage students to communicate orally in different ways (for example, when answering 'whole class' questions, reporting back from group activities as individuals, giving mini presentations).

The times when students can 'legitimately' communicate orally are usually quite restricted and they soon learn the accepted parameters for communication in each teacher's classroom. When we consider just how important talking is to the whole learning process, we begin to realize that the infrequent opportunities offered to most students to engage in subject-related discussion are educationally extremely significant. If teachers totally dominate the classroom, forcing the process of oral communication to become 'one way', then the learning experience for many students is restricted. If students are to understand fully the subject's concepts, ideas and terminology they must regularly engage in talking about geography, as well as listening to the teacher and their peers. The significant point is that talking is often the precursor both to learning and to the production of good quality writing (Williams, 1981; Slater, 1989).

Attention has been given to the manner in which such communication may either stretch student thinking into new areas, or merely repeat a game of rote memorization of facts – which students regurgitate from one geography lesson to the next. The majority of questions teachers ask in class are 'closed' in that only one 'right' answer is possible; often such questions are phrased in such a way that they offer the student very limited opportunities to explore new thoughts and ideas in geography. Similarly many 'recall' questions simply test what the students already know, rather than encouraging new understandings. As Carter (1991) states this use of questioning actually restricts the learning process, as students engage in:

> a guessing game whereby the teacher has the knowledge, and tries through questioning to extract the right answers from the pupils. They in turn reach towards the preferred response, the correct answer. Alternatively they adopt a variety of strategies to keep their heads below the parapet!
>
> (Carter, 1991, p. 1)

But why do teachers pose so many closed questions? There are several reasons for this, some of which relate closely to issues of class management and to our preparedness to take risks. Closed questions are certainly easier to frame than open questions; they can be assessed quickly and are more convenient for keeping academic 'control' of a lesson. A series of one-word answers may also have the advantage of driving the pace of a lesson and they do not threaten the teacher with the possibilities of deviating into areas that he or she has not planned for. By comparison, 'open-ended' questions invite rather more tentative and exploratory answers, which in themselves provide evidence of fresh thinking and new learning. This may, in turn, create management and assessment problems within the geography classroom. Nonetheless, such questions are truly 'educational' in that they push students into higher order thinking and reasoning, often by making them engage in analysis, synthesis, decision-making and the formulation of conclusions. An important consideration is the teacher's intention when using questions – is it to enable students to recall previous learning, or to explore new thoughts?

Roberts (1986) helpfully illustrates the effect of asking closed and open questions in the geography classroom from the perspective of their influence on student thinking (see Figure 8.1). Although both open and closed questions *may* have the ability to make 'high order' cognitive demands on students – that is, they can *both* be used to push students into analytical and evaluative modes of thought rather than merely requiring students to recall a piece of knowledge – it is closed, recall type questions that are most frequently used in the geography classroom. Such questions usually restrict students to recalling previously learnt facts. By contrast open, evaluative questions (which allow students to make sense of new knowledge; to reason, justify and explore their understandings; and to utilize what they already know) are usually posed only infrequently in the geography class.

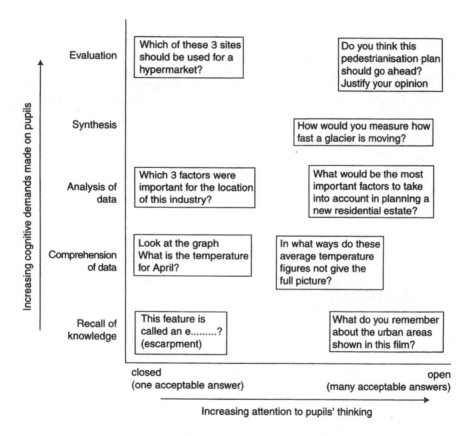

Figure 8.1 *Two dimensions of questioning (Roberts, 1986)*

Marsden (1995) describes what he considers to be the features of good questioning. He reminds geography teachers to:

- ask questions fluently and precisely;
- gear questions to the students' state of readiness;
- involve a wide range of students in the question and answer process;
- focus questions on a wide range of intellectual skills, and not just on recall;

- ask probing questions;

- not accept each answer as having equal validity;

- sensitively redirect questions to allow accurate and relevant answers to emerge; and

- use open-ended as well as closed questions in order to invite creative thought and value judgements.

Asking a high proportion of closed questions, either in oral or written work, may be organizationally convenient in that they enable us to get students to 'do something' without too much fuss – but it is often the case that not much real learning results!

Practical activity 8.1

During a placement in school ask to observe a geography lesson, informing the teacher that [with his or her agreement] you intend to note down the kinds of questions asked.

Refer to Marsden's (1995) list of what he considers to be features of good questioning.

Does the teacher's questioning reflect aspects of the list? If not, can you think of reasons why not? Are there other aspects of 'good questioning' that Marsden does not consider?

2 | THE LANGUAGE OF STUDENTS

If we accept that it is important to give students opportunities to discuss the geography they are learning and to answer thought provoking open-ended questions, what does this imply about the ways in which we think geography should be taught? First, we should encourage students to use language in *exploratory* ways, rather than solely in *transactional* ways. That is, we should allow students to use personal and expressive forms of language (exploratory) which help to reveal what they think, feel and believe. By contrast transactional language, which is more formal and structured, is used to convey factual information and concepts in a logical and ordered sequence. Unfortunately teachers often expect students to be able to produce good quality transactional writing too quickly and with little support. Students must be allowed to 'play' with language to discover new meanings, rather than simply use it to convey final answers. As Lambert and Balderstone suggest:

> Students should be given opportunities to talk in a range of contexts and for a variety of purposes in geography including describing and explaining, negotiating and persuading, exploring and hypothesising, challenging and arguing.
>
> (Lambert and Balderstone, 2000, p. 215)

A strand of research, which has been developed around these ideas, looks at both developing thinking skills and supporting students in analysing how they learn. For example, Leat (1998, 2000), Leat and Nichols (1999) and Leat and Kinninment (2000) have explored the ways in which students 'think about their thinking' (metacognition). These researchers have sought to analyse the language that students use when solving problems and have encouraged students to think about how they learn, so that they can approach subsequent geographical tasks and questions more effectively. Although this work has not yet been extended fully into researching students' writing, it has made some important links between thinking, talking and writing.

We can offer students the opportunity to talk by using role-play and simulation activities and decision-making exercises in geography, most of which will involve group work at some stage (see Chapter 4). Some geography teachers are concerned that such activities may transfer control of the learning process from them to the students. While this is a justifiable concern teachers must accept that it is also the only way in which students will start to learn for themselves, rather than relying directly on the teacher for instruction and guidance. Ensuring that students engage constructively in more independent learning is not always easy and takes time; it is only after the fears of messy and non-directed learning are conquered that students can move towards more independent and valuable forms of learning with language. This is not to say that 'anything goes' – even though students will be offered opportunities to discuss or write freely, properly conducted discussion work or exploratory writing still needs very clearly defined and expressed parameters.

It is easy to assume that when students use geographical vocabulary they fully understand what the terms mean. This becomes a more significant point when students use terms that are in 'everyday' usage but also have a specific, and different, meaning in geography. Examples of such words which have 'double' meanings – which should be explored with students to check their geographical understanding – are terms such as 'city', 'space', 'market', 'joint', 'labour', 'environment', 'energy'. Learning the correct meaning of words within a subject discipline is an important precursor to concept development.

3 FROM TALKING TO WRITING

Many students produce writing that is poorly structured, overly concise and unbalanced, and which is also incapable of conveying complex messages, ideas and thoughts. Although the reasons for this are numerous, often the key to the regular production of unsatisfactory writing lies in the nature of the task originally set by the teacher. We need to consider what, from the students' viewpoint, he or she could reasonably be expected to write, given the tasks we set. If closed questions are asked too regularly, as the focus for writing tasks, students may find it both conceptually difficult, and structurally taxing, to escape from the usual 'one word answer' syndrome when they are attempting to produce a piece of extended writing. Merely stating that their answer to a particular question should be 'at least one side long' gives no help whatsoever! Instead it leaves the mechanisms, techniques and connections necessary for producing high quality extended writing unclear. Only when the steps towards the production of extended writing are mutually understood, and the means of achieving it become readily apparent and easily recalled by the students, will they succeed in creating analytical, explanatory and purposeful extended writing in geography.

Practical activity 8.2.

What types of writing are students asked to undertake in geography?

From your observation of geography classrooms discuss the forms of writing that students are usually asked to complete. How often are different writing activities set for students? To what extent are students asked to write in expressive ways, exploring new ideas, thoughts and feelings?

4 | EXTENDED WRITING AND ASSESSMENT

Geography teachers can employ a number of techniques to improve the quality of their students' written work and help them to produce work that is purposeful, grammatically secure and contains good geographical knowledge and under-standing. One of the main problems geography teachers face is that, at present, the production of high quality extended writing does not seem to be highly valued in geography at Key Stage 3, at GCSE and (some would argue) even within A and AS level examinations. Despite the demand for the completion of externally assessed coursework, the emphasis on students having to produce purposeful extended writing has steadily decreased over recent years. Geography examination papers now tend to require students to write single sentence answers or, if more marks are to be awarded for a more complex answer, space is given for a three or four line response. Only in the (proportionally fewer) 'higher order' questions are students expected to engage in anything that approaches extended writing in the generally accepted sense. Often students are expected to write a concise, transactional set of short sentences or even bullet points to ensure that they convey essential geo-graphical content. The reasons for this relate to assessment. It is 'safer' (in the sense of maintaining reliability) for an examiner to mark a one-word answer than to assess a more complex piece of extended writing. Little, if any, opportunity is given for the type of extended writing that encourages students to formulate a structured argument, to be analytical, to reach conclusions or to display their ability to reason. Many of the classroom activities that students now undertake using geography textbooks (and other published materials) also tend to encourage this narrow approach to writing. Unfortunately, the 'double-page spread' with text, supporting photographs and diagrams, brief comprehension questions and a summary passage for the students to copy, typifies many contemporary geography resources.

So why is it important for students to engage in extended writing in geography? If all examiners need are 'one-word answers' to assess what students know, understand and can do, why ask them to produce more writing? Extended writing compels students to support or justify what they want to say. A one-word answer to a closed question tells us little about the depth of that student's understanding; without the supporting evidence of extended writing or a debriefing session (Leat and Kinninment, 2000; Butt, 2001b) we have few clues to his or her reasoning. Writing provides a key to how he or she understands and develops concepts, how gaps in that student's understanding occur, and how his or her critical thinking is developing. In short, it provides us with clues as to what the next educational steps should be for the creation of that student's greater knowledge and understanding (Black and Wiliam, 1998).

How do we get students to produce high quality extended writing? The straightforward answer might be for us to go back to getting students to write more essays, but like most simple answers this does not convey the whole truth! Good extended writing in geography does not develop of its own accord. It requires careful structuring, scaffolding and practice within the classroom. As Counsell explains, in the context of history education:

> The challenge of helping students to hold on to more than a couple of propositions in their heads at once and do some 'joined up thinking' is rarely addressed. Longer and more open-ended activities abound but students are expected to leap over the abyss of structure, organisation and genre. Not surprisingly, many just fall into the abyss and never get out. Lower-attaining students, by being given over general instructions to 'use the sources', or 'answer the question' or 'plan your answer' are simply being invited to fail. Some teachers therefore conclude that lower attainers cannot construct written analyses or explanations. But they can.'
>
> (Counsell, 1997, p. 7)

We should not view all writing simply as an assessment 'end point': the mere culmination of what students know, understand and can do. Most writing is (or should be) a formative and educational activity. Writing can be used as a pedagogical tool to help students to clarify concepts, make links between ideas and engage in more advanced forms of thinking and learning.

A section of this book is dedicated to assessment and marking (see pages 142–158), however, it is important to state here that the marking of students written work should be sensitively handled if one is to avoid damaging the confidence of reluctant writers. As stated elsewhere:

> [the] over-enthusiastic correction of every mistake of grammar, spelling and punctuation can be extremely disheartening to some pupils and may dissuade them from writing at all. In general, the use of praise and positive teacher comments, where appropriate, may help to encourage the reluctant writer and start a discussion between the teacher and learner about the geography being studied
>
> (Butt, 1997b, p. 163)

4.1 Writing to learn

Too often we assume that the writing process is straightforward and simple. Selecting relevant geographical points, analysing how they fit together, reconvening them into an extended answer, and then successfully writing that answer requires a series of logically structured and correctly sequenced steps. Most of the extended writing tasks we set do not acknowledge this and we often expect students to go straight from the first stage of information gathering to the last stage of successful extended writing in one 'leap'. Occasionally we may concentrate too heavily upon 'the geography' and too little upon the process of students' writing. Without our support students will be encouraged to 'lift' geographical information from (usually) one source and merely write it down.

4.2 Approaching extended writing

Students initially find that achieving high quality extended writing in geography is difficult because they have to 'carry' large amounts of information in their heads (and/or refer to a wide range of different sources) as they attempt to organize their writing. The 'steps' involved in transferring content into writing are numerous and have to be repeatedly practiced before students are able to carry out the process unaided. This activity can be complicated by the fact that:

- new information may be revealed that somehow has to be included;

- old information may need to be rejected in the light of new evidence;

- a new line of argument or analysis may need to be established; and

- some information may not easily 'fit' within the emerging answer and therefore may have to be rejected or reformulated.

At the same time students will need to consider the 'bigger picture' in a piece of extended writing. For example:

- What are the 'big points' that must be emphasized?

- What are the relatively insignificant pieces of information that still need to be included in support of the bigger picture?

Such complexity of structure, organization, genre, audience and analysis is daunting for even the most experienced writer. For the least experienced or less able student these challenges often result in him or her following the easier path of simply copying information or including irrelevant 'padding' in an answer.

Counsell (1997, p. 13) outlines the main problems students face in creating high quality extended writing in Figure 8.2.

4.3 Achieving high quality extended writing

The techniques described below offer some steps towards the production of thoughtful extended writing in geography. Not all of the techniques are uncontroversial – evidence exists that in certain situations teachers and students have not found them supportive to the process of writing. However, they bear consideration when helping students to produce extended writing and (suitably adapted) can be used successfully with any age or ability range. Four techniques are suggested – ordering, card sorting, writing frames and Directed Activities Related to Texts (DARTs).

Ordering

Ordering activities help students to handle data and information confidently before attempting to engage in writing activities. They mirror some of the processes that

---

Memory and construction

Students often need to be offered opportunities to develop the skill of retaining more than one important point in their short-term memory, while making decisions about the status of such pieces of information, and finally attempting to relate these points to each other before writing. Within the context of answering a specific geographical question (or questions) achieving each of these interlinked steps can prove to be problematic for many students.

Relevance and selection

Students can often achieve a workable idea about what is and is not relevant information to be included in an answer. However, they need to develop the means of both selecting, and justifying the selection of different facts or points. Creating a set of basic criteria for the selection of information that will eventually be included in their writing is an important reasoning activity.

Sorting

The process of sorting pieces of information establishes their relevance to a particular question. Classification and sorting are often closely linked; with sorting being a pre-requisite to eventual description, analysis and evaluation. The need to establish patterns and order when sorting, to label information correctly and to use key geographical terms to help in the sorting process, achieves a variety of educational goals. Sorting helps to develop students' thinking skills and is an important stage in marshaling information before they attempt to write.

General and particular

Often students have difficulties in seeing the difference between those points that are general and those that are particular. They need to practice using geographical evidence to support a position taken, defining which are the 'small points' and which the 'larger points' in an argument, and to be clear about which specific points can be raised as generalities. Many students need also to be aware that it is usually not possible to substantiate a general conclusion with a single piece of specific evidence.

The language of discourse

Students often need to develop greater sophistication in the form of their writing, and therefore need to be exposed to a variety of texts. They need to be offered opportunities to create different types of prose, experiment with different 'starters' and 'finishers' for sentences, create connections between sections of text and confidently use simple causal connectives (e.g. 'therefore', 'and so', 'thus', 'as a result'). Indeed, students need to learn the function and use of these and more complicated connectives (e.g. 'despite', 'notwithstanding', 'although') within geography texts.

Figure 8.2 *The main problems students face in creating high quality writing (adapted from Counsell, 1997)*

writers go through before attempting to construct a piece of extended writing – that is selecting pieces of information, isolating key points, restructuring facts into an order that makes most narrative sense, and presenting a final piece of writing that has a clear direction and a message within it. In most cases ordering activities involve supplying a number of 'points' on small pieces of card for students to place in a logical order. By undertaking ordering activities students learn that their own extended writing can be successfully structured through correctly piecing together a series of geographical concepts, ideas and facts which then link together to form a meaningful whole. Ordering activities are only the 'first steps' in producing extended writing because they do not require students to structure a piece of their own writing, or indeed actually to *write* anything. The process is important as a signifier of what students will have to do independently, once they have gathered information from a range of sources. Issues of structure, genre, audience and form will all follow once the basic approach to ordering is achieved.

Card sorting

Card sorting activities provide a helpful extension to the ordering tasks described above. Students have to prioritize a series of points – for example a set of cards describing the effects of using different fuels on the environment, or detailing how damaging different ways of using the rainforest may be – to answer a given question. In so doing, students are undertaking a structuring activity which is very similar to one that immediately precedes the production of good extended writing. By sorting these points the students have achieved a valuable framework for a piece of extended writing (Counsell, 1997). Selecting information is the first stage of the process, followed by prioritising and organizing it, then – if a writing task is actually set – students must produce a synthesis of this information.

Nash (1997), Norton (1999), Leat (1998) and Leat and Nichols (1999) offer similar card sorting activities. These researchers specifically stress that such activities provide a route to effective group work rather than necessarily being extended into requiring individual students to produce a piece of writing. Activities involving sorting, labelling, ranking, and matching words and definitions on cards can all be used to promote discussion and to create a point from which the step into writing is more straight forward.

To make such activities more challenging, ask the students to sort the cards into more than one 'column' to reflect consideration of another question (for example, not just prioritizing the least environmentally damaging fuels to use, but also considering the least costly, or the most convenient). By doing so, they should understand that the construction of a single prioritized order of information is not always the expected outcome. To make the task mirror more accurately the first-hand selection of data, from which the student would then be expected to compose a piece of extended writing, other sources of information can be suggested. These information sources can range from previous whole-class discussion, to teacher-supplied notes, textbooks, photographs and the internet. With younger or less able students it may be important to restrict the range of sources to avoid the risk of the task becoming too complex and difficult.

Providing the information on cards allows students to move text around without them being in danger of writing the 'wrong thing' first or engaging in effort-sapping writing that has then to be discarded. In addition, research has shown that useful student discussion often arises from such sorting and ordering activities, which in turn provides evidence of first order thought and concept clarification (Leat, 1998). However, as Counsell warns:

> Without careful planning, a lot of 'resource-based' or 'enquiry-based' learning can lead to rampant copying, thus failing to develop the very capacities of independent, critical analysis for which it was designed ... If the goal is to help all students to use wider ranges and types of information, in increasingly independent enquiry, the teacher's attention to structure in their thinking must be correspondingly great.
>
> (Counsell, 1997, p. 19)

Card sorting exercises should therefore be used by teachers as opportunities to introduce students to 'texts' from a variety of original sources, to help students to order and structure their thoughts, and to avoid the simple copying of information without comprehension of the concepts contained within it.

Writing frames

Writing frames provide students with the initial structure for a piece of extended writing. There are many forms of writing frames and they can be differentiated according to the perceived strengths and/or weaknesses of the students. They are usually designed to provide either the means of completely structuring the students' writing or to only loosely support the writing process. As with card sorting activities, writing frames provide a simple way of reducing the pressure on the students to complete the variety of tasks necessary to produce good extended writing. Writing frames support and scaffold the organizational process before students start writing so that they can concentrate on making decisions about what to include and where to include it. Students are, therefore, encouraged to come to decisions about 'which facts go where' when writing in an extended fashion, rather than rushing headlong into recording lots of unrelated facts in almost any order. Frames usually contain a variety of 'starters', 'connectives' and 'sentence modifiers' which give students a structure within which they can concentrate on what they want to say, rather than getting lost in the form of the writing (EXEL, 1995). The frame, in certain circumstances, may represent first draft writing that students can then amend and add to.

By getting students to order and structure the geographical information they have been presented with, often from a number of sources, the teacher can make some valuable judgements about how well each student understands the geography. Students should not see writing frames as being fixed and unchangeable – once their confidence in using writing frames grows they should be encouraged to alter the frames to suit a specific purpose and even devise their own (Wray and Lewis, 1994). The writing that ensues from using a writing frame actually supports the assessment process because it gives us an important insight into the thinking processes the student employed before he or she started to write. This signifies whether the difficulties which the student faces when attempting to write in an extended fashion are related to his or her understanding of the geography, or an inability to order this understanding into a meaningful piece of writing, or both. Such assessment opportunities are formative. They help us to understand the next educational steps that students should go through to increase their geographical understanding and skills.

Directed Activities Related to Texts

All of the above activities might also be described as Directed Activities Related to Texts (DARTs). Figure 8.4 helps to explain the range of techniques that might be applied to texts either broadly for 'reconstruction' purposes (that is activities that require students to use a text that has been modified in some way by the teacher), or for 'analytical' purposes (that is an activity that gets them to use text in its original form). In essence DARTs involve students developing their reading skills and focusing on specific aspects of the text.

'Reconstruction' activities	'Analytical' activities
Text completion	Text marking
Sequencing	Labelling
Prediction	Segmenting
Table completion	Table construction
Diagram completion	Diagram construction
	Student generated questions
	Summary

Figure 8.3 *Some DARTS*

Counsell (1997) suggests that some DARTs techniques can be used to enable students to analyse both their own and other people's writing. In situations where students are asked to draft and redraft their writing these strategies may prove particularly useful in suggesting to them where changes may be necessary. They also help the students to understand the importance of order and structure in their writing. In this way students' writing can be used as a teaching resource in a truly formative way.

The following techniques are based on suggestions made by Counsell (1997, p. 38). Try using the instructional phrases to direct students' reading of their own writing:

- Shade all the points you have made about x in green, and all the points about y in red. What do you notice?

- Underline all the points where you directly refer to an information source. Look at how you introduced each point. Compare your wording/writing with your neighbour's.

- Cut up your writing. Make cuts between each paragraph. How easy is it for your neighbour to arrange your paragraphs correctly?

- Find all your 'big points' and underline these in red. Are there places where you needed more 'little points' to support these?

And on work that has been marked, write:

- Read all of my comments in the margin. Can you think of two targets for next time you do a similar piece of work?

- I have underlined four things on this page. Can you work out what they have in common?

- Show me the place in this writing where you stopped writing about the causes and went off the point!

- With which parts of your writing do you think this geographer (quotation) would not agree?

See, also, the work of Westoby (1999) on text sequencing, construction, completion, annotation, and use of DARTs.

5 | AUDIENCE

Recent research has explored the effects of students writing for different audiences in geography, that is, undertaking writing to, or for, someone other than the teacher (for example to an adult, to another student, to a younger child, etc.). The audience for some writing tasks may still be the teacher, but as someone other than an assessor (for example as a peer, as a group member, as a consultant, etc.). Getting students to remove their writing focus away from the 'teacher as assessor' is difficult, but not impossible, and if a realistic audience can be found for students to write for there is some evidence that this changes the form of what they write and the ways in which they understand geography. Some students produce more original, creative and individual pieces of writing – for example, when writing to, or for, audiences such as (say) newspaper readers, television viewers, an MP, a shanty town dweller, or a wood gatherer. Often the most tangible effects of students engaging in such writing processes seen in the classroom comes in the form of increasing work-related discussion, greater student questioning, enhanced perception of an audience's viewpoints, and a clarification of personal values (Butt, 1993, 1998b).

Brownsword (1998) is concerned that students' writing should reveal empathy for non-western cultures and has developed a range of language-based activities designed to promote this. These activities are structured to help students to explore ethical, social and citizenship issues and therefore encourage them not to write solely from a factual, transactional perspective but to engage in using expressive, values-related and affective perspectives. Persuading students of the importance of writing about their own views and reflections, or simply encouraging them to make comparisons between their own and others lifestyles in their geographical writing, can be instrumental in helping them to produce high quality work. On a related subject, Bermingham *et al.* (1999) remind us that all written texts have been produced from a particular perspective and that students should read, analyse and aim to produce writing from various stances and for various purposes. Here the term 'text' is used in its broadest sense – from the written word to videos, pictures and sketches.

McPartland (2001) discusses the use of narrative discourse within the context of using moral dilemmas to help teach geography. He argues that a narrative structure helps students to understand geographical concepts partly because the statements in the discourse are usually arranged in chronological order, have a person recounting the story who is often a central participant in the narrative and tie events in the past to actors in the narrative. Leat (1998) makes a similar point when he considers the importance of a narrative form within the construction of effective Mysteries. He argues that letting students create such narratives for themselves can help them to order and structure geographical events and concepts.

Practical activity 8.3

Plan a lesson that will enable students to carry out some writing for an audience other than the 'teacher as assessor'.

Consider this writing from the following perspectives:

1. the geographical content contained within it;

2. the ability of the writer to engage realistically and convincingly with the audience you (or they) have established.

6 | READING

Students are often not sufficiently supported during reading undertaken in the classroom, a situation that is exacerbated in the context of homework tasks where no teacher support is available. The technique employed by many teachers of getting students to read 'around the class' can lead to short bursts of concentration, nervousness and defensiveness by poor readers who do not want their weakness publicly exposed. When combined with a lack of supportive intervention by the teacher, or in situations where reading is used as a control mechanism rather than a learning activity, the educational value of such reading can be limited. There is also only limited evidence that students gain much from listening to the reading of their peers.

The fundamental problem may lie with the text. Often the 'implied readership' of geography textbooks does not have the reading competence expected by the author – students find it difficult to either understand the text, or to link text to accompanying images, data, maps, diagrams and photographs which have been used to illustrate points. It is easy to be fooled into assuming that if a student can actually read what is written, then he or she *understands* what they have read. Presentation is important; density of text, font size, layout, use of headings may all have an impact on understanding. The readability of the text is an essential consideration – there are a variety of readability formulae that may be applied to texts, such as the Flesch formula, but evaluating readability is not simply a matter of analysing a score generated by such a test. It is an 'art rather than a science' where the teacher makes a judgement based on a knowledge of the students he or she is teaching and on the presentation, grammatical structures, word length, abstraction of concepts and amount of technical vocabulary used in the text. In recent years concern has been expressed that some publishers have tried to make their geography texts more marketable by cutting down on the amount of text they contain, or oversimplifying what is written. This is not an acceptable response to the issue of improving readability – students should be challenged by the texts they read, but they should also be appropriately supported and guided during their efforts to understand such texts.

Students reading texts on their own often find greater difficulties because these texts rarely give clues to their meaning in the same way the spoken word can. For example, written texts (unless read out) do not convey for the student nuances of intonation, stress, inflection and gesture that a teacher can include when talking or reading aloud in class. However, the reader may have an advantage that he or she can go backwards and forwards across a piece of text at his or her own pace to try to aid understanding.

Partical activity 8.4

Using your previous observation of geography classrooms for sources of evidence what kind of texts do you think students usually have to read?

What form does the reading take (students reading to themselves, reading 'around' the class, teacher directed and mediated reading, teacher reading to class, etc.)? How often do different 'types' of reading occur in geography?

How appropriate are the reading tasks established for students?

CONCLUSION

This chapter provides some guidelines about the importance of considering language and communication in the geography classroom. It is important for trainee teachers to realize the uneven nature of the communication process that exists in most teaching and learning, as well as recognizing how geography as a subject discipline may present its own barriers to understanding. By raising one's awareness of the need to allow students to talk in different settings and in response to both open and closed questions, as well as applying supportive activities to enable students to engage in more meaningful writing, language can be used to support the very process of learning. As students become familiar with a range of language and literacy techniques, more advanced forms of organization of information sources can be introduced using a greater breadth of materials, new geographical vocabulary and/or more challenging questions. Students can also be encouraged to analyse their own and other people's writing, possibly as a result of considering the teacher's comments on assessed pieces of extended writing, to alert them to alternative ways of structuring and presenting text. Striking a balance between providing students with overly supportive or formulaic writing structures and leaving them to struggle with poorly directed or open-ended writing tasks is never easy. However, with increasing experience of 'what works', both teacher and student can achieve pleasing results.

The ability to write extended pieces that convey good geographical knowledge and understanding is important not only as an end in itself, but also as a signifier of the processes of thinking that students go through. Critical thinking, reasoning, analysing and decision-making can all be revealed through well-structured and purposeful writing. Indeed, whenever the development of extended writing skills is considered in geography, a key question might be 'Will these activities help to enhance the students' thinking skills?'.

CHAPTER 9

Assessment within geography education

Assessment has always been an integral part of teaching and learning, and good practice in assessment is an important means of improving students' attainment.
(Hopkin et al., 2000, Introduction).

INTRODUCTION

The standards for initial teacher training place considerable emphasis on trainees developing an understanding of assessment in its broadest sense during their period of training. The term assessment is taken to cover areas of monitoring, assessment, recording, reporting, and accountability with reference to children's work and progress. This chapter will explore the many ways in which geography can be assessed by the trainee teacher and some of the advantages and disadvantages of formative and summative assessments, use of portfolios, level descriptions and criteria referenced assessment. It seeks to convey that students should be placed at the centre of the assessment process – a process which requires teachers to make sound and reliable professional judgements about students' attainment on a daily basis. There is also a realization that the application of assessment methods in geography is not straightforward and that these methods need to be varied over time. Different methods are best suited to serve different purposes – some of them educational, some of them bureaucratic.

1   WHAT IS ASSESSMENT FOR?

The most basic definition of what assessment is 'for' usually highlights the measurement of an individual's learning at a particular point, or the gauging of their performance on a particular task. In addition the most useful forms of assessment also seek to improve the future learning of the person being assessed. Assessment therefore involves gathering, interpreting, recording and using information about students' performance on different educational tasks (Harlen *et al.*, 1992). It is important to realize that there is a major difference between assessment *of* learning and assessment *for* learning. A number of possible answers to the question 'What is assessment for?' are therefore listed below:

- to enhance pupils' learning;
- to measure (or possibly raise) standards;

- to check teaching objectives against learning outcomes;
- to recognize and plan for pupils' learning needs;
- to place pupils against different descriptors of achievement;
- to discover what pupils know, understand and can do;
- to help plan future learning objectives;
- to help pupils to devise personal targets;
- to evaluate teacher effectiveness and performance;
- to motivate teachers and pupils.

As Lambert reminds us, assessment by teachers and awarding bodies (which largely replaced examination boards in 1997) has traditionally been seen as 'an inevitable and essential part of the education process' (Lambert, 1997, p. 255). However, assessment should not simply be about end of course, or end of unit, testing where students receive acknowledgement of their attainment on the previous work studied in the form of a single mark or grade. If this is the only form of assessment applied a few students inevitably carry away the 'glittering prizes', whilst the majority measure themselves by degrees of failure against the performance of the very best. All too often assessment implies that we must focus too quickly on what children are *not* capable of, rather than celebrating what they *can* do. In a more rounded assessment system the process should be 'two way' in that the student should not merely be a passive recipient of a fixed judgement made about his or her attainment, but be regularly included in discussions about the assessment information gathered and the ways forward for their future learning. Not only is this a process of the teacher 'getting to know' the student in educational terms, but also of the student more fully understanding the process of teaching, learning, assessment and improving attainment.

2 | RECENT DEVELOPMENTS IN ASSESSMENT

The Education Reform Act of 1988 represented something of a watershed in terms of assessment practice in England and Wales due to the resultant implementation of a National Curriculum. Previously governments had viewed assessment, and indeed the construction and delivery of school curricula in general, as a professional matter to be determined largely by teachers themselves. Admittedly, external examinations at ages 16 and 18 were already controlled by examination boards and were therefore largely outside the influence of practising teachers, but education and assessment to the age of 14 was very much within the domain of the schools – particularly following the wholesale removal of the 11+ examination from most LEAs as a result of the comprehensivization of schools. The National Curriculum initially changed this by providing a very detailed specification of what should be taught in each subject from ages 5 to 16, and by focusing attention on both the methods and levels of assessment at the end of each of the Key Stages. By centralizing the assessment of all students it was hoped that the collection of information about the educational performance of teachers, students and schools would be possible, on which national standards could be measured.

One of the largest developments in assessment practice was the forced ascendancy of teacher assessment. It soon became apparent in the early 1990s that national testing, as a means of collecting accurate data on student attainment across four Key Stages in each curriculum subject, would be both unwieldy and prohibitively expensive. However, the government of the day still wanted to collect reliable national data on student performance that could be used to compare the educational performance of schools and monitor standards. Therefore foundation subjects, such as geography, avoided the imposition of Standard Assessment Tasks (SATs) which were reserved for the core subjects of English, Mathematics and Science. In geography, teachers were charged with the responsibility of providing a 'level' for each student's attainment at the end of Key Stage 3. These levels were determined as a 'best fit' against published level descriptions and were to be decided by a process of teacher assessment. Such teacher assessment became pivotal to the planning and evaluation of lessons, to the provision and recording of information about student progress, to the construction of future learning activities and to the eventual professional judgement of student attainment at the end of the Key Stage. As a result teacher assessment has now achieved a greater status, recognition and importance than at any other time. However, the consistency of the assessment standards applied by different teachers in different schools is an issue. Geography departments were not alone in their struggle to cope with the shift in the national assessment system in the early days of the National Curriculum, a situation quickly reported by OFSTED (1993a, 1993b). Very little money, or guidance, was being directed towards supporting teacher assessment in these early days, particularly compared to the very large amounts being directed towards testing the core subjects. It is still unrealisitic to expect that teacher assessment will ever create unambiguous national standards of student assessment, even with the help of supporting materials from ACAC (1996), ACCAC (1997), SCAA (1996a, 1996b) and its replacement organization the QCA; however, if a high level of consistency in judgements is achieved between schools such assessments will gain widespread credibility.

External (or public) examinations have also witnessed major structural changes. The General Certificate of Secondary Education (GCSE) replaced both the GCE Ordinary Level (O level) and Certificate of Secondary Education (CSE) in 1986, ending over twenty years of a two tier examination system at age 16. Encapsulated within the GCSE is the belief that a national assessment system could be devised that recognized and rewarded 'positive achievement', rather than simply striving to divide the academic 'sheep' from the 'goats'. The aim of creating a unified examination to serve virtually all abilities and of removing the difference in esteem that existed between the O level (for the 'most able' 20 per cent of the population) and CSE (for the 'middle ability', or next 40 per cent) was only partly achieved. The subsequent introduction of 'tiered papers' for different abilities within the GCSE and the creation of Part 1 General National Vocational Qualifications (GNVQs) in 1998 served to broaden options at 14, but raised questions about the status and comparability of these assessments. In addition the Certificate of Achievement (CoA), a qualification designed to offer certification to school leavers who would not be expected to achieve GCSEs, was also introduced in the same year (Flinders, 1998). Whilst this broadening of academic and vocational pathways is of benefit to students' education, the creation of further options at age 14 simply reduced the number of students choosing geography after Key Stage 3.

Within the 16–19 age range the GCE Advanced level (A level) has provided the 'gold standard' qualification for university entrance for many years. Criticized for apparent over-specialization the A level has resisted attempts at fundamental reform on numerous occasions, the most recent being those of the Higginson Report (DES, 1988) and Dearing Review (1996). However, change has occurred – most A levels are now modular rather than linear in form following reforms to most subject specifications in the late 1990s. Modular courses are taught in separate modules (three in AS and a further three in A2) which are assessed at points through the course, rather than all at the end of the entire course. From September 2000 new A level and Advanced Subsidiary (AS) level examinations were introduced for geography by all awarding bodies, reducing the total number of geography specifications offered at this level. All geography students now study an assessed AS level in their first year, progressing to A2 and the award of the full A level in their second year. This has meant that the majority of students now have a broader educational experience at the start of their post-16 education, studying around five AS levels. This usually narrows to three A levels for the majority of students in their final year. Additionally an Advanced Extension Award (AEA) was announced in March 1999 as a 'world class test' for the most able eighteen-year-olds, set against international standards benchmarked by the International Baccalaureate Organisation.

Both the GCSE and A/AS level examinations have specifications set against criteria. In geography these are the GCSE National Criteria for Geography and A and AS level Subject Criteria for Geography (QCA, 1999c). The aim of these criteria is to standardize the construction of specifications for geography between awarding bodies and to create a 'bridge' between norm and criterion referenced methods of assessment (see p. 152). Each set of criteria broadly indicates the aims and objectives for the specifications; assessment weightings for knowledge, skills and understanding; geographical content and concepts; and the range of spatial scales to be studied. The development of geographical enquiry skills, and their assessment through coursework (usually fieldwork), is also expected at both levels.

Recently educationists have questioned whether a 14–16, followed by a 16–19, configuration of national external assessment is still sensible even though compulsory schooling ends at the age of 16. With around 70 per cent of students 'staying on' in full time education after the completion of GCSEs it appears more appropriate to have a 14–19 orientation to the curriculum, rather than concentrating students' efforts on an 'intermediate' assessment at age 16. The growth of vocational qualifications within the 14–19 curriculum, such as the General National Vocational Qualifications (GNVQs) and more recently the Vocational A Levels, has created further pressures for such a re-orientation. Unfortunately geography currently appears to be marginalized within Key Stage 4, pressured on both sides by various academic and vocational options. Some geography teachers therefore have the less than tantalizing choice of maybe offering students 'short courses' in geography at GCSE, or putting their efforts into promoting Leisure and Tourism qualifications, in an attempt to convey some form of geography education post-14 (see Rawling, 1997).

3 | ASSESSMENT IN THE TYPICAL (GEOGRAPHY) CLASSROOM

Research evidence tends to suggest that teachers do not use assessment in the most helpful ways to advance student learning. Black and Wiliam (1998) note that in the typical classroom assessment feedback from the teacher, either orally or in writing, tends to be overly generous and unfocused giving students little real support in improving their learning. Feedback also tends to be used for managerial or social purposes, rather than for highlighting specific learning goals. In assessing written work, teachers regularly seem more concerned with filling their markbooks with grades than meeting the educational imperative of improving learning – they focus too readily on students' presentation and length of answers, rather than on content and learning. In addition teachers only rarely meet to discuss and improve their assessment practices, preferring to keep such matters in the 'black box' of the classroom away from investigation, challenge and possible change.

Black and Wiliam (1998) suggest a variety of ways in which assessment practice could be improved. Central to this is the encouragement of a 'culture of success' in which students understand that they will have to face challenging and taxing educational tasks, but that they also are expected to take risks and to make mistakes. Assessment should point students towards explicit learning goals without making negative comparisons with the work of other students in the classroom. Much of the improvement in students' attainment relies on them taking responsibility for their own learning and assessment performances – to encourage this it is suggested that students should feel confident about expressing their problems orally and that they should develop competence in self assessment, analysing and expressing what they can do as well as what they can't! Once students begin to understand the criteria for success in geography they have moved a considerable way towards improving their attainment. From the teachers' perspective effective lesson planning and the establishment of clear and achievable learning objectives for each lesson are key.

Practical activity 9.1

1. Complete an audit of the range of different assessment methods regularly used within a geography department at Key Stage 3. Do one or two methods of assessment dominate? What effect does this have on the process of making both formative and summative assessment decisions?

2. What kind of assessment information is gathered by geography teachers? To what use is it put? Are these mainly educational uses, bureaucratic uses, or a mixture of both?

3.1 The role of level descriptions

Following the Dearing Report (1994) on the National Curriculum each of the Subject Orders were slimmed down to ease their complexity, content loading and over-prescription. Programmes of study were simplified and clarified, whilst in geography a single attainment target was created from the five which had previously existed. Importantly, the 183 statements of attainment, that had proved so hard to assess, were replaced by a system of eight level descriptions, with an additional level for 'exceptional performance'.

Level descriptions describe the types and range of performance, and expected attainment, at a particular level within an attainment target. They are descriptive criteria of what a student should know, understand and be able to do to achieve a given level in each curriculum subject. Level descriptions therefore represent an attempt to state national criteria, and to establish national standards, for the assessment of students. In geography they refer to particular skills, enquiries, places, patterns, processes and themes and are broadly progressive as one moves from one level to the next. As geography is a synthesizing and integrative subject care must be taken not to disaggregate the levels in an effort to 'fine tune' student assessment. The important consideration is achieving a 'best fit' – where the students' whole performance in terms of their skills, place knowledge and understanding of geographical themes is assessed.

The major issue surrounding the application of level descriptions is their interpretation against students' work. Teacher assessment of this kind is never wholly objective and straightforward – the work that a geography teacher in a particular school assesses as being of a certain level may be assessed differently by another teacher in a different school. Hence the difficulties of achieving national standards. However, as Balderstone reminds us:

> Teachers' knowledge of the level descriptions, and understanding of what they mean in relation to students' work, will increase with experience. One of the most effective ways of gaining this experience is to discuss students' work and achievements with other teachers. This, together with reaching agreement about what evidence we might expect to find of progress through the levels, is the approach to take.
>
> (Balderstone, 2000, p. 10)

In addition the publication of support materials featuring examples of students' work and how they might be assessed, such as the Exemplification of Standards at Key Stage 3 (SCAA, 1996a) and web-based exemplification materials which accompany the most recent version of the Geography National Curriculum (DfEE/ QCA, 1999a), have helped to promote some consistency in teacher assessment.

Gipps (1994) suggests that teacher assessments of the kind seen in the National Curriculum are credible and that although they may never achieve the highest standards of *reliability* and *objectivity* they do exhibit aspects of *comparability*. That is, they show a professional and consistent approach by teachers which links to a common understanding of the levels, rather than a more narrowly bureaucratic approach associated with testing. Unfortunately the level descriptions, which tend to describe 'steps' of difference between the levels rather than a gradual 'incline', are not presented in a particularly 'student friendly' language. The descriptions therefore need to be interpreted with the students before they can become partners in the process of assessment.

3.2 Planning for assessment

All lesson plans should take account of the assessment of learning. The National Curriculum Subject Orders are each designed with assessment in mind, such that lesson plans can be constructed to show an awareness of the programme of study, of the learning objectives and outcomes desired, as well as an appreciation of how these will be assessed. Opportunities for assessment are closely linked to the statement of learning objectives and should therefore be considered at the start of the process of lesson planning, not 'tacked on' as an afterthought. Unfortunately recent inspection evidence in geography suggests that assessment is insufficiently integrated into such planning (Butt and Smith, 1998; OFSTED, 1996, 1999a). Standards of performance against which the students' efforts can be measured, usually in the form of assessment criteria, should also be stated at the outset.

With any planned assessment, be it for a whole class end of unit assessment or a national examination, there are important considerations of validity and reliability. In essence these terms allude to the fairness of the assessment – validity refers to whether the assessment methods actually provide the assessor with information about what he or she wants to assess, reliability refers to whether the assessment is standardized and therefore repeatable with comparable results on other occasions with a similar population.

It is essential that assessment should be planned for the short, medium and long term (see Hopkin and Telfer, 2000). In this way teachers can take account of students' progression against the geography curriculum and a wide range of assessment activities can be planned to give students the opportunities to show what they know, understand and can do (see Figure 9.1)

In essence long-term assessment planning is about assessment policy, where decisions are made in the geography department concerning the type and frequency of assessments, taking into account whole school policies for (say) end of year reporting and half termly gradings (Hopkin and Telfer, 2000). Medium-term assessment strategies anchor the informal day-to-day judgements made about students' performance by providing opportunities to assess in greater depth, such as through the provision of extended enquiry tasks, end of unit tests or special assessment occasions. The QCA schemes of work for geography at Key Stage 3 (QCA, 2000) provide a range of progressive units which aim to advance student achievement and create a framework for medium-term assessment. They also give guidelines for expectations of students' attainment at the end of each unit and can be used alongside SCAA's (1996a) 'Exemplification of Standards at Key Stage 3: Geography' to standardize assessment decisions. Short term assessment planning relates to the learning objectives stated within each lesson plan – the evidence for this can be collected formally and informally during each lesson, as explained in the following section.

The Optional Tests and Tasks (SCAA, 1996b; ACCAC, 1997) can be used to provide assessment evidence and assist teachers in making judgements of students' levels of attainment. Their detailed marking schemes and assessment criteria help to develop an understanding of student progression and achievement, whilst the tasks themselves act as useful models on which to base further assessed activities and mark schemes.

3.3 Marking students' work

The day-to-day marking of students' work provides a vital dialogue between the teacher and the learner. Many different forms of marking are used within education – each has its own conventions of communication, having been devised for the

	Planning for progression: learning objectives	Planning for progression: attainment and target setting
Long term	• Learning objectives for the key stage are general and closely related to the programme of study or GCSE syllabus, i.e. knowledge, understanding and skills. • To promote progression over the Key Stage, decisions focus on how the programme of study/ syllabus can be divided into topics or study units, and when these are planned. For example, a spiral approach to the Key Stage plan helps students revisit, develop and extend their knowledge, concepts and skills.	• The level descriptions in geography are designed as benchmarks against which to assess students' attainment over Key Stage 3 as a whole. • Level descriptions are useful as a focus for long-term evaluation of how successful the curriculum has been in promoting learning and providing opportunities for students to show their attainments. • This helps to set departmental targets and to make decisions about where to focus next to raise achievement and 'standards'.
Medium term	• Here progression is concerned with the development of knowledge, understanding and skills within a topic or unit. • The focus is on planning sequences of learning objectives that will help support students' progress, e.g. by broadening and deepening their knowledge and understanding, and relating these objectives to assessment. • Evaluation at the end of the unit helps focus on the progress students have made	• Key decisions focus on identifying assessment opportunities to match the learning objectives. These should be developmental, to match progression over the unit as a whole. • Here the level descriptions are less useful although they may help in deciding the level of demand of activities and the pitch of assessment. • Student self-assessment and target setting help support their progress towards the next stages in their learning.
Short term	• Progression in individual lessons is concerned with the (often small) steps students make in the development of knowledge, understanding and skills. • Planning is focused on deciding on specific objectives, activities and opportunities for assessment, and on differentiation. • So progression is an integral part of teaching and learning, related to deciding strategies for individuals and groups, assessing and monitoring progress and deciding future objectives.	• Assessment within lessons can be based on a range of informal and more formal strategies, such as observing and talking to students and marking their work. • The focus is on using information gained from these assessments to decide the next step in their learning, in other words supporting progression at the most important level. • Here the level descriptions are of little value, since they relate to the Key Stage as a whole and the steps between them are large.

Figure 9.1 *Progression in objectives and attainment (Hopkin et al., 2000)*

different purposes of motivating, informing or censuring the individual who receives the information. What is important is that the student understands what the communication is 'saying' from the teacher's perspective and, more importantly, how he or she can improve their performance in the future. Whatever 'marks' are placed on a student's work they are most helpful if they both assess what has been attained, as well as help the student to understand what is required of them to perform and learn better in the future.

Hopkin (2000, p. 39) helpfully outlines the main teacher activity when adopting formative assessment strategies in the classroom as follows:

- watching and listening to students as they work;

- questioning, discussing or reviewing work with students;

- marking students' work, perhaps alongside them;

- students reflecting on and assessing their own work;

- agreeing 'what next' with students, that is, short-term targets to improve their work.

It is worthwhile considering when marking students' work how your assessment of their performance will have consequences for their future learning (what Gipps (1994) refers to as 'consequential validity'). That is, will your marking be 'valid' in that it helps the students to improve their learning in the future? A further interesting consideration arises as to whether choosing *not* to mark a particular piece of the students' work, or marking it in a different way, creates any significant consequence for their future learning. It is salutary to think that one's marking may not be having any effect whatsoever on the learning process of the students! Thus, how do we make sure that our marking *does* have a formative effect on student learning (Figure 9.2)?

Marking is a time consuming and sometimes tedious activity for many teachers. If it has no point – that is, if it has no 'consequential validity' in changing the ways in which students learn and perform in their assessments – then it is a fruitless exercise. However, good, reliable assessment information is very highly valued and sought after. Heads of Department and inspectors are interested in how students perform, parents are often anxious to know how their child is progressing and the students themselves value the feedback that marking provides. Most geography departments have a marking policy which outlines for teachers, students and parents the principles by which work is assessed, monitored, recorded and reported upon. Such policies seek to ensure consistency in assessment practice and usually convey a commitment to the principles of formative assessment. They sometimes address issues of manageability of assessment by making statements about how frequently students' work should be marked, the kinds of grades and comments that will be added, and the assessment criteria that will be applied.

3.4 'High stakes' and 'low stakes' assessment

External examinations, such as for GCSEs, A and AS levels, are often termed 'high stakes' assessments in that their results are used for the bureaucratic purpose of selecting future (educational) pathways for students. Examination results can be easily constructed into league tables from which individual schools' and teachers'

1. The criteria against which students' work is assessed should be clearly communicated and understood. Both 'assessor' and assessed' should be 'talking the same assessment language'. The assessment criteria should link back to the learning objectives stated for the lesson.
2. The reason why marks have been awarded (or withheld) should be made clear to the student. What the marks are awarded for should therefore be mutually understood. Often teachers award marks for attainment and/or effort. (But how does a teacher know what effort a student has really made on a piece of assessed work? Can we compare one students' efforts with another? What does it mean to a student to be awarded high effort marks but low attainment marks; or vice versa?)
3. What and how you are going to mark, needs to have been considered when planning the lesson. Will you concentrate on the students' grasp of geographical content? Or skills? Will you give credit for presentation? Will marks be taken away for poor spelling, punctuation and grammar? Do you intend to provide a written comment on each piece of work? To 'say' what? Is the student expected to respond to your comment? Will he or she understand what is being communicated?
4. The next educational steps should be apparent to the student. He or she should know, from the comments and marks on a piece of assessed work, what has to be done to progress in terms of learning, attainment, and assessment.
5. At the end of the assessment process the teacher should be confident about why he or she has awarded each particular mark to each student. It is a professional responsibility to be able to account for one's marking – to know, and to be able to explain or justify, why *this* mark has been given to *this* piece of work.

It is not necessary to mark every new piece of work in the same way, or to the same depth. At times you may wish to concentrate on giving feedback and suggesting improvements, on setting targets, on spelling, punctuation and grammar, on redrafting a piece of writing, on correcting errors, or merely checking that the work has been completed. There is a danger of over assessment if everything the student does is closely assessed, particularly if that assessment is all encompassing with respect to each of the points raised above. Some of the work produced by students merely has to be 'acknowledged' by the teacher as having been completed, usually by placing a 'tick' next to it. The *focus* for the assessment should vary at times and any change of assessment focus should be made clear to the students. It is better to assess less work to a high standard, than to mark all work superficially. Many geography departments also devise 'key assessment tasks' to assess the main aspects of a unit of work studied by the students.

Figure 9.2 *Some considerations when marking students' work*

performances can be compared. As a consequence there is a temptation for many teachers to 'teach to the test' or to skew the educational experience of students towards the 'successful' completion of a summative assessment at the end of a course. There are numerous examples of the assessment 'tail' wagging the curriculum 'dog', where teachers gear their teaching narrowly towards ensuring that their eventual league table standing is enhanced. For example some teachers admit to concentrating on trying to improve the examination performance of grade C/D borderline students as these results will 'count' significantly in league tables of proportions of A to C grades achieved at GCSE. As a consequence candidates who are expected to achieve 'straight' A, B or C grades are given less attention as they are already reasonably safely 'banked' in terms of their future examination performance. Other effects of 'high stakes' assessments may not be immediately

> **Certification** – the provision of an award, usually as a paper qualification, for performance in given assessment(s).
> **Diagnostic assessment** – assessment which targets particular learning difficulties faced by the student so that future teaching and learning activities can be designed to counter these.
> **Evaluation** – the use of assessment information to appraise some aspect of the teaching and learning process. This might be an appraisal of the assessment task itself, of the teaching previously carried out, or of the learning that has resulted as witnessed by assessment results.
> **Informal assessment** – part of the classroom routine, for example, observing students as they work questioning them or through discussion.
> **Formal assessment** – an 'occasion' set up internally or externally. Examples would range from a short test or special assessment task to public examinations.
> **Formative assessment** – using formally or informally collected information about students' learning to plan and support future learning.
> **Summative assessment** – using assessment information, usually from a variety of tasks, to produce a statement of what a student knows, understands and can do.
> **Teacher assessment** – the continuing process of assessment through which teachers monitor and record student progress. The information gathered is used both to support future student learning and eventually to make a summative judgement of student progress. At Key Stage 3, judgements about national curriculum levels are based on teacher assessment.

Figure 9.3 *Some assessment terminology (adapted from Hopkin et al., 2000)*

apparent but do tend to affect the educational experience of students in various ways – in geography this may mean that 'examination' classes are more rushed, that less discussion and open-ended learning takes place, that fieldwork is only experienced if it directly contributes to examination coursework, that games, role plays and simulations are avoided (particularly if they will take more than one lesson to complete), that 'case study' examples are learned by rote and that photocopied materials may simply be passed to students to learn.

'Low stakes' assessments are usually those that are made by teachers on a day-to-day basis. These are often formative, having been designed to support students' future learning, and seek to encourage the learner to correct mistakes revealed through assessment. Their purpose is therefore wholly educational – unlike summative assessments the point is not to compare each student's performance with that of his or her peers, but to determine what the next educational steps should be for both the learner and the teacher. Low stakes assessments can be extremely varied, ranging from the assessed presentation of a group work task, to a piece of single project work, or to an extended writing exercise.

3.5 Norm referenced and criterion referenced assessments

The 'traditional' forms of assessment, those used for high stakes external examinations such as GCSE and A levels, are generally norm referenced. Here a cohort of students are tested and then ascribed a grade related to the marks they have gained. The students' work is judged in comparison with that of the other students who have sat the same examination; no pre determined fixed standard exists for particular grades. For example, the whole population of students who have been examined may ultimately be divided up such that the top 10 per cent of marks are given a grade 'A' and the bottom 10 per cent 'fail'. The awarding of particular grades depends on the performance of the *whole* population of students taking the test – therefore in a 'strong' year, when the candidates are mostly 'able' and perform well in the test, a particular student may only be awarded, say, a grade 'B' for an examination performance that in a 'weak' year might be capable of earning him or her a grade 'A'! Therefore grading is determined by the (usually normal, or bell shaped) distribution of marks awarded for the entire population of examination entrants. Inevitably a percentage of students will always fail in such a norm referenced assessment system, even given the albeit unlikely event that they all perform extremely well in their examinations.

By contrast a criterion referenced system of assessment appears fairer. Here the standards of performance are 'fixed' into a set of written criteria before the assessment takes place. If a particular student, on assessment, matches a particular criteria for performance and attainment he or she will be awarded with the grade that is ascribed to that criteria. It therefore does not matter how other students taking the assessment perform – any number of students who meet a given criteria can be awarded the grade which accompanies it. As Butt states: 'Criteria-referenced assessment is based on acknowledging positive achievement related to learning objectives' (Butt, 2000b, p. 21).

It is important to realize that although criterion referenced assessment systems appear to be the fairest, both criterion and norm referenced assessments can be applied well or badly. In geography it is often very difficult to provide a criterion for the assessment of each piece of content, or skill, such that when criteria are devised and applied they often need to refer to previously established norms to make the assessment process work.

In essence the National Curriculum level descriptions are criteria for assessment and can be used in both a formative and summative way – however, like any assessment which seeks to serve two different purposes, this creates tensions and difficulties. As Lambert and Balderstone comment in their reflections on the attempt to create a single, criteria referenced system to meet all assessment purposes in the National Curriculum:

> To this day, it is still far from clear exactly how so-called National Curriculum 'Teacher Assessment' should operate in order to fulfil a formative role at the same time as providing a single, summative attainment level for reporting to parents or other schools and teachers.
>
> (Lambert and Balderstone, 2000, p. 338)

4 | MONITORING, RECORDING AND REPORTING ASSESSMENTS

The monitoring, recording and reporting of assessment information must consider two important questions:

1. Is the process of monitoring, recording and reporting manageable, consistent and understandable?

2. Does the information collected impact positively on the process of teaching and learning?

In essence these are considerations of purpose. It is only sensible to spend time and effort monitoring, recording and reporting assessment information if it is going to have some positive impact on the educational process. Mark books full of grades, comments and symbols may look impressive, but if the data recorded serves little or no purpose what is the point of painstakingly collecting it?

Whatever system is used to record assessment information – and there are many different types – it should ideally be capable of:

- providing accurate information about each student's knowledge, understanding and skills in geography that can be readily understood by students, teachers and parents;

- simple aggregation into a synoptic assessment of each students' level(s) of attainment;

- reflecting a variety of modes of assessment, each of which give specific information on different aspects of each student's attainment;

- creation into a form that can usefully be reported to parents' evenings, department meetings, profiles of achievement, etc.;

- flexibility, such that valid and reliable assessment information can be extracted for different audiences at different times (assessment information that is 'fit for purpose').

It is worthwhile remembering that perhaps the most powerful and substantial record of each student's daily performance is often carried in the teacher's head. Here the impressions, observations, feelings, and attitudes of the teacher to each student, based on their classroom presence (both academic and behavioural), are amassed in a holistic form. Teachers add to this 'assessment record' every time they teach, modifying it slightly each day as new ephemeral evidence is presented to them in the classroom.

5 | THE USE OF PORTFOLIOS

Portfolios can provide a means of collecting a sample of students' work in geography which exemplify the standards of work produced in a school or department (Howes, 1996, 2000). These portfolios can then be used as a basis on which to make level judgements in geography at Key Stage 3 and can provide evidence for monitoring progression in achievement. Although there is no obligation to collect students' work in this way, the resulting portfolios, either of the work of single students or of a group of students whose work exemplifies attainment of a particular level, help to support the 'levelling' process. Portfolios can be used in combination with exemplification materials produced by SCAA (1996a) to help to determine standards of student performance.

A range of different types of portfolios exist (after Howes, 2000):

- *geography department portfolio, Key Stage 'levels' portfolio* – designed to provide exemplars of students' work completed on a range of different activities against which consistent judgements of performance can be made. Such portfolios therefore exemplify the geography department's beliefs about the standards which need to be achieved for the award of a particular level. Departmental portfolios are helpful in the process of differentiating between work judged to be at the borderline between two levels. The work contained within the portfolio should have been assessed collectively by members of the geography department at an agreement trail, so as to ensure that teacher assessment standards are comparable across the whole department.

- *Individual student portfolios* – frequently updated portfolios, where a small set of exemplars of a particular student's achievements are kept. Such portfolios should see a 'turnover' of work and be used to support summative assessments of performance, or as a discussion document to be used with the student, other teachers and/or parents to help the formative development of that student.

- *Class portfolios* – to provide a record of the activities and achievements of a particular class and to aid the curriculum review process. Common assessment activities, used across all the geography classes within a year group, might be collected into a class portfolio to enable comparisons across teaching groups.

Portfolios have a range of audiences and purposes and can (Howes, 2000, p. 63):

- serve as a reference point for all teachers in promoting and supporting consistent judgements both during a Key Stage and at the end of a Key Stage;

- be used as a focus for moderation between schools;

- support new colleagues in informing their understanding and judgements;

- remove the pressure on individual teachers to build up their own collection of work to support their judgements;

- demonstrate to others (e.g. parents, other teachers, students, governors, OFSTED) the agreed standards of work within the school;

- exemplify progression and support evaluation and review of the school's geography curriculum;

- include work from a small number of 'case study' students, showing a range of work and attainment, for example, Levels 3, 5 and 7.

To be most useful, the materials collected in portfolios should have attached a comment sheet on which the geography teacher who has selected the work may record the context or focus for the sample. In addition annotations recording significant features of the performance of each student on this task, a brief summary to show how this work has fulfilled (or not achieved) expectations, and an indication of how or why the teacher's judgement has been made are all useful contributions to the portfolio. Obviously there is a danger that recording such information can become time consuming and unwieldy – it is therefore advisable to only collect a few pieces of exemplar materials, but to annotate these carefully. Often students are asked to complete self evaluation slips that can be included in personal portfolios (see Figure 9.4) which can act as a stimulus for discussions between the student and teacher with the aim of achieving formative assessment.

Student's name: _____ Date: _____

Investigation title: _____
_____

Did you understand what you had to do? _____
_____

What did you find difficult? _____
_____
_____

What did you enjoy? _____
_____
_____

Do you understand the teacher's comments and/or mark? _____
_____

What do you have to do to make progress in the future? _____
_____

Figure 9.4 *The student's geography self-evaluation sheet (from the John Kyrle High School) (Hopkin et al., 2000)*

Portfolios have the added advantage that they provide a transferable record of a student's work should he or she move class, or schools; they provide evidence for OFSTED inspectors of work undertaken, assessment policy, student involvement in assessment and standards achieved; and can support beginning teachers or new colleagues in the assessment judgements they make.

Practical activity 9.2

1. With a partner who teaches in another school collect a range of assessed pieces of work from four students which you think exemplify two adjacent levels within Key Stage 3. Check these pieces against the level descriptions to decide upon which level you think they 'best fit'. How useful were these exemplars, and the assessment tasks from which they were derived, in helping to determine the levels achieved by the students? How might these assessment tasks be improved upon, or added to, to act as more accurate signifiers of levels attainment?

2. Look at the level descriptions for geography at Levels 5 and 7. What sort of assessment activities would you need to devise to accurately assess attainment during Key Stage 3 against these level descriptions? What are the most

> appropriate assessment opportunities needed to cover the range of knowledge, understanding and skills expected in geography at Key Stage 3?

CONCLUSION

Black and Wiliam, in a major research paper reviewing the recent literature on teacher assessment, conclude that student learning responds most effectively to frequent formative assessment. Of equal importance is the ability of students to reflect on their own academic performance and to be able to picture their learning in terms of what they need to do to perform better. Unfortunately, the current day-to-day assessment practices in the classroom do not generally address either of these goals because (after Black and Wiliam, 1998):

- superficial rote learning often takes place, with classroom assessment based on the recall of details of knowledge which students soon forget;

- teachers fail to review the forms of assessment used, do not discuss assessment practices with other teachers and rarely reflect on what is being assessed;

- there is an over-emphasis on grading and an under-emphasis on learning;

- there is a tendency to use normative rather than criterion-referenced assessment systems;

- teachers emphasize competition through their assessment methods, rather than personal achievement and performance;

- assessment methods tend to reinforce perceptions of failure among the less able, leading to de-motivation and a loss of confidence in their ability to learn; and

- dominance of external, summative testing is still the norm.

It is always worth remembering that assessment is best defined as an 'art' rather than a 'science'. As such, as Hopkin *et al.* state:

> Objectivity is almost certainly impossible in any form of assessment. The whole process of assessing children is dependent on the subjective judgements of teachers and examiners, albeit using objective criteria.
>
> (Hopkin *et al.*, 2000, p. 20)

Assessment requires effective professional judgement, skill, competence and confidence – the latter, in particular, to adjust earlier judgements made about students' attainments and abilities, and to value the need to make positive comments as much as negative ones (Lambert, 1997). Because of the difficulties surrounding the selection, application and interpretation of the results gained by using various assessment instruments it is worthwhile reminding ourselves of their fallibility. This is partly a result of 'user error' but also due to the high, and unrealistic, expectations we still have of summative assessment systems.

In essence our view of assessment is often heavily influenced by our view of intelligence. If one believes that students' abilities and intelligences are largely fixed at birth, then the role of the teacher is merely to prepare them for assessments where the results are, to a greater or lesser extent, already determined by their genes. If, however, your view is that teachers can 'make a difference', and that intelligence is not fixed and immutable, then the results of students' assessments are not pre determined. As Lambert and Balderstone (2000) point out, adopting this view affects the whole way in which you teach – students will no longer be labelled as (say) passive, less able, recipients of your teaching, but as active learners who can – with help and support – improve their intelligences and by so doing enhance their assessment performance. Using assessment evidence to try to determine the attainment, or indeed the ability, of students is fraught with dangers – not least because it is too often assumed that the relationship between performance, attainment and ability is simple, linear and straightforward. Using a single assessment tool in an attempt to understand the complexities of such factors of intelligence is almost certain to fail. Rather we must be guided by a set of assessment principles in our attempts to get to know students better.

Much has changed within the 'assessment industry' over the past decade. Formative teacher assessment, with its aim of improving students' learning, has achieved a significant status within the whole process of education. Geography teachers are, in general, clearer about the reasons why effective planning should incorporate the use of specific learning objectives, assessment criteria and assessment methods. Assessment information gathered from such lessons should inform future planning and enable individual students to improve upon their educational performance.

CHAPTER 10

The role of ICT in the teaching and learning of geography[2]

ICT is more than just another teaching tool. Its potential for improving the quality and standards of pupils' education is significant. Equally, its potential is considerable for supporting teachers, both in their everyday classroom role ... and in their continuing training and development.

(DfEE/QCA, 1999b)

Despite the hype and the range of articles imploring teachers to use the technology, it is vital that ICT be used only where it does add value to the geography.

(Hassell, 2000a p. 89)

INTRODUCTION

It is currently a statutory requirement that all trainee teachers successfully follow a National Curriculum in Information and Communications Technology[2] (ICT) in ITT (DfEE, 1998a), and pass an ICT skills test, before they can be awarded QTS and start their teaching career. Given the importance ascribed to the use of ICT in the classroom it is essential that trainee geography teachers are conversant with both research and practice in this area. Recent governments have, quite rightly, felt that the educational world has rather 'dragged its feet' with respect to fully embracing the use of new technologies – although it is readily apparent why this reticence has occurred within many schools and departments, as teachers suffer the 'innovations fatigue' associated with having to implement yet more government initiatives (Hargreaves, 1994). However, ICT is pervasive in society and many feel there is 'a duty to ensure that pupils leave school prepared for life in the technological world of the twenty-first century' (Hassell, 2000a, p. 81). In addition ICT is now central within the study of geography itself, as a consequence of its influence on globalization, the growth in the use of satellite imagery and the development of GIS (Geographic Information Systems).

---

[2] The term Information and Communication Technology (ICT), as used within this chapter, encompasses a wide range of technologies including microcomputers (portable and desktop), software packages (word processors, databases, speadsheets), input devices (keyboards), output devices (monitors, printers), and storage devices (CD-ROMs). It also can refer to tape recorders, fax machines, telephones, video machines, satellite televisions and overhead projectors.

1   A BRIEF HISTORY OF THE USE OF ICT IN GEOGRAPHY AND GEOGRAPHY EDUCATION

The introduction of the requirement that all trainees follow a National Curriculum in ICT in ITT (DfEE, 1998a) during their initial teacher training was the culmination of a drive by successive governments in recent years to make the teaching profession more technologically proficient. Mention had previously been made in some initial teacher training circulars that trainees should become proficient in their use of educational technology, including computers (see DFE, 1992). However not all such pronouncements on training have been unequivocal with respect to ICT use (see Fisher, 2000). Therefore the publication of the ICT in ITT National Curriculum (DfEE, 1998a), combined with the introduction of ICT training for existing teachers under the National Lottery's 'New Opportunities Fund', represented a major step towards ensuring that all teachers would become competent in the use of new technologies. Teachers and their students are now required to both learn 'about' and 'with' computers, as a direct result of the government's drive to make all education technologically enhanced. (It is perhaps worth acknowledging that the government's intention is to spend around £1 billion on the development of the educational use of computers.)

The launch of the National Curriculum in schools heralded the first coordinated steps towards making the use of ICT a statutory requirement of education in each curriculum subject, even though Information Technology was to exist later as a National Curriculum subject in its own right (DFE 1995a; DfEE/QCA, 1999b). In geography all three versions of the Geography National Curriculum (GNC) (DES, 1991; DFE, 1995; DfEE/QCA, 1999a) have contained some reference to the use of ICT in the study of geography, becoming more prescriptive in successive documents. This increasing prescription has also been witnessed in the revisions of GCSE, A and AS level specifications for geography, where a compulsory requirement to assess the use of ICT in the context of geography now exists.

1.1   Computers in universities

In the 1960s and 1970s many university geography departments became increasingly interested in using large mainframe computers as an aid to data handling, particularly given the 'conceptual revolution' which was driving many geographers into using more quantitative means of analysing and interpreting data. Geographers made use of computer-based data handling software, cartographic packages, statistical programs and modelling software in their attempts to advance their discipline. Later the use of remote sensing equipment, which created satellite images of large expanses of the earth's surface via computer technology, provided geographers with another powerful tool; whilst the development of Geographic Information Systems (GIS), which use computer-based technology to display and analyse multivariate data spatially, is perhaps the current acme in both the educational and commercial application of geography related technology. Recently Global Positioning Systems (GPS), which can be utilized in the form of small hand held devices, have been suggested as useful additions to fieldwork in locating grid references or latitude and longitude of any location in the field.

The impact of these new technologies on many aspects of the study of physical, human and environmental geography has been profound. Not only have they provided the tools to change the *ways* in which geography is studied, but also the very *content* of geography as a subject. If we consider just one geographical theme, that of industrial geography, we can see how pervasive the effects of introducing new technologies have been – for example, they have radically changed the proportions of employment within different industrial sectors, the possession of technology-related skills has become increasingly important within the industrial labour force, and production and structural changes brought about by using such technology have altered the preferred locations of certain industries. The impacts of telecommuting, the growth of call centres and the rise of e-commerce are also having profound influences on industrial and economic geography.

1.2 Computers in schools

The history of computer use in geography education in secondary schools is telling. A number of 'false dawns' have occurred – despite many confident predictions about the ways in which computer-aided learning (CAL) would dramatically revolutionize the teaching of geography. Like most innovations computers have had a number of pioneers and converts, but many geography teachers have watched from the sidelines, not getting involved.

In schools the impact of advances made in university geography departments through the use of computers were at first negligible. Although teachers were aware of the progress being made on the research frontiers of geography using new technologies the machines that were involved in making these advances were too expensive, too complicated and too unwieldy to be easily transferred to the geography classroom. Only with the advent of the 'microcomputer' in the late 1970s and early 1980s did computer-based learning in school geography departments become a possibility (see Midgley and Walker, 1985; Fox and Tapsfield, 1986; Watson, 1984). Kent (1992) and Jackson (2000) illustrate how the use of computers in geography education grew in the 1980s, highlighting the establishment of a regular Computer Page and software reviews in *Teaching Geography* from 1983, the growth of computer simulations in geography and the publication of case studies detailing how computers could be used in the geography classroom.

Initially, many geography teachers were 'technophobes' who either did not wish to devote the necessary time to learning how to use new technology, doubted its relevance to school geography, or that feared a loss of classroom control might result from its use. Many teachers argued that they had managed to teach effectively for years without using ICT, so why bother? (Hassell, 2000a). Geography teachers questioned whether their involvement with computers was being encouraged primarily to enable them to help educate a new generation of technologically proficient labour, or to incorporate new forms of pedagogy, or for subject related reasons – if the latter was the case many geography teachers felt that they could teach geography more efficiently by using 'tried and tested' methods, rather than by adopting new technologies to help them. This situation is largely changing – as a result of the greater use of personal computers in the home, through the development of the internet and the more significant role that such technologies now play in everybody's lives. Coupled with this has been the realization that a subject such as geography, which attempts to educate about the world around us, can make significant use of computer-based technologies and cannot ignore the impact of technology on many aspects of its subject content.

A major impetus on the uptake of computer use in geography education stemmed from the Geography and IT Support Project coordinated by both the Geographical Association (GA) and National Council for Educational Technology (NCET, now the British Educational Communications and Technology Agency or BECTa). Partly funded by the DfE this project helped four secondary subjects clarify their relationship with ICT and produce materials and INSET activities to broaden the dissemination of new practice. In 1994 the GA and NCET produced a booklet outlining students' entitlements to ICT within geography (NCET/GA, 1994). This was an attempt to clarify the aspects of ICT use which students could reasonably expect to gain from their geographical education.

The expectations on schools to produce a skilled, flexible, computer-literate labour force capable of sustaining, advancing or repairing our national economy are now clear. The necessity to remain internationally competitive, mainly through the application of a technologically advanced 'information economy', is agreed upon by all major political parties. In addition the aim to create a self sustaining 'learning society' has also been expressed, where access to information is enhanced by the use of new technologies. Today's social, cultural, educational and economic world has rapidly 'moved on', partly as a result of the influences of these new technologies, unfortunately schools have not progressed structurally or procedurally at the same pace and are now being charged with a responsibility for which they are not wholly equipped. This is partly due to the lack of a clear governmental vision, or strategy, for the implementation of ICT into education in the early and mid 1990s (although governments have not been nervous about spending money on this 'problem'!). Since 1997 a more systematic range of initiatives was put in place building upon the proposals of the Independent ICT in Schools Commission (1997) which established development targets for the following five years in a consultation paper (DfEE, 1998b). The National Grid for Learning (NGfL) was established to ensure that these targets are achieved.

1.3   The National Grid for Learning (NGfL)

The National Grid for Learning (NGfL) has four main functions – to enhance training in ICT, to improve infrastructure in schools, to set up websites, and to launch a range of smaller initiatives. The Grid connects all educational institutions to the internet. In terms of its training functions the ICT National Curriculum for ITT is one of the major initiatives, whilst the opportunities for existing teachers to train in the use of ICT under the aegis of the 'New Opportunities Fund' (NOF) is the other. Schools can only deliver ICT within their curricula if they have the necessary hard and software to do so and money is being centrally provided, some of it 'matched' by LEA funding, to enhance the schools' technological infrastructure. The NGfL website (www.ngfl.gov.uk) contains much information, advice and materials to support learning, as does the Virtual Teacher Centre (vtc.ngfl.gov.uk) supported by BECTa. The smaller initiatives aim to enhance teacher efficiency through their application of new technologies, new software and access to data.

Beyond the government initiatives such as the NGfL there are a number of EU sponsored projects for research and development of ICT use in education. In geography education two such projects – 'Eurogame' and HERODOT, which trains and supports geography teachers in their use of the internet – are worthy of mention (see Jackson, 2000).

Pupils studying geography are entitled to use ICT:	When undertaking these activities in geography:	ICT can contribute by making possible:
• to enhance their skills of geographical enquiry	• collecting, investigating and questioning data from primary (fieldwork) and secondary sources • undertaking a broad enquiry approach to a topic	*The use of:* • large amounts of data (e.g. data handling packages, CD-ROM and data otherwise difficult to obtain (e.g. data-logging) • a wide range of ICT techniques and approaches (e.g. creating and selecting maps, graphs for a report)
• to gain access to a wide range of geographical knowledge and information sources	• drawing on appropriate sources to obtain factual information, ideas and stimuli relating to place, physical, human and environmental topics	*Access to:* • new sources about places and environments (e.g. newspaper on CD-ROM); different ways of viewing the world (e.g. remote sensing); moving images, sound, first-hand contact (e.g. CD-ROM, e-mail); instantaneous images and information (e.g. fax, remote sensing)
• to deepen their understanding of environmental and spatial relatinships	• analysing change over time, locational decisions and people/environment inter-relationship	*Insight into:* • relationships otherwise inaccessible to pupils (e.g. modelling packages) and monitoring change over time (e.g. logging weather information)
• to experience alternative images of people, place and environment	• developing awareness and knowledge of other cultures, places and societies and creatively presenting one's own 'sense of place'	*Access to:* • real images views, and first-hand contact (e.g. e-mail, CD-ROM, video disk); creative ways of mixing sound, text and images (e.g. multimedia, word-processing, graphics)
• to consider the wider impact of ICT on people, place and environment	• studying specific examples e.g. changes in lifestyle, environmental impacts and locational consequences	• pupil knowledge and awareness of ICT use and applications in work and society

Figure 10.1 *A pupil's entitlement in ICT through geography (Lambert and Balderstone, 2000)*

1.4 The ICT National Curriculum in ITT

It is worthwhile focusing upon the ICT National Curriculum in ITT (DfEE, 1998a). Because all trainees have to address successfully this curriculum in the context of their own subject it is written as a generic document. It concentrates on when and how to use ICT effectively within teaching – although it obviously has to be interpreted by each curriculum subject with respect to its most sensible application. Written in two sections it details aspects of effective teaching and assessment using ICT (in effect, the pedagogical implications of ICT use), and the trainee's personal knowledge and understanding of, and competence with, ICT (the trainee's personal ICT capabilities). There are around 120 specific requirements within the ICT National Curriculum which means that within an intensive PGCE course finding the time to meet all of these requirements – particularly for trainees who are not initially *au fait* with ICT or who have other key considerations within their training – can prove problematic. Even for the many geography graduates who enter initial teacher training believing themselves to be competent in their personal use and understanding of ICT there may be issues concerning which aspects of skills, knowledge and understanding the ICT in ITT National Curriculum deems most appropriate.

All ITT courses should audit trainees' levels of ICT competence on entry, with the results being placed into the contexts of Sections A and B in the ICT National Curriculum for ITT such that personal targets and expectations can be clarified. The content and structure of these sections is interesting in terms of ITT, as Fisher points out when sounding the following cautionary note:

> The various sub-sections of Section A are all prefaced with the phrase 'trainees must be taught...' This implies that there is a body of knowledge about the appropriate use of computers in geography teaching, which is commonly known by ITE lecturers and school-based colleagues, and which can unproblematically be passed on to student teachers ... But [there] is not a systematic, theorized approach to the use of computers in the subject. Hence, it remains true that much of what is currently known about the sound educational use of computers should be regarded as tentative and provisional.
> (Fisher, 2000, p. 59)

Section B details a range of personal computing skills expected of the trainee. It is vital to remember that any skills training in ICT is of little value if those skills are not regularly used in the period following training and if the training is decontextualized. If one's ICT development is not set within the context of personal use, or within a real educational setting to enhance the teaching and learning of geography, it will be largely ineffectual. Perhaps one of the major issues currently facing ICT training in ITT is the problem that many geography mentors in schools are themselves not yet fully competent in using the technologies, or do not understand their pedagogical implications, in the geography classroom. There is still a large variability in schools' state of preparedness for the use of ICT, as well as problems of restricted access to computers, and of ageing hard and software. This has inevitably placed some pressures on trainees to lead, rather than to learn, with respect to the use of ICT in geography departments.

2	TEACHING GEOGRAPHY USING ICT

As teachers of geography our prime concern should be that students actually learn *geography*. This sounds self-evident, but it is a statement worthy of further consideration when the issue of ICT use in the teaching of geography is raised. Can we always be confident that we are primarily 'teaching geography' through the medium of ICT within the geography classroom? Or are we predominantly teaching ICT skills, with comparatively little geographical knowledge and understanding being learnt? The answers to these questions are not always straightforward and should be the focus of lesson evaluations.

The GNC (DfEE/QCA, 1999a) makes explicit reference to the use of ICT in geography teaching at Key Stage 3. In the section on 'Geographical enquiry and skills' the requirement is for pupils to be taught 'to select and use secondary sources of evidence' with particular reference to 'ICT-based sources [for example from the internet]' (p. 22). In addition they should use ICT to draw maps and plans at a range of scales (for example, using mapping software to plot the distribution of shops and services in a town centre), as well as communicating in different ways (writing a report about an environmental issue, exchanging fieldwork data using email) and include ICT in their development of decision-making skills (using a spreadsheet to help find the best location for a superstore). Marginal notes instruct the geography teacher that ICT can also be used to support fieldwork, perhaps by using a digital camera to record appropriate images, or to obtain Earth observation, satellite and other information about rainforest depletion and sustainable use. A number of opportunities for ICT use are also highlighted in the 'Breadth of Study' section which details the geographical themes students should cover in Key Stage 3.

Each statutory subject Order in the National Curriculum also makes clear that ICT should be used across the curriculum in the following manner:

1. Pupils should be given opportunities to apply and develop their ICT capability through the use of ICT tools to support their learning in all subjects (with the exception of physical education at Key Stages 1 and 2).

2. Pupils should be given opportunities to support their work by being taught to:

   a. find things out from a variety of sources, selecting and synthesising the information to meet their needs and developing an ability to question its accuracy, bias and plausibility;

   b. develop their ideas using ICT tools to amend and refine their work and enhance its quality and accuracy;

   c. exchange and share information, both directly and through electronic media;

   d. review, modify and evaluate their work, reflecting critically on its quality, as it progresses.

(DfEE/QCA, 1999a, p. 40)

Unfortunately the use of ICT in geography, and many other curriculum subjects, is still piecemeal. Lewis (1999) notes that the pedagogical thinking behind the introduction of new technologies is often limited, whilst Watson (2000) concludes that many geographers need considerable convincing that ICT will directly support their pedagogy before they are willing to adopt it. This tends to suggest that ICT is currently used as an occasional resource, rather than being viewed as central to many aspects of teaching and learning in geography. This, as Jackson (2000) notes, is a situation that will be increasingly debated as the nature of teaching and learning changes in a society where the new information age empowers individuals to access a greater range of resources and information. Conventional approaches to education will be transformed by distance, virtual and networked models of learning using new technologies.

Lambert and Balderstone (2000) highlight the belief that ICT has the potential to enhance students' skills of geographical enquiry. To meet this potential often requires two conditions to be met:

1. Geography teachers need to improve their own understanding and competence in the power of information technology to support enquiry methods (such as collecting, recording, analysing and presenting data in a variety of forms – text, maps, tables and diagrams).

2. Students need to develop their ICT skills beyond the basics of data handling (such as an ability to conduct a sound geographical enquiry utilizing information skills such as selection, evaluation, interpretation and presentation of appropriate data).

Like all other sources of (geographical) information, the data which is provided through ICT needs to be carefully interpreted and evaluated. Here the medium of ICT can be a helpful focus for the development of essential enquiry skills such as defining questions, finding information, assessing the relevance of information, and presenting it in the most appropriate forms to answer the questions set. An enquiry approach – which is central to the GNC and its assessment – is encouraged within the application of new technologies in geography education (see Fisher, 2000; NCET/GA, 1994). In this respect a good software program may actually have the capacity to provide and support virtually all aspects of an enquiry. Nonetheless, Fisher (2000) is aware of some of the pitfalls of using new technologies when conducting enquiry learning:

> If enquiry is inadequately conceptualised as an approach, then simply adding ICT is not likely to improve matters. Indeed, there is a danger that using new technology can make matters worse, as it may create a superficial impression that something more sophisticated is happening, when in reality it is not.
>
> (Fisher, 2000, p. 60)

Students need to be able to address each of the points below when carrying out an enquiry, and also have the competency to use appropriate technology in doing so (after Lambert and Balderstone, 2000 and Matthews, 1998):

- What question or enquiry am I trying to answer? [**defining**]

- What sort of information do I need? (topic, theme, area of study) [**planning**]

- What will be the most likely source of this information (internet, CD-ROM, software, other)? What search words should I use? What search engines are most appropriate? What sites are most appropriate? [**planning**]

- What information have I found? [**searching**]

- How useful is the information gathered? (checks for bias, reliability, accuracy) [**analysing, evaluating, selecting, refining**]

- How do I filter, refine, synthesize, organize and present this information? (drafting, printing) [**selecting, refining, organizing, presenting**]

Freeman (1997) concentrates on the ways in which the IT National Curriculum (DfEE/QCA, 1999b) for schools can combine with geographical education to mutual benefit. She highlights many aspects of data handling and communication (such as searching sources for relevant information, amending data, using data handling packages for processing and analysis, and for presenting and displaying information to different audiences); and measuring, controlling and modelling (such as measuring and recording variables, exploring and creating models, and predicting the effects of changing variables in a model) which are important in the learning of geography. For geographers ICT can therefore provide the essential tools for (say) environmental monitoring and data logging, for recording information during fieldwork (where laptops can be employed), or for creating presentations and web pages of various types (see Taylor, 2001; Hassell, 2000b). The complementary nature of many IT and geographical skills in pursuing enquiries is also noted by Freeman. Some examples are given in Figure 10.2.

A useful source of practical information in the form of case studies on the use of ICT to enhance geography can be found in Hassell and Warner (1995).

Practical activity 10.1

Plan, prepare and teach a lesson (or series of lessons) which incorporates the use of ICT using the model in Figure 10.3.

How valuable is the model in structuring and helping to manage a geography lesson using ICT? What are the main areas where difficulties occur for the beginning teacher?

How might the model be improved?

As with any aspect of geography education the teacher has to be critically reflective in his or her evaluation of the learning achieved by students when they are using ICT. New technologies have the ability to make students 'look busy' as they push keyboard buttons or print out information, but what is the quality of the geography being learnt? Too often students can become engaged in 'electronic plagiarism' – the unquestioning lifting and printing of screen text without fully understanding what it says – or can scan and jump between pages without considering their content. Blind faith in the capabilities of new technology to provide a panacea for learning geography is as damaging as expecting textbooks to provide 'teacher proof' geographical understanding, or believing that all fieldwork is motivational.

Two particular technologies perhaps require special attention with respect to their potential for enhancing geography education. First, Geographic Information Systems (GIS), with their ability to overlay spatial data onto maps and permit the

Geography context	IT element
Shopping survey. Collecting data on functions. Analysing information to explore shopping hierarchies from a questionnaire and functions survey.	Collecting data, entering data onto computer, interrogating the data and displaying it in various ways.
Journey to school. The relationship between distance, method of transport and time taken.	Use a spreadsheet to enter data and sort it. Look for patterns in the data.
Using a simple database/GIS package to display spatial information as an aid to decision-making about the environmental impact of building houses in a woodland area.	Interrogating and displaying data to obtain information on thematic maps.
Investigate an environmental issue within an economically developing country as a simple role playing exercise, e.g. in the Sahel.	Using a simulation to explore patterns and relationships.
Explain the causes and effects of flooding using a flood hydrograph.	Using a spreadsheet to model the pattern of rainfall and river flow during a storm.
Exploring a global development database to compare levels of economic and welfare development, to identify patterns and relationships between different indicators.	Interrogate a large database, display the information on graphs or maps.
Industrial location – a decision-making exercise on possible locations of a new hypermarket or hotel.	Use a simulation program or a spreadsheet to model the most appropriate location based on different criteria.
A newsroom simulation as a stimulus to investigating an issue from different standpoints. For example defending a rainforest.	Using a word processing or DTP package to present geographical information from different standpoints for an audience.
Collecting fieldwork data on river flow and cross sections.	Using a laptop computer for collecting data and entering it onto a spreadsheet to work out cross sectional area and discharge.
Using UK census data to identify geographical patterns in the home region.	Using a CD-ROM, interrogate a large database and display the information on thematic maps.

Figure 10.2 *IT uses in geography enquiries (based on Freeman, 1997)*

investigation of spatial distribution patterns, enable fundamental aspects of geography to be brought into the classroom. The advantages of using digital maps is that they enable the user to manipulate and explore data relatively easily in his or her attempt to discover patterns. GIS is now widely used in the commercial world for such purposes and therefore its use in the geography classroom may not only be

Managing your first ICT lesson

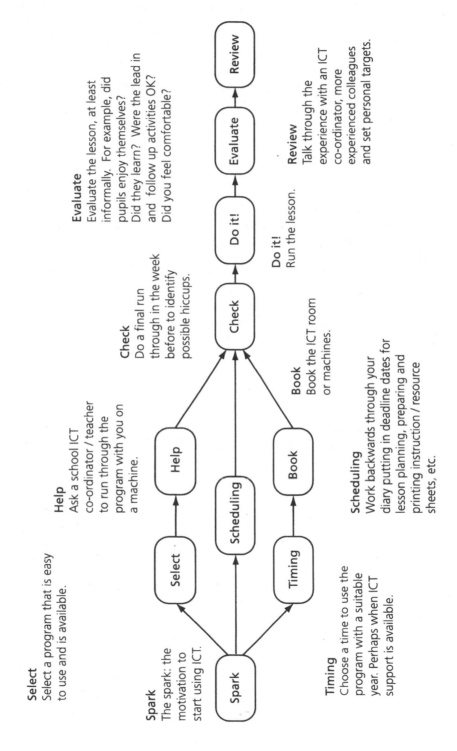

Select
Select a program that is easy to use and is available.

Spark
The spark: the motivation to start using ICT.

Timing
Choose a time to use the program with a suitable year. Perhaps when ICT support is available.

Help
Ask a school ICT co-ordinator / teacher to run through the program with you on a machine.

Check
Do a final run through in the week before to identify possible hiccups.

Scheduling
Work backwards through your diary putting in deadline dates for lesson planning, preparing and printing instruction / resource sheets, etc.

Book
Book the ICT room or machines.

Do it!
Run the lesson.

Evaluate
Evaluate the lesson, at least informally. For example, did pupils enjoy themselves? Did they learn? Were the lead in and follow up activities OK? Did you feel comfortable?

Review
Talk through the experience with an ICT co-ordinator, more experienced colleagues and set personal targets.

Figure 10.3 *Managing your first ICT lesson (Lambert and Balderstone, 2000)*

promoting good geography education, but also enhancing the vocational side of the curriculum. Second, the internet is a huge resource which should be carefully tapped by geography educationists. Jackson notes the almost exponential rise in the number of internet connections from schools in the last years of the 1990s and details the ability of the internet to

> access a variety of resources such as websites with international data, e-mail and chatroom facilities, and live web cameras showing everything from volcanic eruptions to game park watering holes in Africa.
>
> (Jackson, 2000, p. 156).

There is now an almost unimaginable amount of information on the World Wide Web (WWW), much of it geographical in nature, and the potential to 'take' children to people and places they would not normally have contact with in the geography classroom (Grey, 2001). The pedagogical implications are huge – not least in terms of the quality, validity and nature of the information students have access to, how this information can be used to ensure good geographical learning, and what role the geography teacher has in facilitating the process either as pedagogue, supporter or co-learner! Perhaps some of the biggest practical considerations involve gaining access to machines capable of linking to the internet, the time taken to make the links, the undesirable nature of some of the materials that students may access, the time taken to download images, and the readability of some of the text (see Donert, 1997). One of the, as yet, underused aspects of the net is the potential of email to link students to their peers in other countries for the purpose of exploring geography.

3 | ICT RESOURCES – THE GOOD, THE BAD AND THE UGLY

There is no denying the attractiveness and apparent power that many ICT-based resources offer the teacher and learner of geography. However, the educational potential that some commercial organizations claim for their software may be hard to realize and the initial 'buzz factor' that much new technology generates may not be easily transferable into effective learning. Unfortunately much of the geographical software currently available either does not transfer well into the GNC (or specifications for GCSE, A and AS levels) or is biased, requiring considerable 'mediation' by teachers before it is useable in the geography classroom. The very nature of new technologies, which enable one to skim, page hop, browse and print sections with ease, often encourages rather uncritical and passive learning when exactly the opposite is required!

A wide range of software is now commercially available to geography teachers to help them to teach about, or to model, aspects of geography such as the hydrological cycle, industrial location, population changes and mapping. However, the geographical and pedagogical quality of these programs is highly variable. Some practical evaluative questions need to be asked to discover whether the software, CD-ROM, internet site or other form of technological 'package' is suitable for use in the geography classroom:

1. Are the computers I have available for teaching purposes suitable to 'run' this package in a straightforward manner?

2. Is the package easy to use? Will I have to teach/learn new ICT skills?

3. Is the content of the package – the text, pictures, sound, video – fit for the purpose of teaching and learning this particular aspect of geography?

4. Does the package primarily provide new content, enhance skills, or offer models/simulations (or all three)?

5. Are the activities included in the package suitable for the students I intend to use it with? Will I have to provide other support materials? Will I need to involve other staff (e.g. IT coordinator)?

6. How will I, and my students, use this package? What is the most appropriate learning style (directed, structured, open, free)? How should students be grouped? Is differentiation possible?

7. Does the package provide anything, in terms of valuable educational experience, that other geographical teaching resources do not?

8. How will I evaluate the outcome of the lesson and whether my learning objectives have been successfully achieved?

Practical activity 10.2

Use the questions above to evaluate a piece of geographical software, an internet site, or the use of a piece of hardware within your geography department.

Getting information from sources such as CD-ROMs and the internet is often not too problematic – but getting students to evaluate the usefulness, accuracy, and geographical significance of this information is an important aspect of their geographical learning. Students should therefore use ICT to learn how to question information. This changes the role of the teacher from the 'fount of all knowledge', a rather outdated concept particularly with the myriad sources of information now available and the advent of more 'modern' pedagogical approaches, to a facilitator who helps students handle, question, probe and evaluate information. A reappraisal of the teacher's role as *the* subject expert may be timely; however this is not an argument for the removal of the teacher and his or her replacement by a computer – an event which is both unlikely and potentially extremely hazardous!

Interestingly, the few commercially produced games which have a strong geographical context reveal what may be possible in terms of enhancing students' concept development in geography. Often students can handle much more detailed and abstract concepts than we give them credit for in our day-to-day teaching of geography. Hassell (2000a), for example, considers the impact of the game SIMCITY (Electronic Arts, 1990) on children's decision-making with respect to an urban planning simulation. Most children will quite quickly understand how the 'model' works and are soon able to understand what types of planning decisions they will have to make to 'win', given the parameters of the game. They gain instant feedback about the impact of their decisions and can decide for themselves how their choice of different land uses either 'compliment' or 'conflict' with each other in this model of urban structure and process. It is salutory to think that we may be teaching students, often in rather uncritical ways, about models of urban structure such as those of Burgess (1925), Hoyt (1939) and Harris and Ullman (1945), when they have already interacted with a more sophisticated, conceptually- advanced model of urban structure some five or six years earlier by playing SIMCITY.

It is helpful to have an idea of what a well equipped geography department should have in terms of its ICT hardware and software. Hassell (2000a) provides a list of these facilities, noting that this list will change as new technologies appear. Alongside specific geography software and CD-ROMs he would expect geography departments to possess:

- generic ICT facilities, including printers and multimedia computers with word processing, database, spreadsheet, DTP and authoring tools;

- an internet browser with associated on-line and email services;

- a digital camera;

- geography specific facilities such as CD-ROM electronic atlas and encyclopaedia, geographical modelling software, GIS with digital map data; data logging weather station, and map and statistical databases.

4 | ICT IN THE CONTEXT OF GEOGRAPHY ITT

Evidence from Secondary Geography Inspections of ITT (Tapsfield, 2001) indicate some important factors in the preparation of trainees to become efficient users of ICT in their geography teaching. Teacher training institutions have a key responsibility in ensuring that trainees develop ICT skills, use these skills in their teaching, and understand how ICT can enhance students' learning of geography. Many do so by initially auditing and profiling trainees' skills and achievements, often in combination with some form of assignment, and subsequently setting targets for their personal and professional development of ICT use in geography education.

Despite the generally improving provision and access to ICT facilities in HEIs and schools, and the increase in computer ownership by trainees, there are still problems with the availability of good, up-to-date geography software (although a loans scheme run by BECTa has partly alleviated some of these difficulties). However, the most important issue still remains the planning of opportunities to use ICT with students which promotes good geographical learning. When based on considerations of students' entitlements and learning outcomes in both ICT and geography, combined with careful and skilful selection of information such that bias is avoided or countered, the results of using ICT in the geography classroom can be impressive. Nonetheless, often trainees are expected to progress too much through self study and almost any experience of ICT use in the geography class-room may still be considered beneficial by some mentors and tutors, without a critical appraisal of how effective the provision of ICT was to the learning experience in geography. In conclusion good teaching strategies in ICT and geography are not always made apparent to trainees.

To counter this Tapsfield (2001) suggests a checklist for providers to evaluate their ICT provision which may be of interest to trainees as a statement of entitlement:

- Do all partners understand what constitutes good ICT practice in geography?

- Do trainers present good role models of effective ICT use in their own teaching?

- Do course materials offer tangible exemplars of good geography practice for trainees and mentors?

- Do trainees observe in schools a good range of teaching strategies with ICT?

- Are all trainees required to plan and teach a series of lessons involving ICT?

- Are trainees involved in professional ICT use beyond resource creation?

- Does training consider educational issues around ICT use, e.g. inclusion?

- Are ICT audits checked and targets revised during the course?

- Do ICT profiles include evaluations of trainees' teaching and pupils' learning?

- Are trainees' lessons using ICT formally observed and evaluated?

CONCLUSION

The use of ICT in the geography classroom is no longer an option, but a statutory necessity. Societies worldwide are in a phase of rapid technological change for which future generations of students must be prepared and equipped. Geography is itself subject to huge changes as a result of this global 'technological revolution' – both in terms of shifts in its content and in the use of new technologies and skills for its study.

Nevertheless, on the 'bottom line' still remains a basic pedagogical question for those who teach geography – will students learn geography more effectively if they use ICT? The answer to this question, if one reflects on the responses given by many currently serving geography teachers to a recent survey of IT use in schools (DfEE, 1997b), appears to be 'no'. This survey found that only 10 per cent of geography teachers regularly use new technologies in their teaching. The current reluctance of the majority of teachers to embrace ICT partly explains the emphasis placed upon the possession of ICT skills in advertisements for virtually all geography teaching posts.

From a geography education perspective ICT can support many aspects of teaching and learning. According to Hassell (2000a) it can be used to

- collect, keep and use individual or class collected data;

- monitor the environment;

- explore and extract relevant information;

- create, edit, manipulate and use appropriate maps, diagrams and graphs;

- investigate, develop and present geographical ideas;
- predict and solve problems;
- help make decisions.

However, ICT should only be used if it enhances good geography and therefore the 'trivial' use of technology ('using ICT for ICT's sake') must be avoided. In essence, ICT should be integral to geography education only if it can provide an effective means of actualizing the learning objectives planned for the lesson, if it is time and effort efficient, and if students have some opportunities to reflect upon the usefulness of the technology in helping them to learn geography.

What is required is a new generation of geography teachers who are not only confident in their personal ICT capabilities and who are willing to continually update their skills, but who are also fully aware of the pedagogic implications and practicalities of ICT use in their subject. Benyon (1993) adds a further requirement – that teachers should also be technologically literate inasmuch that they fully appreciate *why* new technologies should be used in the wider social, cultural, economic and political setting, rather than simply understanding *how* such technologies can be used.

CHAPTER 11

Geography, cross-curricular themes and values education[3]

Whatever the claims of geography for a curriculum place in its own right, the urgency of the task [preparing for a better world] requires a clear commitment to the wider aims of education.

(Carter, 2000, p. 188)

INTRODUCTION

This chapter focuses upon the contribution which geography education can make to the teaching of cross-curricular themes as well as exploring the importance of incorporating a values dimension into the study of geography. The cross-curricular themes considered here are: the development of the spiritual, moral, social and cultural dimensions (SMSC); citizenship; key skills; education for sustainable development; and personal, social and health education (PSHE). These themes have been selected because of their 'official' link to the National Curriculum, having been set out in general terms in the handbooks for primary and secondary teachers and in the GNC (DfEE/QCA, 1999a) – other themes, such as environmental education (EE), development education and economic and industrial understanding (EIU), are also mentioned. Issues of 'race' and gender within geography education are also briefly considered within this chapter.

During the late 1980s the main concern amongst education policy makers was the perceived inability of state schools to provide children with appropriate subject knowledge, understanding and skills. This resulted in the passing of the Education Reform Act in 1988 and the creation of the first National Curriculum for England and Wales – a curriculum which could be centrally defined and assessed. Once established, the focus of government attention shifted away from the curriculum and towards the standards of teaching, learning and assessment within schools. The newly formed inspection agency, OFSTED, was used to supply evidence of such standards at the local, regional and national scale. The period from the mid 1990s until the start of the new millennium saw another shift in focus, largely brought about by the election of a New Labour government, whereby the development of students as citizens was considered to be increasingly important. As Broadfoot *et al.* (2000) state:

---

[3] This chapter draws upon material previously published by the author as 'Finding its place: contextualising citizenship within the geography curriculum (in Lambert, D. and Machon, P. (eds) (2001) *Citizenship through Second Geography*, London: RoutledgeFalmer, pp. 68–84).

In the late 1990s anxiety was being expressed about the pupils themselves, their apparent lack in many cases of moral and civic values and consequent indiscipline inside and outside school. The specific teaching of 'citizenship' was widely advocated

(Broadfoot *et al.*, 2000, p. 72)

For many years the attitude of the Department for Education and Employment (DfEE), and of its previous incarnations, had at best been ambivalent towards the promotion of cross curricular themes in schools. This attitude contrasted sharply with that held within education departments in many other countries, particularly with respect to the teaching of citizenship and human rights education (see Machon and Walkington, 2000). The New Labour government understandably wished to shape the National Curriculum it had inherited in 1997 to reflect its own particular educational policies and concerns. This led to the establishment of a 'New Agenda' for education which sought to introduce a range of cross-curricular themes into schools, whilst keeping the subject-based structure of the National Curriculum largely intact. The only subject to be added to the National Curriculum was Citizenship, which was to be studied at Key Stages 3 and 4 from September 2002 – other themes were mostly expected to be permeated through existing subjects.

One of the major issues addressed by the QCA's review of the National Curriculum for 2000 was how to incorporate new initiatives into a ten subject curriculum which was still believed to be overloaded by many teachers. The Dearing Review (Dearing, 1993, 1994, 1996) had managed to slim down the statutory curriculum – but despite the insistence of successive governments that the National Curriculum subjects alone could not provide a sufficiently broad and balanced education for young people, teachers still perceived the National Curriculum as the 'whole curriculum'. Unfortunately, the early 1990s had seen a damaging 'false start' in efforts to integrate cross curricular themes into the curriculum. The National Curriculum Council (NCC) had devised five cross curricular themes to be included within the National Curriculum, but the government of the day had reacted nervously towards what it saw as an attempt by the education establishment to hijack proceedings (Graham and Tytler, 1993, p. 20).

1 | THE DILEMMA OF CROSS CURRICULARITY

Geography teachers face a number of concerns regarding whether or not to promote cross-curricular themes. The content of the Geography National Curriculum (DfEE/QCA, 1999a), with its physical, human and environmental themes, its use of enquiry methods and its insistence on the development of a wide range of related skills and values, is well placed to contribute to many of the cross curricular dimensions of the curriculum. Indeed geography is already expected to deliver aspects of citizenship, environmental education and sustainable development within its own subject Order.

However, strong opinions exist about whether geographers should become involved. For example, Walford is clear in his views:

Far better, perhaps, for geographers not to be deflected from what they do better; providing a sound base of world knowledge, stimulating interest in places near and far, and getting pupils to appreciate the wonder and diversity of the world in both its physical and human manifestations ... It is tempting to tailor teaching to passing governmental initiatives, but they may not prove to be a dependable long-term base!

(Walford, 2000, p. 302)

2 | SPIRITUAL, MORAL, SOCIAL AND CULTURAL DEVELOPMENT THROUGH GEOGRAPHY (SMSC)

Geography can provide considerable scope for the development of spiritual, moral, social and cultural (SMSC) aspects of education. Given the previous (over) emphasis on subject content within the original GNC (DES, 1991) recent curriculum revisions have promoted a greater emphasis on exploring SMSC dimensions.

2.1 Spiritual development

The 'official' examples given of geography's opportunities for promoting spiritual development refer to helping students to reflect on their experiences of imposing natural landscapes, dramatic environments and photographs of the world from space (DfEE/QCA, 1999a, p. 8). The previous aims for geography education, stated in the Final Report of the GNC, incorporated a significant steer towards spirituality in the statement that geography should:

> b. foster their [the students] sense of wonder at the beauty of the world around them.
>
> (DES, 1990)

Similar words were used by SCAA (now QCA) in their statement that children's spiritual development, and their education in general, would be lacking if they were not able to 'be moved by feelings of awe and wonder at the beauty of the world we live in' (SCAA, 1995, p. 5). Although many children's immediate world may *not* be a thing of spiritual beauty, geography teachers can play a part in helping them to appreciate other worlds and different aspects of spirituality. For example, geography can show how people in contrasting environments should be valued for their diversity and individuality, and how students can value themselves and their backgrounds whilst also seeking to expand their spiritual horizons.

2.2 Moral development

The GNC focuses on geography's potential contribution to students' moral development by highlighting some of the impacts of their, and other people's, actions. Students are asked to consider the consequences of dropping litter, or to reflect upon environmental issues such as global warming, where our current needs have to be balanced against those of future generations (DfEE/QCA, 1999a, p. 8). However, moral issues are composed of a complex combination of values, beliefs, attitudes and behaviours and may have different expressions in different societies.

Bound within this is the influence of custom, culture, law and religion. As geographers we may, within case studies of other countries or regions, touch upon many aspects of morality. In certain circumstances the moral dimension of geography education may be expressly confronted through the introduction of moral dilemmas (see 'The values dimension in geography and cross curricular education', p. 189).

It is not always easy to introduce a moral dimension into geography; either because of the nature of the content being studied (it is difficult to have a moral insight into plate tectonics, for example), or because of the stage of intellectual development and values system that may be held by the students. The resolution of moral questions can be extremely sensitive and raise implications for the teaching styles adopted and the role of the teacher. Enabling students to express their values, attitudes and beliefs in response to controversial issues in geography will certainly help their moral development, as will persuading students that life choices have consequences (for themselves, others and the planet) for which they should increasingly take responsibility. We must guard against any teaching that is, to use Lambert's phrase, 'morally careless' – nonetheless, the careful exploration and extension of students' systems of values which will guide their moral behaviour is certainly possible within geography (see McPartland, 2001).

2.3 Social development

Aspects of social development and education can be provided through geography fieldwork, particularly if it is of a residential nature. More broadly, understanding the ways in which societies function, as well as understanding one's 'place' within society, is central to many aspects of human and social geography. In the GNC this is expressed through examples of students investigating the impact of transport changes in a local area, or considering how differences in development can alter the quality of life of different people (DfEE/QCA, 1999a, p. 8). With its direct links to welfare, cultural and humanistic geography the social dimension is extremely significant within the study of geography. Students need to appreciate how societies work such that they can play an active, responsible and fulfilling role within them. Importantly the values which shape our societies are constantly changing, often in quite subtle ways, and students should learn to recognize and evaluate the processes that impact upon the society around them. The very education that students receive is the result of the influences of various powerful groups and individuals within society, be they broadly political, religious, cultural or economic.

Geographer's explorations of the social dimension will almost certainly overlap with studies of citizenship. At its most diverse this may lead to considerations of our role as citizens in supporting or rejecting the interests of others in society, in participating in the democratic process, understanding the law, respecting diversity (cultural, sexual, religious), and striving for social justice.

2.4 Cultural development

Culture may be defined as the beliefs, traditions, symbols, ideas and values which influence behaviour and social structure within a particular group (Butt, 2000a). In cultural geography this is typified by studies of how human activities are determined by culture, which then has an expression within both landscape and environment. As such the definition of the cultural dimension is quite broad – it can encompass 'high culture' (art, music, literature), but more often refers to the ways in which the culture we live in influences us (and vice versa). Central to this may be cultural understandings of one's identity, sense of belonging, and worth, which in turn influence how we all respond and react to other cultures.

In the GNC (DfEE/QCA, 1999a) the cultural development of students is described in terms of students finding out about traditions and activities within families in developing countries, or investigating the ways in which their school's local environment reflects the culture of its inhabitants (p. 8). In geography education, the concept of 'cultural literacy', which was originally espoused by Hirsch (1987), was debated around the time of the creation of the first GNC (DES, 1991). In essence this outlines the knowledge that everyone should possess to be able to operate and communicate effectively (hence 'literacy') within their national culture – the cultural history, language, assumptions and understandings that makes one a 'member' of a national culture. However, the concept has limitations in that it can be applied as an attempt to 'fix' cultural (and geographical) references to one point in time and to reach a consensus on aspects of national culture (see Dowgill and Lambert, 1992).

3 | CITIZENSHIP

As with any of the cross-curricular themes finding the most appropriate balance between either single-mindedly promoting geography *per se* in schools, or using it as a vehicle for citizenship education, is not easy. Most geographers would argue that a part of their discipline, by the very nature of its subject content, has always involved considerations of citizenship – but what kind of citizenship, and where does this fit within a changing geography curriculum? Finding the 'common ground' between both 'subjects' is problematic, although this is essential if we are to avoid injudiciously forcing the two together, possibly to the detriment of both.

The GNC (DfEE/QCA 1999a, p. 8) states that geography can play a significant part in promoting citizenship through:

- developing pupils' knowledge and understanding of the institutions and systems that influence their lives and communities, and how to participate in decision-making, for example, in relation to a local planning issue;

- providing opportunities for pupils to reflect upon and discuss topical social, environmental, economic and political issues;

- developing pupils' knowledge and understanding about the diverse national, regional, religious, and ethnic identities in the United Kingdom and the wider world;

- developing pupils' understanding of the world as a global community and the issues and challenges of global interdependence and responsibility.

In November 1997, David Blunkett, then Secretary of State for Education in the New Labour government, announced the creation of an advisory group to strengthen the education for democracy and citizenship in schools – an act largely driven by fears about the political apathy and disengagement of young people. The group was chaired by Professor Bernard Crick, one of Blunkett's previous tutors, whose recommendations were incorporated into the review of the National Curriculum for 2000 (Crick, 2000). The definition of citizenship agreed upon by the group focused on social and moral responsibility, community involvement and political literacy highlighting the importance of a local and national perspective as well as 'an awareness of world affairs and global issues'.

Section 7.5 of the Crick Report highlighted the prospective role of geography in promoting citizenship education as follows:

> In Geography, the emphasis of place, space and environment and the study of places, themes and issues from the local to the global, offers significant opportunities to learn about conflicts and concerns, to extend knowledge about political groupings and the activities of pressure groups and voluntary bodies to evaluate the consequences for people, places and environments of decision-making. There is a particular opportunity to understand how people and places are inextricably linked and interdependent, thus to learn about and experience citizenship from the local to the global. The process of enquiry in geography, as in History, can also contribute to pupils' development of the understanding, skills and confidence needed to take informed action. Pupil involvement in fieldwork can enhance such learning and despite the pressure of the timetable, many schools in Key Stage 3 have Environmental Studies programmes.
>
> (QCA, 1998b, p. 53)

Machon and Walkington (2000) believe that geography and citizenship share a number of values and attitudes, concepts and skills, as outlined in Figure 11.1.

Values and attitudes	Concepts	Skills
• social justice	• interdependence	• critical thinking
• a sense of place	• sustainability	• decision-making
• a sense of community	• change	• reflection
• empathy	• place	
• respects and values diversity	• cultural diversity	

Figure 11.1 *Common themes between geography and citizenship (Machon and Walkington, 2000)*

They also highlight the QCA's intention that citizenship education should enable students to think and behave independently and critically. The Final Report (QCA, 1998b, p. 13) makes clear that citizenship education 'is not just knowledge of citizenship and civic society; it also implies developing values, skills and understanding'. This point is taken further by Lambert and Balderstone who argue that:

> Critical enquiry in geography encourages pupils to assess the validity of different value positions, resolve the differences between these and their own positions, and consider the limitations of stereotypical views. It can therefore make a significant contribution to education for citizenship.
>
> (Lambert and Balderstone, 2000, p. 318)

Unfortunately, the lack of experience that most geography teachers have of political education may limit the promotion of citizenship through geography (Machon and Walkington, 2000; Lambert and Machon, 2001). The Citizenship document clearly establishes that students should become active citizens and, by implication, that active learning methods should be employed to achieve this goal. Many geographical themes can be taught from a citizenship perspective – the active and enquiry learning approaches favoured by geographers helping to promote involvement. There is some evidence that geography teachers who focus narrowly on the teaching of geographical content tend to adopt more didactic methods, whilst those concerned with developing citizenship are more open and participatory in the teaching and learning styles that they seek to adopt (see Walkington, 1999). Such methods are also central to the teaching of environmental, development and sustainability issues through geography (see *Teaching Geography*, 2001; Oxfam, 1997). Walkington's (1999) research amongst primary geographers has a resonance at secondary level, where both geography and citizenship can be successfully combined to focus on key themes (such as interdependence, sustainability, social justice and equity), methodologies (enquiry, role play, simulations), skills (decision-making, critical thinking) and values and attitudes (empathy).

Schools have the option of delivering Citizenship either through existing subjects – such as geography and history – or as a 'discrete' subject utilizing 5 per cent of curriculum time. There are growing concerns for the security of geography's position in the curriculum post-14 if the latter option is taken by schools. The optional status of geography (and history) at Key Stage 4 may tempt curriculum designers to create option banks in Year 9 that may severely restrict, or even remove, the possibility of students choosing geography as one of their GCSEs. Worryingly, Rawling (2000a) reports that in the Republic of Ireland similar efforts to broaden the lower secondary curriculum have already meant the removal of geography from school timetables, to be replaced by aspects of social, political and technological education.

4   KEY SKILLS

The key skills stated within the National Curriculum are as follows:

- communication
- application of numbers
- IT
- working with others
- improving own learning and performance
- problem-solving.

Each of these is accompanied by a brief example of how geography can contribute to the promotion of such skills in the GNC (DfEE/QCA, 1999a). Other sections of this book highlight some of their influences on geography education and do not need to be repeated here.

5 | EDUCATION FOR SUSTAINABLE DEVELOPMENT

Education for sustainable development is often linked to futures education (see Chapter 3), environmental education and development education, as well as a variety of geographical themes in the National Curriculum. However, it can be argued that almost all aspects of schooling should contribute to education for sustainable development. Ideas about what actually constitutes 'sustainable development' are contested – but it is clear that there are no simple answers that societies can adopt to ensure that future generations will avoid problems related to the exhaustion of finite resources and the creation of environmental pollution. The complexity of the factors which need to be considered in any attempt to achieve global sustainability are numerous – be they social, economic, ecological or political. Nonetheless, if one believes that our current scale of resource use is unsustainable then we surely cannot teach students that the mere maintenance of the status quo is acceptable, for by definition this will eventually mean that substantial numbers of people will suffer. (It is, of course, a moot point that this is already the situation in many developing countries.) Many governments appear conscious of the forces which make the achievement of global sustainability unlikely and only a few have started to address the problems of wasteful and careless use of resources seriously. Unfortunately, the impact of the resulting conferences and international laws has proved largely negligible. Elected governments, who are in office for relatively short periods of time, do not wish to engage in long-term environmental controls which make them unpopular with businesses and industries. Indeed, such measures often appear to run contrary to the national interest. Despite this the Brundtland Report (WCED, 1987) and the Rio Convention in 1992 have had some impact on international resource conservation, the adoption of sustainable practices, pollution control, education and the establishment of parameters for future action (Agenda 21).

The current GNC (DfEE/QCA, 1999a) promotes the teaching of sustainable development within 'Knowledge and understanding of environmental change and sustainable development' where section 5b states that pupils should be taught to 'explore the idea of sustainable development and recognise its implications for people, places and environments and for their own lives' (p. 23). There is also an additional requirement, stated in the 'Learning across the National Curriculum' section, that geography should adopt a role of:

- developing pupils' knowledge and understanding of the concept of sustainable development and the skills to act upon this understanding [for example, as part of a local Agenda 21 initiative]

- developing pupils' knowledge and understanding of key concepts of sustainable development, such as interdependence, quality of life and diversity

- developing pupils' skills of critical enquiry and an ability to handle and interpret information

- exploring values and attitudes about complex issues, such as resource use and global development.

(DfEE/QCA, 1999a, p. 9)

In the past, ideas about development have focused narrowly on concepts of economic growth and generally disregarded considerations of costs in terms of social and environmental damage. Achieving a shift in thinking towards sustainability is not straightforward. Sustainability is complex – emphasizing the need to improve economic and social well being, whilst simultaneously protecting the biosphere on which life depends, is fraught with difficulties. However, this is the only way to ensure that future generations inherit environmental and material wealth comparable to current generations. People have never yet, at a large scale, found it possible to live in a fully sustainable way, even when resources have been plentiful. It is therefore misleading to present such prospects to students, who must be made aware that individually and collectively they will face a variety of difficult options concerning sustainability.

Hicks believes that:

> Working towards a sustainable future requires production planned to meet human needs together with a more just distribution of resources. It means reducing the harmful effects of industry and new technology, challenging company policies that are dangerous to people and the environment, stopping aid programmes that are inappropriate and damaging, reducing over-consumption and waste, restraining population growth, distinguishing clearly between wants and needs, and organising locally, nationally and internationally for appropriate change.
>
> (Hicks, 1994, p. 5)

But how does the geography teacher interpret these not inconsiderable challenges within the geography classroom? Some would advocate that we should 'change hearts and minds', such that students are led to a 'commitment to action' (Calder and Smith, 1993, Huckle and Sterling, 1996). Others state that teachers should simply 'teach values for sustainable living' (Tilbury, 1997). The current commitment of geography education to teaching about sustainability is questioned by some, particularly given the restrictive nature of the curriculum through which state education occurs. For example, Morgan (2000b) argues that 'the desire to teach geography for a 'sustainable society' – a more inclusive and socially just society – is stifled by established approaches to teaching in geography' (p. 169). Other notes of caution are also apparent – Walford (2000) expresses the view that 'the proposals to encourage students to be positive about 'sustainable development' are, at present, [also] vague, relatively unresourced and untried' (p. 302). Thus behind each of the assertions that sustainable development should be taught through geography, lurk not inconsiderable questions as to what the learning objectives for such teaching might look like, particularly given the contested nature of what sustainable development actually is.

Perhaps a way forward exists through the careful exploration of values positions – by encouraging students to undertake exercises in values analysis and clarification in response to issues surrounding sustainability (see 'The values dimension in geography and cross-curricular education', p. 189). Students (and their busy teachers) will find it difficult to actually *change* the societies in which they live, or those at larger spatial scales – this is not to say that they should not try, but there are realistic limits to the roles and responsibilities of both parties. As Lambert and Balderstone warn:

> Their [the teachers'] achievable aim is to change the individuals they teach, principally by enabling them to respond to issues, and each other, more intelligently. If success at

this individual level also leads to more informed personal choices and behaviours, it could also contribute to the creation of a better world. But the main interest of the teacher is with the pupil. Pupils and teachers have a relationship which in many ways is unequal: they are not just joint 'participants' in an imagined common struggle.

(Lambert and Balderstone, 2000, p. 374).

6 PERSONAL, SOCIAL AND HEALTH EDUCATION (PSHE)

PSHE, which may be considered as a combination of cross-curricular themes, is believed by many to be an essential element of students' education within the predominantly subject-based National Curriculum. Most schools have chosen to deliver PSHE via form tutors due to the practical difficulties of permeating it within subjects.

With the introduction of Curriculum 2000 PSHE has an enhanced status at Key Stages 3 and 4, although it still remains non-statutory. Some aspects of PSHE may be delivered through geography education, or by geography teachers, but are not considered here as they are often tangental to the main work of geography departments.

7 ENVIRONMENTAL EDUCATION

Job (1997) explains that the last three decades has seen a burgeoning of initiatives concerning education *about, from* or *for* the environment; initiatives in which geography education has often featured prominently. In the 1970s, discrete curricula in Environmental Science and Environmental Studies emerged, whilst the arrival of the National Curriculum saw the development of a cross-curricular theme in Environmental Education (EE) (NCC, 1990a). Currently there are numerous overlaps between initiatives for education for sustainable development and EE – both of which have a significant interface with environmental aspects of geography.

Within the GNC (DfEE/QCA, 1999a) mention is made of environmental issues in the programmes of study for Key Stage 3, where students should be taught to 'describe and explain environmental change [for example deforestation, soil erosion] and recognize different ways of managing it' (p. 23). The geographical themes also include 'environmental issues' (6j) which focus on the planning and management of environments.

Although EE is concerned with themes such as sustainability, population growth, pollution control, habitat destruction and resource management – all of which environmental geographers may also pursue – it occupies a specific curricular niche, for unlike geography education it is not primarily interested in the *spatial* dimensions of these phenomena. When it was formalized into the National Curriculum, EE projected a largely technological view of the potential solutions to the environmental crises faced by people. This also involved helping students to know and understand how environments are shaped, to appreciate the vulnerability of certain environments, and to consider opportunities to protect and manage environments. However, more recent interpretations of EE stress the importance of incorporating a political, economic, ideological and values perspective within considerations of environmental problems. Geography should incorporate an holistic appreciation of the world in which the component parts of the environment – that is the biosphere, atmosphere and geosphere – are clearly represented. Whether these should be portrayed from a mainly anthropocentric or ecocentric perspective is debatable.

Little guidance has been forthcoming about exactly how the environmental dimension should be delivered in the school curriculum, even at the basic level of whether it should be a cross-curricular theme or a separate curriculum subject. The teaching of EE was partly supported by publications from DfEE (1993b), SCAA (1996c) and the Panel for Education for Sustainable Development (1998), but these have not constituted a unified approach to its delivery. Tilbury (1993, 1997) argues that confusion has partly arisen because EE has historically lacked close definition, being used to encompass a diverse range of educational aims related to the environment. Various definitions of environmental ideologies exist (ranging from the 'technocentric' to the 'ecocentric') on which different strands of EE have been built. These can be explored through the summaries provided by Job (1996, 1997), O'Riordan (1981), and Fien (1993). Here distinctions vary between the values adopted and the means of effecting change, distinctions that can be usefully investigated through geography (see Figure 11.2).

Each of the ideological perspectives on the environment has an accompanying educational perspective. Thus forms of education *about, from* or *for* the environment – that is, teaching about environmental matters in the classroom (*about* the environment), venturing out into the field (*from* the environment), or using education in a practical way to help solve environmental problems (*for* the environment) – each have ideological roots. However, as Fien (1993) comments (cited in Job, 1997), 'Education *about* and *through* the environment are valuable only in so far as they are used to promote skills and knowledge to support the transformative intentions of education *for* the environment'.

Some would draw attention to the largely apolitical teaching about the environment under the banner of EE in the 1970s and 1980s, compared to the aim of achieving a more active, participatory involvement in resolving environmental problems suggested in certain government documentation (NCC, 1990a) and by particular educationists (Greig *et al.*, 1987; Tilbury, 1993, 1997; Fien, 1993; Huckle, 1994). As Job concludes:

> proponents of environmental education for the environment recognise the dichotomy between a curriculum which generally seeks to pass on the prevailing culture and economic values, and an environmental viewpoint which see the existing political and economic structures as fundamentally incompatible with a sustainable view of global ecology.
>
> (Job, 1997, p. 150)

Practical activity 11.1

To what extent should environmental education continue to be delivered through geography (and other subjects) as a cross-curricular theme? Is there a case for giving environmental education greater curricular status as a 'subject' in its own right?

Selected issues	Technocentric	Shallow green	Ecocentric (deep green)
River management	Channel engineering (straightening, levees, dredging, etc.) to increase flow rate and channel capacity. Dams upstream to hold back floodwater.	Maintain present channels and protect floodplain development but control water and sediment input to the channel through catchment management.	Allow catchment vegetation to revert to a more natural state to increase interception and infiltration. Avoid/clear development on floodplains and allow river to flood. Restore natural channel forms and bank vegetation.
Coastal erosion and flooding	Protection using hard defences where cost benefit justifies expenditure.	Soft defences, beach nourishment, sediment recycling, offshore structures to control wave environment and sediment movement	Allow erosion to occur in order to maintain sediment supply to whole coastal system. Retreat from eroding or flood-prone coasts.
Eutrophication	Chemical treatment of effluent to reduce nutrient concentrations.	Use biological methods to mop up excess nutrients from agricultural runoff and sewage.	Avoid artificial fertilisers and return nutrients in crop, animal and human wastes to the soil by composting.
Acidification	Liming acid lakes. Dispersing acid gas emissions through building higher chimney stacks.	Scrubbers and catalytic converters to reduce acid gas emissions from burning fossil fuels.	Change to renewable energy and energy conservation to avoid acid gas emissions from fossil-fuel burning.

Figure 11.2 *Environmental viewpoints on specific geographical issues (Job, 1997, p.152)*

What are the main areas of mutual strength in environmental and geography education? How might both forms of education combine in a beneficial way?

8 DEVELOPMENT EDUCATION AND ECONOMIC AND INDUSTRIAL UNDERSTANDING (EIU)

Development Education explores aspects of economic and social developmsent at different spatial scales, thus enabling students to gain an awareness of development issues and to understand concepts of social justice. It stresses the importance of participation in one's society and emphasizes the development of skills and attitudes, as well as knowledge and understanding. The themes covered within development education are diverse and often holistic – themes which can be overlooked within a subject-based curriculum. Many of the educational materials produced by Development Education Centres (DECs) stress the importance of active, decision-making and enquiry led learning which assume the existence of a 'democratic' classroom.

Development Education commonly overlaps with six broad areas of geography education – global viewpoints and interrelationships, unity of the human race, role of the learner in the study of school geography, justice, provision of a skills base, and attention to the real world (see Robinson and Serf, 1997). Importantly development is seen to be a factor concerning both the developed and developing worlds.

Practical activity 11.2

How should geographers define 'development education'?
In what ways can geography education convey to students the importance of developing a sense of their own 'global citizenship'?

Economic and Industrial Understanding (EIU) was established as a cross curricular theme within the original conception of the National Curriculum (NCC, 1990b). In its initial design it involved the study of financial decision-making, economic roles (producers, consumers and citizens), government economic policy, and the impact of economic activity on the environment. For geographers many of these themes have direct relevance in human geography at Key Stages 3 and 4 (NCC, 1992a). The Geography Schools and Industry Project (GSIP) developed curriculum ideas and materials relating to EIU before the National Curriculum was established (see Corney, 1985, 1992).

9 | 'RACE' AND GENDER

Issues of 'race' and gender in geography education are inevitably linked with considerations of bias and stereotyping. To some extent stereotyping is an unavoidable aspect of human nature, for in order to understand the complex world around us we need to simplify, select and generalize information about it. As geographers we perhaps face the problem of stereotyping more than most – we therefore have to be particularly sensitive to the issues that surround it, for behind every generalization sits a stereotype (Marsden, 1995).

Marsden (1995, p. 120) believes the main characteristics of stereotypes reveal:

- false and/or distorted information;
- over-simplified and undifferentiated thinking;

- favourable impressions of certain groups; and

- attitudinal rigidity.

The term 'race' is a socially constructed, rather than scientific, term and is not used by anthropologists to describe the human species, although it still has a common acceptance within literature and society. It has been applied to classify people who share common characteristics (be they physical, ethnic, social or cultural), as well as a specific geographical origin. The Commission for Racial Equality (CRE), in defining the characteristics of a 'racial group', refer to skin colour; nationality; ethnicity; shared history; cultural tradition; common geographical origins; descent from common ancestors; a common language; literature and religion; and being either a minority or majority within a larger community (CRE, 1989). Often the terms 'race' and 'ethnicity' are used rather loosely or interchangeably. This is a mistake as 'race' is a broadly biological definition whereas ethnicity is culturally defined – as such one can not change one's race, but can alter one's ethnicity (Grosvenor, 1999).

Racism, as perhaps the most insidious form of stereotyping, has a number of common facets. The characteristics of different groups of people are usually ascribed narrowly to their heredity – physical differences are given particularly heightened social or moral significance and may be placed into some form of hierarchy, whilst such differences are reinforced by spurious warnings about 'cross breeding' and the supposed dangers of creating 'racial impurity'.

Recently the interface between 'race' and geography education has become the focus for renewed concern, with calls for the latter to critically reflect upon the contribution of geography to multicultural education (see Morgan and Lambert, 2001). Unfortunately issues of 'race' have been marginalized in the geography curriculum of England and Wales over the last decade, with a lack of involvement, challenge and taken-for-grantedness typifying the approach of many geography departments. Indeed, at present:

> School geography tends to ignore questions of racialisation, emptying out the racia-lised meanings attached to processes of economic and social change in favour of a relatively abstract body of knowledge that counts as 'the geography curriculum'.
>
> [Morgan and Lambert, 2001, p. 244]

In the latter part of the twentieth century 'gender and geography' became a theme for serious academic consideration in many university geography departments. Investigating the various roles and responsibilities of the sexes saw research in geography concentrate on issues such as unequal access to employment, differentials in earnings, property ownership, lifestyle, transport, variations in educational provision and power. Much of this work challenged the 'gendered' assumptions about the roles of the different sexes, which narrowly linked women to domestic roles and men to the world of paid employment. Within geography education current concerns with gender issues tend to focus on the casual assumption that male and female lived experience is equal. Women have often been largely 'invisible' in many geography resources (for example, many texts convey an impression that 'people' share common lifestyles and experiences, whereas in fact male and female lifestyles are often very different). Interest in gender issues in education has recently been stimulated by the differences in boys and girls assessed performance. Examination statistics at the end of the last century clearly showed that whilst boys outnumbered girls in candidate entries for GCSE and A/AS levels in geography they achieved marginally poorer results. A similar situation is revealed at Key Stage 3 from data gathered on levels achieved in geography (see Butt, 2001a).

Much of the work on gender and geography education in the 1970s, 80s and early 90s concentrated upon the issue of gender bias in geographical teaching materials, particularly textbooks. Publishers have become sensitive to the ways in which women are represented, the use of language, and the problems of sexism and gender bias, particularly in the visual images used in geography texts. Nonetheless, there is still an issue regarding the *content* within the written text itself and what the author chooses to focus upon. Here analysis is less straightforward, compared to counting the number of males and females shown in photographs.

10 | THE VALUES DIMENSION IN GEOGRAPHY AND CROSS-CURRICULAR EDUCATION

Much of the day-to-day teaching of geography, and indeed of many cross-curricular themes, directly explores students' values and attitudes. For many teachers this is the most important aspect of their teaching and provides a basis for their whole philosophy of education. Although some geography teachers do not wish to engage in any teaching about controversial issues, for fear of possible accusations of indoctrination, one can not avoid the fact that geography is value-laden and therefore can not be taught in an entirely value free (or value neutral) way.

Values education can be defined as being concerned with the exploration of human qualities and principles: in essence the belief that certain things, phenomena and patterns of behaviour are more worthwhile than others. In recent years some have considered that the most productive forms of geography education have been those which have sought to combine and balance the cognitive and affective aims of education, as typified through values education (Fien, 1996; Huckle, 1980; 1983; Slater, 1994, 1996a). Here geography education is ultimately called upon to help to redress the social, economic and political imbalances of the world by helping children to adopt values associated with social justice and democracy (Butt, 2000a). It is important to realize that education itself is not 'value neutral', it draws upon the dominant values of the society and culture in which it is practiced and seeks to establish priorities based on these values. However, in so doing it tends to reflect the values of the most powerful educational and political decision makers (Fien, 1996).

Fien (1996) has attempted to define the values which are most applicable to geography education, namely those which are consistent with the creation of a democratic society, as follows:

- positive self image

- acceptance of, and respect for, others

- compassion and kindness

- open mindedness
- respect for human rights
- concern for justice
- commitment to sustainable development
- willingness to be involved.

He also stresses that implicit within such values education in geography should be the development of children's capacity to clarify their own views, beliefs, attitudes and opinions about geographical issues (see Rokeach, 1973 for an explanation of the differences between beliefs, attitudes and values). This clarification process will inevitably involve the ability to analyse and evaluate information and come to some form of reasoned decision – aspects of which are contained within the enquiry process in geography.

For some years geography education has expressed the importance of the values dimension within the education of students, particularly within the Schools Council Geography 16–19 Project established in 1976 at the University of London's Institute of Education. The aims of the Project emphasized the need to involve teachers in the curriculum development of geography materials which would show a distinct 'route for enquiry' as well as a values dimension. There are a number of valid approaches to values education, each seeking to explore a particular aspect of affective learning. These are sometimes arranged along a continuum starting at one end with 'values inculcation', which means that students are encouraged to learn a predetermined set of values given by the teacher, and progressing to 'values clarification', which acknowledges that students have an already developed values system that may need to be explored further in relation to their own, and others, behaviour. A final stage may be the actualization of these clarified values by the student taking some form of action to influence a particular social or environmental issue.

If we utilize the 'hierarchy' of approaches to values education, as described by Lambert and Balderstone (2000), we can describe the ways in which geography teachers may integrate these into their lesson planning.

There is a reasonably clear distinction between those geography materials that embrace a need for students to clarify their own values and those that do not. In some cases where the materials (or the teacher) attempt such values education in an ill considered, or careless, way they may actually do more harm than good to children's geography education. Marsden (1995) draws an important distinction between forms of geography education that could be considered to be either 'issues permeated', 'issues based' or 'issues dominated'. He expresses his concern about the dangers of proselytizing the 'issues' over and above the 'geography', such that certain controversial issues merely become the focus for values indoctrination in the classroom. In addition, if an issue is explored without cognitive and affective rigour, students may simply be expected to 'offer an opinion' which may then be casually accepted by the teacher without further analysis or question. The process by which students confront controversial issues is extremely important – they should learn how to analyse and clarify their own and other people's values, but the focus should be on learning *how* to evaluate, rather than on *what* to value.

Confronting controversial issues in the geography classroom can be attempted in

Aspect of values education	Definition	Example in geography education
Values inculcation	Students adopt a predetermined set of values.	Direct teacher exposition of a preferred values position, e.g. telling students that destruction of tropical rainforests is indefensible. *Drawbacks*? Teacher indoctrination of values.
Values analysis (see Fien and Slater, 1985; Huckle, 1981; Marsden, 1995)	Students undertake rational discussion and logical analysis of evidence to investigate issues. Students make defensible value judgements.	Teacher supports students in their decision-making process, but leaves them to make their own final judgements e.g. role plays and public enquiry simulations to appreciate the values positions of people involved in planning decisions. *Drawbacks*? Desire for consensus, continued promotion of cognitive over affective learning, creation of false confidence in the democratic process.
Moral reasoning (see Kohlberg, 1976; Marsden, 1995)	Students discuss reasons for values positions to encourage growth of their moral reasoning abilities.	Teacher enables students to discuss a moral issue offering evidence and encouraging empathy with the different groups and individuals involved. Teacher introduces questions to lift students onto higher levels of moral reasoning during their small group discussions e.g. moral dilemmas presented to students to resolve through debate in small groups. Dilemmas are often in the form of stories or small geographical case studies, each containing a conflict about what is 'right' and 'wrong' in respect of a decision to be made. *Drawbacks*? Assumptions that students pass through a set of hierarchical stages before reaching a final stage of 'moral autonomy'. Expectation that teachers can ask appropriate questions to advance students' moral reasoning and that all teachers have achieved a stage of 'moral autonomy' themselves.
Values clarification (Huckle, 1981; Fien and Slater, 1985; Slater, 1980, 1994)	Students become aware of their own values in relation to the behaviour of themselves and others.	Teacher encourages students to clarify their own position on an issue and to defend this. In so doing, students explore their own values, feelings and behaviour, as well as

Continued

		those of others. Students directed towards analysing the process by which they (and others) adopt values and the consequences of holding certain values e.g. through role plays and simulations, through brainstorming about an environmental conservation issue with student responses being grouped for later analysis, through students expressing their level of agreement with banks of statements about moral values to create a 'personal values clarification scale'. *Drawbacks?* Adoption of a role does not always encourage clarification of one's own values. Concentration on the clarification of the values of others, rather than on one's own values. View that all values are a matter of individual choice and that each value position adopted is equally acceptable.
Action learning	Students take action on social and environmental issues having previously analysed and clarified their values position.	Teacher enables students to analyse and clarify their own values in relation to an issue and provides avenues through which these values may be expressed e.g. students acting in relation to a social or environmental issue in the school environment or local area such as conservation, recycling or litter. Or fundraising, or letter writing. *Drawbacks?* Involvement in issues can be conducted in damaging and morally careless ways if not fully explored through values analysis and clarification

Figure 11.3 *Aspects of values education possible within geography lessons (after Lambert and Balderstone, 2000)*

a variety of ways. The teacher can either take a position of near neutrality, such as being an impartial chair of a debate, or can make his or her views known to the class. He or she could present a range of different views, or adopt a completely contrary stance ('Devil's Advocate') to that expressed by the students or the teaching materials. Each of these approaches has particular benefits and drawbacks in terms of their efficacy in promoting values education. Students are often adept at working out what their teacher's views are and may attempt to comply with these, therefore reinforcing an acceptance of the status quo. They are also skilled in presenting teachers with what they know to be 'acceptable' values statements and positions, which they would rarely adopt outside the geography classroom.

Some approaches to 'teaching values' may have the damaging effect of actually reinforcing the students' existing prejudices, rather than opening them up to analysis and clarification. Perhaps a major danger is the risk of conveying an impression that all issues or questions have a 'right answer' (often students wrongly believe that the teacher is the gatekeeper of all 'right answers'!), or that all issues can be resolved by accepting a 'grey area' somewhere between 'black and white' polar opinions. Nonetheless there are considerable benefits in introducing controversial issues into the teaching of geography – students will often express views and solutions that the teacher has not considered, more students may engage in discussions than is usually the case, communication skills can be developed, and students can learn to respect the opinions of others. When used skillfully the introduction of conflicting information, or the adoption of a contrary position, can force students into considering that there are rarely set answers to controversial questions.

Whatever approach one chooses to adopt when confronting controversial issues in the geography classroom it is important that an atmosphere of trust and acceptance is conveyed. Only if this is achieved will students feel confident that they can explore their own values in front of the teacher and their peers in an arena where mutual respect is afforded. The exploration of values is often the most sensitive and difficult aspect of teaching, for not all students will be comfortable in expressing their beliefs, views, attitudes and values in the classroom.

CONCLUSION

Rawling (2000b) recognizes that the twenty-first century has started with a profound emphasis on the 'New Agenda' within education in England and Wales, pursued by a government often more concerned with the development of cross curricular themes than with traditional subjects. It has always been possible to view education from such an inter disciplinary or cross curricular perspective – geographers have to become more aware of this and position their subject carefully within the curriculum in order to ensure that its unique educational perspective is still realized.

At the launch of the National Curriculum in the early 1990s supporters of 'whole curriculum' planning regretted what they believed to be the demotion of cross curricular activity in favour of a subject-based curriculum (Marsden, 1995). Whilst the dominance of academic subjects in the curriculum still exists, the 'hold' of the non core subjects has considerably weakened in recent years. Geography currently walks a tightrope – it has much to offer within many of the cross-curricular themes, but by so doing it may paradoxically weaken its own curricular position and become a prime candidate for removal or downgrading within Key Stage 4. The prospect of only three years of compulsory geography education (at Key Stage 3), preceded and followed by a very uncertain geographical experience for the majority of students, is not a healthy one for the subject.

CHAPTER 12

The future for the reflective geography teacher

Geography, I believe, has a future. It will be a future determined not only by curriculum developers and teachers, not only by academics and environmentalists, not only by politicians and the public. It will be a future determined by the way children perceive our knowledge base and the sensitivity and utility it offers to a worthwhile understanding of the world...

(Slater, 1995, p. 6)

'As a young man my fondest dream was to become a geographer. However ... I thought deeply about the matter and concluded it was far too difficult a subject. With some reluctance I turned to Physics as a substitute.

(Albert Einstein, cited in Carter, 1999)

INTRODUCTION

This concluding chapter aims to achieve two purposes. First, it will consider how the trainee geography teacher should view his or her current and future professional life as a reflective practitioner empowered to 'make things happen'. Second, it will explore the 'possible futures' in which new teachers of geography may soon be working, both in terms of their professional development as NQTs and from the perspective of how geography education is currently changing. The chapter therefore attempts to draw together key aspects of each of the previous chapters into an overall conclusion.

1 BEING A REFLECTIVE PRACTITIONER

The intense activity associated with the period of initial teacher training soon ends and successful trainees quickly find themselves within geography departments as Newly Qualified Teachers (NQTs) at the start of the first year of their teaching career. However, one's education as a beginning teacher does not stop at the point of transition from being a trainee to becoming a full-time teacher. The use of the word 'initial' in the phrase 'initial teacher training' is deliberate, for this is only the *start* of a process of professional development and continued learning that should accompany the teacher throughout his or her professional life. Indeed the QTS acquired at the end of ITT is provisional on the successful completion of a first year within the classroom – a year in which trainees will again be expected to meet targets, evaluate their practice and advance professionally.

During your initial training you will have been expected to be 'reflective' – that is, you will have been required to critically consider the ways in which your teaching skills are developing. You will have been helped in this process by the support and guidance of trained mentor teachers in schools and tutors in your university department. Ideally they will have combined to ensure that you maximize your potential as a beginning teacher.

Once you start to teach in your first full-time post similar guidance should be forthcoming from a named induction tutor, or mentor, in your school. However, the extent of such guidance may be variable; evidence suggests that schools view induction in different ways despite a clear requirement that they provide support structured around the Career Entry Profile (CEP) completed at the end of ITT. Some schools rather unhelpfully consider that you are now 'trained' and therefore should be able to cope with all the rigours of the classroom on your own. This is partly why the abilities you have developed as a reflective practitioner during your ITT programme are essential – they help you to think and act as a professionally responsible individual. It is crucial that all teachers have this ability to critically reflect on their practice if they are to remain effective (see Kent, 2000). No one wants teachers who are content merely to 'coast' and who will not 'push' themselves to give of their professional best. Coasting tends to lead to low expectations and declining standards amongst students – it is typified by a lack of challenge and stimulus in the geography classroom. Getting the balance right is essential. Whilst coasting is unacceptable it is equally wrong to expect teachers to continually drive themselves onwards to meet new challenges, at risk to their health and personal relationships. The short-sighted creation of meaningless targets, which needlessly increase competitiveness without raising standards, only serve to increase one's stress, anxiety, tiredness and inability to cope. Unfortunately, many teachers in today's staffrooms show signs of exactly this abuse.

Conducting successful lesson evaluations, which utilize clear criteria that define what constitutes an effective lesson in a particular context, is a feature of sound reflective practice. Evaluations should not stop just because the period of one's ITT has finished. The focus for evaluation broadly remains the same throughout your entire teaching career – whether your students are learning is the prime consideration, rather than how well you think you are 'performing' as a teacher. The QTS Standards attempt, with some degree of success, to identify the knowledge, understanding, skills and values of effective teaching largely from this perspective of encouraging purposeful learning (Lambert and Balderstone, 2000).

Critical reflection is therefore essential to the process of learning how to teach and to maintaining one's teaching abilities during an entire career in the profession. However, the term 'reflection' is regularly overused within teacher education and often very loosely applied – it has been wrongly placed by some training institutions at the very cornerstone of all aspects of teacher education, elevated to a position of almost talismanic importance. In addition, what some trainees understand by reflection may not be helpful to their development, particularly if the process of reflection is merely used to justify poor practice or the meeting of mediocre standards. Effective reflection should be critical and set against established criteria or standards; it should involve target setting and be challenging without being unnecessarily threatening. The key element in good reflective practice is the ability to actually *change* aspects of one's teaching that are not up to standard. The impetus for this change should come from secure and impartial evidence, based on observation of current practice. Whilst effective change is the desired endpoint of critical reflection it is not helpful to reflect too negatively or emotionally on one's perceived lack of capabilities or fears. In extreme cases this may result in a form of 'teaching paralysis' – where students continue to be offered an unchanging and uninspired diet of worksheets or note taking simply because the teacher incorrectly perceives that 'this is all I can do with this group'! You will also already be aware of the unhelpful 'collusion' that sometimes occurs within teaching and learning whereby the teacher sets undemanding, easily achievable tasks which give the appearance of engaging students in a busy working atmosphere – say, colouring in maps or completing wordsearches – whilst actually providing little intellectual stimulus or prospect for educational advancement. Low student expectations soon result from this kind of teaching, which the teacher finds increasingly difficult to draw students away from. In some cases this results in the teacher simply 'child minding', rather than establishing sound learning experiences in geography education.

Evaluation and critical reflection are closely linked. Importantly they should not represent 'end points' in a process, as both should occur with an aim of improving teaching and learning. Therefore they are only valuable if their findings are fed back into the educational context in an effort to change future practice. In this way evaluation and critical reflection are similar to formative assessment – their role is to enable more effective learning to take place. To have greatest impact the evaluative/reflective process should be ongoing and regular.

Key questions need to be posed in one's reflection, some of which may need support from a tutor or mentor who can provide a critical and objective edge to the process:

- What should I reflect upon?

- Why should I reflect upon this?

- What action should I now take to resolve the situation?

- How will I judge whether this action has been effective?

Inevitably during the period of ITT critical reflection is regularly focused on elements of one's ability to teach and the impact of this teaching on students' learning. The Standards direct this process reasonably effectively. However, reflection should not be too narrowly concentrated on teaching performance to the detriment of reviewing other aspects of professional competence. One aspect of reflection (and lesson evaluation) which is not considered as fully as it might be, given the immediacy of the 'performance' of the teacher being scrutinized, concerns subject knowledge and application. The importance of teaching and learning 'good geography' is fundamental, but often somewhat forgotten in evaluating the act of 'teaching children'. It is essential that what is taught under the heading of 'geography' is accurate, meaningful, up-to-date and accessible. This implies that all geography teachers should keep abreast of developments within their subject and consider how these apply to the particular curriculum and/or specifications they teach. Many beginning teachers have a distinct advantage here in that they are usually recent graduates in geography and therefore may be at a more advanced stage of subject appreciation than the teachers they are working with; however, other beginning teachers may feel that the rather piecemeal or overly selective content of their joint honours, or 'geography-based', degrees set them at a distinct disadvantage!

Looking to the future it may be important for many NQTs to consider the objectives Kent (2000) states for his book *Reflective Practice in Geography Teaching*, for although these objectives are targeted at the experienced geography teacher they also have a resonance for the geography NQT. In essence, these encourage and challenge geography teachers to (after Kent, 2000, p. vii):

- achieve a critical understanding of the literature and concepts of geography education;

- stimulate their interest and enjoyment in teaching geography so that they continue with personal and professional development;

- develop as autonomous, reflectively thinking individuals, capable of taking a leading role in education, most often but not always in geography education;

- achieve professionally relevant knowledge, understanding, skills and values.

2 | THE TTA CAREER ENTRY PROFILE (CEP)

The CEP is a brief summative record of your achievements during your period of initial teacher training. It serves to identify your strengths at the point when you were awarded QTS, but also states your priorities for professional development during your first year of teaching as a NQT. The CEP is designed to enable your new school to establish a programme of induction for your first year of teaching. It is a requirement that all training institutions provide their trainees with a completed CEP at the end of the ITT course.

The CEP is presented in a slim wallet folder comprised of two sections: notes for guidance about completing the profile (including a complete set of Standards for the award of QTS), and the profile itself (in three sections: A to C). The main section of the profile consists of a statement of your experiences, achievements and areas for development – this provides a basis for the creation of a programme of induction with your induction mentor. The CEP should therefore be used to set out an agenda of personal targets for the induction year and therefore, ideally, represents a seamless progression from initial training to continued professional development. It is usually completed at, or near, the end of your training and comprises a series of brief statements agreed by you and your ITT provider set against the QTS Standards. The school in which you have gained your first teaching post complete, with you, the section on targets and an action plan for the induction period. Success criteria need to be established at this stage.

The CEP is often completed as a final summative document, the Standards having already been used formatively throughout your period of training on other profiles or assessment documents. Whatever form of the Standards you have used with your mentor and tutor during ITT you should be clear how these translate to the CEP in terms of the actual Standards.

3 | FURTHER PROFESSIONAL DEVELOPMENT

Once you have become a serving teacher there are a wide range of professional development courses and qualifications that will be made available to you. These may be 'award bearing' courses, such as diplomas, certificates, taught masters degrees or research degrees (such as M.Phil or PhD) in different aspects of education. Schools and LEAs provide many of the day-to-day professional development courses, although they may involve the use of individual education consultants who provide aspects of professional training. Certificated courses are usually provided by Schools or Departments of Education in HEIs where standards are moderated by a system of external examiners and inspectors. Such courses are usually available on either a part-time or full-time basis.

The TTA is central to the development of a single framework for teacher qualifications which has accepted national standards. The structure within which such professional development occurs currently looks as follows:

1. QTS – for all teachers employed in maintained schools.

2. Advanced Skills Teacher – for experienced classroom teachers.

3. National Professional Qualification for Subject Leader (NPQSL) – for teachers with subject leadership roles (e.g. Head of Geography Department).

4. Standards for Special Educational Needs Co-Ordinators (SENCOs) – for teachers with responsibility for SEN.

5. National Professional Qualification for Headship (NPQH) – for current and aspiring headteachers.

The original reasons for devising this national framework of standards between 1994 and 1998 (with SEN teachers' standards added in 1999) – to define teacher expertise in specific roles – still remain. However, the role of the TTA as the body charged with the responsibility for formulating and managing these standards appears to be changing. Indeed some commentators believe that 'at present the significance of the TTA appears to be diminishing before our eyes as its' purpose becomes displaced either to the GTC or relocated at the DfEE' (Mahony and Hextall, 2000, p. 3).

The Circular 4/98 standards, which were being revised at the time of writing, will almost certainly maintain their regulatory and quality assurance function in whatever guise they eventually reappear. The four main reasons for their existence (after Mahony and Hextall, 2000, p. 34) have not gone away, namely:

1. to ensure quality and consistency in a context where a variety of diverse routes into teaching have been established;

2. to meet the desire of central government to establish greater control of ITT, fuelled partly by distrust of 'education professionals';

3. to reflect the increasing use of standards in other spheres of the public sector and in other countries;

4. to provide a procedural basis for the external inspection of ITT.

In practice, all standards inevitably experience amendment and interpretation at the level of practice. The ITT standards had previously been criticized for implying that only one acceptable 'model' of teaching exists for the beginning teacher. Criticism has also occurred because of their technicist approach to teacher education, their lack of values and for creating the impression that effective teachers should primarily be concerned with producing a skilled and internationally competitive workforce. Broader values and concerns, involving personal/professional development and the pastoral care of children, tended to be downplayed. Arguably the standards have had a positive impact on the process of personal target setting, planning, monitoring of performance and the clarification of professional roles. However, it would be surprising if the national standards framework did not also continue to fulfil an inspecting and policing function in future years. This mirrors the shift in practice in the public sector in recent years, as described by Hartley (1997), where 'the high trust *professional acceptability* of the 1960s and 1970s gave way in the 1980s to low trust *public accountability*; and this public accountability has been set subsequently within an almost Darwinian *market accountability*' (p. 143).

4 | THE ROLE OF RESEARCH

It is increasingly clear that teachers need to be more aware of current educational research and its implications for their classroom practice. ITT makes reference to the need for trainees to take account of such research, whilst teachers have recently been encouraged by the DfEE/DfES to engage in their own classroom-based action research, supported by higher education institutions, through applying for Best Practice Research Scholarships (BPRS). Assertions about the importance of educational research lie at the heart of considerations that teaching is, in essence, a research-based profession (Hargreaves, 1998). In geography education some efforts have recently been made to introduce teachers to relevant research findings which they can relate to their own classroom context, such that their professional development is kept fresh and up-to-date (for example the *Theory into Practice* series published by the Geographical Association since 1999).

As Kent (2000) states, too often valuable research findings fail to reach a wider audience who would benefit from them. However, there are questions about the 'maturity' of much of the research conducted within geography education (see Figure 12.1), despite the dramatic increase in the amount of research published within this field internationally over the past 30 years (Gerber and Williams, 2000).

Although the research culture in geography education may be largely held at the 'incipient stage' this does not imply that such research is necessarily of poor quality. What is significant is that the majority of researchers tend not to attract substantial amounts of money to conduct their work, are not closely integrated within a wider research community, and do not enjoy a well developed and respected international infrastructure of conferences and journals. Nonetheless, the current agenda for research within geography education is comparatively clear – according to Gerber and Williams (2000) this agenda encompasses: the development of policy in geographical education, learning and teaching in geographical education, geography curriculum development, assessment and evaluation in

Incipient stage	Intermediate stage	Mature stage
Individuals researching in isolation	Intra-institutional groups	International groups
Idiosyncratic and changing substantive focuses	Stable substantive focuses though subject to personnel changes	Enduring substantive focuses that are unaffected by personnel changes
Unfunded	Funded by local and national organizations	Funded by international organizations
Unsupported by a professional body	Supported on the margins of a national professional body	Central to the work of an international body
Dominated by immediate practical issues	Linking practical and theoretical issues	Dominated by universal theoretical issues
Focused largely on a single sector of a national education system	Focused on more than one sector of a national education system	Focused on lifelong learning in an international context
Undeveloped specialist geographical education research language	Emergence of a specialist geographical education research language	Use of a sophisticated geographical education research language
Absence of textbooks on geographical education research	Introductory textbooks on geographical education research	An array of established textbooks on geographical education research
Lacking close ties with conventional educational disciplines	Developing ties with a number of educational research disciplines	Closely integrated into the educational research community
Lacking any subdiscipline strengths within geographical education	Emergent subdiscipline strengths within geographical education	Established subdiscipline communities within research in geographical education
No infrastructure of research-focused symposia, conferences, web pages, journals and other publications	Developing nationally based infrastructure of research-focused symposia, conferences, web pages, journals and other publications	Well developed international infrastructure comprising symposia, conferences, web pages, journals and other publications
Few opportunities for training in research in geographical education	Limited national opportunities for training in research in geographical education	Many international opportunities for training in research in geographical education

Figure 12.1 *Stages of growth in the culture of research in geographical education (Kent, 2000)*

geography, teaching resources, technology in geographical education, geographical education in differing social contexts, and geographical and environmental education. Roberts (2000b) largely concurs, but provides a re-conception of such research focused upon the role of learners, teachers and contexts for learning within geography education.

The future directions for educational research, and its impact on classroom practice, are not straightforward. The role of research has been debated and contested with respect to its priorities, its relevance, the extent to which it should involve 'user groups', and its expected outcomes (Rudduck and McIntyre, 1998). There are a number of 'big questions' still to be resolved, both within geography education itself and with reference to the role and function research should play in answering these questions. Should research always be applied to the resolution of problems in the geography classroom, or does it have a function in helping us to explore broader parameters – often from a more ideological perspective? Roberts is clear in her understanding of the issues when she states:

> The role of research in supporting teaching and learning in geography is greater than providing information on what works in the classroom. It also has a role in challenging assumptions, in identifying underpinning values and in asking critical questions about purposes. Research into geographical education can help us see things differently and freshly. It can empower teachers to construct their own understandings, to clarify their own values and to have professional confidence to make changes in classroom practices!
>
> (Roberts, 2000b, p. 293).

Warf (1999), within the context of the United States, draws our attention to the barriers between geographers in higher education and those involved in ITT and school teaching. He focuses upon research as the primary concern of academic geographers, whilst teaching (at whatever level) is 'frequently assumed to be easy or minimally important' (p. 586). Significantly the lack of communication between schools and universities is striking and merely serves to fuel the stereotype that research within geography education is 'insufficiently rigorous', 'out of touch with contemporary intellectual trends within the discipline' and 'largely an interrogation of the self evident' (p. 587).

5 | GEOGRAPHY EDUCATION AND THE FUTURE

Whilst it is impossible to predict the future in any walk of life – and this is particularly true of education – it is important to have some idea of the processes which tend to shape future outcomes. In Chapters 2 and 3 it was noted that a variety of factors affect (geography) education at any one time – namely the prevailing philosophies of education, the existing subject paradigms within higher education, the economic climate and the political complexion of the government of the day. This final section will seek to convey a tentative vision of the future, bearing in mind the shifting influences on geography education of academic geographers (predominantly in the 1960s and early 1970s), curriculum developers (late 1970s and early 1980s) and centralized government (late 1980s to date). By understanding the reasons why change is happening it may be possible to have a positive influence upon that change.

5.1 Geography in schools

Geography education in schools is currently weakest, or perhaps least coherent, at its points of interface between Key Stages and sectors (Carter, 1999). The most evident curriculum disconnection occurs between Key Stages 2 and 3, at the point where students have already experienced six of their nine years of compulsory geography education (Chapman, 2001). Unfortunately, many secondary teachers appear unwilling or unable to take account of their students' previous educational experience, often starting their geography teaching from too 'low' a level in Key Stage 3 (OFSTED, 1998). This is undoubtedly a problem of continuity and progression – of teachers not knowing enough about where their students are 'coming from' or 'going to' in educational terms, despite the presence of the GNC. The solution to this problem may eventually arise through more rigorous cross phase liaison, 'bridging' projects in geography, combined target setting between schools and a greater dialogue between the phases via professional associations such as the GA (Chapman, 2001; Wood, 2001).

The future problems for geography education in the 14–19 curriculum are also very apparent, but of a different nature. The optional status of geography at Key Stage 4, created specifically to make room for a mandatory 'core' of subjects and the New Agenda, removes the entitlement that students should have to a broad and balanced education (as originally promised by the National Curriculum). Many students now follow neither geography, nor history, at this level and therefore have a very limited experience of the Humanities at the end of their compulsory schooling. Entry numbers for geography GCSE and A level have steadily declined following the Dearing Review (Dearing, 1993, 1994, 1996), as a direct result of the re-establishment of geography's optional status post 14 (see Westaway and Rawling, 2001) (see Figure 12.2). The wider effects of this weakening of the Humanities may not have been fully considered by the government, for as Carter (1999) argues 'where will citizenship education come from post 14 or post 16 if students have given up geography and history?'

1995	1996	1997	1998	1999	2000
295,229	302,298	290,201	265,573	257,294	251,605

(a)

1995	1996	1997	1998	1999	2000
43,426	42,786	42,641	44,881	42,181	37,112

(b)

Figure 12.2 *(a) Examination entries for GCSE Geography 1995–2000 (b) Examination entries for A level Geography 1995–2000 (QCA, 2001)*

The very conception of the 14–19 curriculum, the future of the GSCE and the performance of the new A/AS levels and Vocational A levels will all have an impact on the future curriculum health of geography. This state of affairs is largely the result of the current hierarchical conception of the curriculum, which prioritizes and rewards so called 'core' subjects to the detriment of others. Whether the majority of students will be given the options necessary to pursue geography to degree level, if they so wish, is yet to be seen.

The two major reviews of the National Curriculum, Dearing's in 1995 and the QCA review for 2000, have therefore resulted in a slimmer, more manageable GNC but one which faces greater curriculum competition from vocational, National Curriculum and non National Curriculum subjects post 14. As a result geography exhibits declining status within the curriculum and caters for reduced student numbers. Worryingly, many geography teachers do not appear to have acknowledged the current flexibility of their subject curriculum and seem content to maintain its existing status quo. With New Labour not intending to lead a further subject-based review of the National Curriculum in 2005 there are dangers that the school geography curriculum may now be enshrined in a rather traditional, static and lifeless form.

Practical activity 12.1

What might be the priorities for a future review of the 14–19 curriculum from a geographer's perspective?

How might we define the contribution of geography to the development of students' academic and vocational skills and abilities within this age range? How should an entitlement to geography education be structured? Ideally, what might the range of geographical courses and qualifications looks like within the 14–19 curriculum?

5.2 Political influences

With regard to future political influences on geography education Marsden is understandably cautious, particularly in the light of the depressing events of the 1980s and early 1990s which he refers to as 'Decades of Disillusion' (Marsden, 1995). He reflects upon a time when political views on education radically altered from a *laissez-faire* approach towards an interventionist stance, reaching a nadir when:

> Thatcherist ideology brought in its train instability, confrontation, buck-passing and a strident moralism, not least in the negative stereotyping of the educational professions by right-wing politicians and press. In the approach to the millennium, educational progress will undoubtedly be checked, not least by a flight of teachers from the profession, if we do not return some stability (psychological as well as curricular), common-sense judgements and decent human relationships.
>
> (Marsden, 1995, p. 206)

Others have come to similar conclusions with respect to recent political involvement in education:

> During the last decade or so there has been a sustained attack on teachers and teaching by politicians and others through the popular media. The sub-text has been that teaching has failed young people and failed society.
>
> (Carter, 1999, p. 296)

Whilst some of the extremes envisioned by Marsden have not yet come to fruition, the general thrust of what he said in the mid 1990s still has a certain resonance today under a second New Labour government. The importance placed upon

'Education, Education, Education' at the start of Labour's first term of office in 1997 has been broadly translated into a desire for state education to create a future labour force which needs 'brains not brawn' and which will embrace the use of new technologies. This government has also sought to achieve the old ideals of using education to achieve emancipation from social exclusion for particular groups of disaffected youngsters (Toynbee and Walker, 2001). At the start of the twenty-first century Labour has fortunately inherited from the Tories two trends – improving GCSE and A level results and an expansion of higher education in colleges and universities. One third of 18–19 year olds in England and Wales now enter higher education – creating a student population of just over one million – nonetheless, almost seven million adults in the UK still lack the levels of literacy and numeracy typical of an average eleven-year-old.

Labour has flirted with the idea of setting up American-style 'charter schools' offering specialist subject curricula and implementing part selection of students. The most recent Green Paper (DfEE, 2001) suggests that 50 per cent of all secondary schools will now become 'specialist schools', although no plans currently exist for any such schools to have a predominantly Humanities focus to their curriculum. Labour is also strongly following the Tory line of trying to involve private businesses in funding state education in public private partnerships (PPPs) and has continued to apply right-wing policies on school improvement – utilizing standards, targets, inspections and performance indicators to effect change. It has, however, drawn back from the excesses of completely dismantling LEAs and using companies to supply, inspect and pay teachers following its disastrous attempts at so doing in Islington during its first term. At the time of the general election in June 2001 Labour's then Secretary of State for Education, David Blunkett, was one of the longest serving Education Secretaries in history. During his time in office he had 'abolished assisted places at private schools, established new City Academies, slimmed the national curriculum, brigaded schools in poor areas into Education Action Zones, started Fresh Start and tested and tested again' (Toynbee and Walker, 2001, p. 47). Legislation to introduce literacy and numeracy hours in primary schools – with their notable impact on geography education at this level – had also been passed, waiving the demands of the National Curriculum. Unfortunately, despite rafts of new initiatives the divisions between the academic performance of children from the highest and lowest socio-economic classes still appears to be widening in many LEAs.

But what will be the political impact on geography in schools? New Labour appears to be maintaining a more pragmatic, less ideological approach to education at the start of the new millennium. This has resulted in a curious mix of 'autonomy and control' within educational policy, which has subsequently transferred to the classroom. This government appears to have less of an interest in individual subjects, such as geography, than previous governments, concentrating more on its 'New Agenda' of PSHE, citizenship, creative and cultural education and sustainable development education. These themes cut *across* subject divisions and may ultimately damage geography's identity and marginalize its contribution to the curriculum.

Against this backdrop of educational change a degree of curriculum stability has been achieved within geography education. Nonetheless, the future for subjects like geography will not be determined solely by education professionals, as was the case before the advent of the National Curriculum. Politicians, educationists and a variety of 'others' (from parents to industrialists) will all have their input within educational partnerships and forums of different types, the power base and influence subtly shifting between each of the players involved. Significantly, education is now, more than ever before, at political centre stage. As Carter (1999) asserts 'political interference with the curriculum seems here to stay'.

> ### Practical activity 12.2
>
> Consider the major policy initiatives within education at the present time.
>
> How does geography education 'fit' within these policies? Does the current geography curriculum match such policies closely? If not, consider whether it should.
>
> Are there dangers in geographers strongly promoting their subject's unique contribution to the curriculum, without regard for the directional changes currently evident within educational policy?

5.3   Higher education influences

Geographers within higher education have recently commented on the significant gaps which have now occurred between the geography taught in schools and that which is promulgated by university departments. This is potentially one of the most serious challenges facing geography in the twenty-first century.

During the 'conceptual revolution' of the 1960s geography departments in higher education had a significant influence on the development of school geography through curriculum development conferences, such as those held at Madingley Hall, and through resultant publications (see Chorley and Haggett, 1965, 1967). By contrast, the creation of the GNC twenty-five years later saw no widespread dialogue between the two sectors, indeed many observers refer to the 'de-coupling' of schools from higher education which has caused a dangerous fragmentation of the geographic community (see Goudie 1993; Bradford, 1996; Machon and Ranger, 1996; Rawling and Daugherty, 1996; Unwin, 1996; Lambert, 2001). Efforts have been made to draw the communities together again – for example the bi-annual COBRIG conferences at Oxford University which started in 1994 – for the need to maintain coherence within the subject is clear. Some would argue that the introduction of the National Curriculum has, in part, intensified the split between schools and higher education. Teachers were forced to concentrate their efforts on restructuring their geography courses for the 5–14 age range following the launch of the GNC and less upon the development of their subject at GCSE and A level, where subject content has traditionally been more heavily influenced by university academics. The number of textbooks for schools written by academics has declined, due perhaps to increased demands on their time to produce higher status research articles, whilst the number of A level geography examiners drawn from the university sector has also fallen (Unwin, 1996). Along with the conceptual shifts currently affecting the discipline within university geography departments, which do not transfer easily to schools, this has led to less interest being shown by teachers in developments at the research frontiers of the subject. Only a few texts have recently attempted to bridge this divide (see Rawling and Daugherty, 1996; Kent, 2000, Bale, 2001).

Geography in higher education in the UK is, in the main, a vibrant, dynamic and healthy subject – although one which is currently prone to fragmentation. It is a discipline that can provide answers to contemporary questions, be they social, economic, political or environmental, and which enables its students to gain a wide variety of transferable skills. Geographers provide a unique spatial perspective on many problems and are currently at the forefront of research into climate and environment change, globalization, sustainability and resource use. However, geographers in higher education have recently had little impact on the form and function of their subject at National Curriculum, GCSE, A or AS levels – indeed some commentators believe that recently-devised post-16 specifications for geography are already almost twenty years out of date. The only forces which draw school and university geography together arise from subject associations (such as the GA, RGS-IBG and COBRIG), or from individuals or small groups producing innovative textbooks, teaching resources and curricular materials.

As a result geography as a school subject has not recently been redefined in modern form. The National Curriculum GWG failed to achieve such a (re)definition either to the satisfaction of geography teachers, or indeed of the membership of the working group itself, at the start of the 1990s. Subsequent subject reviews have merely served to slightly modify the existing geography curriculum. If the parent discipline in universities becomes increasingly divorced from its school roots there are real fears for the long-term future of the subject at all levels. Unfortunately, many of the contemporary, stable and exciting developments in university geography have found difficulty in achieving more than a foothold in school geography. Examples of such developments are numerous: the growth of GIS, globalization, the renewed interest in global politics, cultural geography, geographical modelling, new regional approaches, the significance of environmental change and its management. Arguably all of these themes have a place in school geography at all levels, but are currently not strongly represented in most schools. The previous rigidity of the National Curriculum, and of GCSE and A level specifications have served to restrict the growth of school geography in this respect.

Evidence of dislocation is witnessed in a variety of ways:

- the conceptual content of A Level Geography specifications/syllabuses has remained largely unaltered since the mid 1970s;

- geographers in schools are not invited to challenge models, laws and theories which have been removed from (or heavily critiqued within) geography at university level some years ago;

- confusion, or a lack of information, exists in schools about which strand(s) of university geography to pursue;

- the lack of consensus within university geography about major philosophical, methodological and ideological issues has left school teachers struggling to keep pace with academic changes;

- fragmentation, compartmentalization and subdivision within university geography threatens geography's unity and long-term existence.

In the future we should, as Stoddart (1987) stated well over a decade ago, seek to draw together school and university geography in providing a balanced sense of the 'real' (relating to places), the 'unified' (linking physical and human geography) and the 'committed' (addressing large-scale human problems). The current fragmentation of geography at university level, and its tight curricular frameworks within schools, makes any common way forward difficult. What may be needed are 'mediators' who can encourage 'new geographies' and unifying principles to filter into schools. HEI tutors who already have links with both school and university geography departments might provide the necessary connections.

6 | GEOGRAPHY WITHIN OUR FUTURE SOCIETY

Does geography education prepare children for the society they will face in the future? Does it take into account – and have something significant to say about – the major social changes wrought by economic restructuring, changing technologies, the drive for international competitiveness and the shifts in employment prospects in the UK and beyond? In short, will geography and geography education present an agenda that can be taken seriously by children and adults in the twenty-first century? (see Warf, 1999; Massey, 2001).

Education in the twenty-first century will have to address a number of big questions and concepts. Arguably, the most significant of these include consideration of issues such as globalization, social justice, population growth, sustainability, interdependence, inequality and poverty. Each curriculum subject will have a role to play in educating students about how they might understand and address these issues in the future, both individually and collectively – geography can surely claim to have a very important perspective on these issues too. Unfortunately, the GNC currently gives little indication of a dynamic relationship between geography and society, forcing radical geographers to support more 'adjectival' educations (such as environmental education, peace education, development education) which appear better placed to enable students to explore how the world works and how it might be changed (Huckle, 1997). Huckle therefore believes that:

> School geography is in urgent need of reform. After a decade or more of largely pragmatic development at the bidding of politicians and dominant interests within the subject community, it is now time to acknowledge that the subject has distanced itself from change in society and from those developments in academic geography and curriculum theory which could be used to enable us to better meet our ideals. We need to return to professionalism in geography education and debate the new social, theoretical and pedagogical challenges with re-discovered energy and enthusiasm.
> (Huckle, 1997, p. 249–50)

It is a moot point as to whether our curriculum is adequately constructed to confront the demands of 'education for the future'. Is a subject based curriculum, with or without geography, the best way forward? Do we need to create new links between subjects and stimulate greater curriculum dialogue? Indeed, is our current curriculum flexible enough to be able to deal with educating children to take their place, as well as rise to new demands, in a rapidly changing world? If we fix our focus specifically upon geography we might question how relevant the theories, models and concepts currently being taught within our discipline are – we may be approaching a time when 'school geography will become cluttered with dead information and outdated theory' (Carter, 1999).

What *is* clear is that when geography teachers are constantly expected to enforce major shifts in education policy, rather than being given space to concentrate on teaching and curriculum development, the future for geography looks bleak. The model of curriculum development originally introduced by the National Curriculum, with its tight time scales, lack of consultation and political tampering, should never be repeated. It is essential that geography regains the 'high ground' in curricular and educational terms, seeking out its intellectual roots and finding stability in commonly accepted aims and objectives. These developments can not simply be left to 'others' who have a greater influence on state education – school geography must be debated and restructured in association with geographers in higher education and with an input from educational research findings.

Practical activity 12.3

Who, or what, currently defines geography's contribution to the curriculum?
Ideally, who should be the 'key players' in the process of defining geography's form, content and contribution within the curriculum?

CONCLUSION

Very considerable changes have affected geography education in the last quarter century. Governments have taken a more interventionist stance, the influence of LEAs has reduced, the National Curriculum has been imposed and revised, and the academic and vocational pathways through 14–19 education significantly altered. The accountability of teachers and the extent to which their work is directed by new policies has increased, a process partly driven by the extended use of inspection evidence. Centralization and consolidation has meant that control has become easier for the state, whilst the growth of educational quangos has accelerated the pace of change without a corresponding increase in the accountability of official bodies. Many geography teachers feel that their professional status has been undermined.

The public perception of geography and geographers needs to be advanced. At present many members of the general public have a confused and dated view of the subject. In addition there are no academic geographers who are well known and courted by the media, unlike academics in many other subjects who are 'high profile', respected and publicly consulted. Geography must escape its damaging image as a narrowly utilitarian subject, interested solely in low level knowledge of 'capes and bays', capital cities, rivers and landscapes. This image of geography is unhelpfully sustained by the fondness of the press to only focus on horror stories of childrens' lack of locational knowledge. The ability of the subject to create a deeper critical understanding of place, space and environment should be realized. For the first time geography should be considered important, even controversial, enough to warrant an informed national debate about its contribution within and beyond education.

However, the future may not look entirely gloomy. Geography still occupies a reasonably popular and strong position in English and Welsh schools compared to its standing in schools in other developed and developing countries. It is still recognized within the National Curriculum and there are substantial (if declining) numbers of candidates who opt to study the subject at GCSE and A and AS level. In higher education geography courses are also popular, producing graduates who are currently amongst the most employable of any subject discipline. Within HEIs the geography community is largely united and productive, with a core of individuals contributing strongly to international research and publication in geography education. What must be achieved by geographers, as Marsh (1997) makes clear, is our inclusion in policy formulation and strategic planning within education, not merely as an 'interest group', or even as 'stakeholders', but as a group of ultimate 'decision makers'. Too long has the geographic community been merely 'allowed in' on consultations about their subject's educational future, rather than setting the agenda and shaping its outcome.

REFERENCES

ACAC (1996) *Consistency in Teacher Assessment: Exemplification of Standards, Geography, Key Stage 3*. Cardiff: ACAC.

ACCAC (1997) *Consistency in Teacher Assessment: Optional Tests and Tasks – Key Stage 3, Geography*. Cardiff: ACCAC.

Adey, P. and Shayer, M. (1994) *Really Raising Standards*. London: Routledge.

Andrews, R. (ed.) (1989) *Narrative and Argument*. Milton Keynes: Open University Press.

Balchin, W. and Coleman, A. (1973) Graphicacy should be the fourth ace in the pack. In Bale, J., Graves, N. and Walford, R. (eds) *Perspectives in Geographical Education*. Edinburgh: Oliver and Boyd, pp. 78–86.

Balderstone, D. (2000) Beyond testing? Issues for teacher assessment in geography? In Hopkin, J., Telfer S. and Butt, G. (eds) *Assessment in Practice: Raising Standards in Secondary Geography*. Sheffield: Geographical Association, pp. 9–15.

Bale, J. (2001) *Sportscapes*. Sheffield: Geographical Association.

Barker, S., Brooks, V., March, K. and Swatton, P. (1995) *Initial Teacher Education in Secondary Schools*. Warwick: University of Warwick and AUT.

Barratt Hacking, E. (1998) Editorial: The value of research in teaching geography. *Teaching Geography*, 23 (2) p. 60.

Battersby, J. (1995) *Teaching Geography at Key Stage 3*. Cambridge: Chris Kington.

Battersby, J. (1997) Differentiation in teaching and learning geography. In Tilbury, D, and Williams, M. (eds) *Teaching and Learning Geography*. London: Routledge, pp. 69–79.

Battersby, J. (2000) Does differentiation provide access to an entitlement curriculum for all pupils? In Fisher C. and Binns T. (eds) *Issues in Geography Teaching*. London: RoutledgeFalmer, pp. 69–79.

Bennetts, T. (1995) Continuity and progression, *Teaching Geography*, 20 (2), pp. 75–9.

Bennetts, T. (1996) Progression and differentiation. In Bailey, P. and Fox, P. (eds) *Geography Teachers' Handbook*. Sheffield: GA, pp. 81–93.

Benton, P. and O'Brien T. (eds) (2000) *Special Needs and the Beginning Teacher*. London: Continuum.

Benyon J. (1993) Technological literacy: where do we all go from here? In Benjon, J., and MacKay H. (eds) *Computers into Classrooms: More Questions Than Answers*. London: Falmer, pp. 94–115.

Bermingham, S., Slater, F. and Yangopoulos, S. (1999) Multiple texts, alternative texts, multiple readings, alternative readings, *Teaching Geography*, 24 (4), pp. 160–4.

Binns, A. (1996) School geography: the key questions for discussion. In Rawling, E. and Daugherty, R. (eds) *Geography into the Twenty-First Century*. Chichester. Wiley, pp. 37–56:

Black, P. and Wiliam, D. (1998) *Inside the Black Box: Raising Standards Through Classroom Assessment*. Cambridge: University of Cambridge School of Education and the Assessment Reform Group.

Blades, M. and Spencer, C. (1986) Map use by young children, *Geography*, 71, pp. 47–52.

Blades, M. and Spencer, C. (1988) How do children find their way through familiar and unfamiliar environments?, *Environmental Education and Information*, 7 (1), pp. 7–14.

Bland, K., Chambers, D., Donert K. and Thomas, T. (1996) Fieldwork. In Bailey, P. and Fox P. (eds) *Geography Teachers' Handbook*. Sheffield: GA, pp. 165–75.

Bloom. B. (1964) *Taxonomy of Educational Objectives. The Classification of Educational Goals*. New York: David McKay.

Boardman, D. (1983) *Graphicacy and Geography Teaching*. London: Croom Helm.

Boardman, D. (ed.) (1986a) *Handbook for Geography Teachers*. Sheffield: Geographical Association.

Boardman, D. (1986b) Map reading skills. In Boardman, D. (ed.) *Handbook for Geography Teachers*. Sheffield: Geographical Association, pp. 123–9.

Boardman, D. (1988) *The Impact of a Curriculum Project: Geography and the Young School Leaver*. Birmingham: Educational Review, University of Birmingham.

Boardman, D. (1989) The development of graphicacy: children's understanding of maps, *Geography*, 74 (4), pp. 321–31.

Boardman, D. and McPartland, M. (1993a) A hundred years of geography teaching: innovation and change, 1970–82, *Teaching Geography*, 18 (3), pp. 117–20.

Boardman, D. and McPartland, M. (1993b) A hundred years of geography teaching: towards centralisation. 1983–93, *Teaching Geography*, 18 (3), pp. 159–62.

Bradford, M. (1996) Geography at the secondary/higher education interface: change through diversity. In Rawling, E. and Daugherty, R. (eds) *Geography into the Twenty-First Century*, Chichester: Wiley, pp. 277–88.

Broadfoot, P., Osborn, M., Planel, C. and Sharpe, K. (2000) *Promoting Quality in Learning: Does England Have the Answer?* London: Cassell.

Brown, S. and Smith, M. (2000) The secondary/tertiary interface. In Kent, A. (ed.) *Reflective Practice in Geography Teaching*. London: Philip Chapman Publishing, pp. 262–75.

Brownsword, R. (1998) Developing empathy through language, *Teaching Geography*, 23 (1), pp. 16–21.

Bruner, J. (1960) *The Process of Education*. Cambridge, MA: Harvard University Press.

Burgess, E.W. (1925) *The Growth of the City*. The City, pp. 47–62.

Butt, G. (1991) Have we got a video today? *Teaching Geography*, 16 (2), pp. 51–5.

Butt, G. (1993) The effects of audience centred teaching on children's writing in Geography, *International Research in Geographical and Environmental Education*, 2 (1), pp. 11–24.

Butt, G. (1996) Developments in geography 14–19: a changing system. In Rawling, E. and Daugherty, R. (eds) *Geography into the Twenty-First Century*. Chichester: Wiley, pp. 173–93.

Butt, G. (1997a) *An Investigation into the Dynamics of the National Curriculum Geography Working Group (1989–1990)*. Unpublished PhD thesis University of Birmingham.

Butt, G. (1997b) Language and learning in geography. In Tilbury, D. and Williams, M. (eds) *Teaching and Learning Geography*. London: Routledge, pp. 154–67.

Butt, G. (1998a) *Birmingham: Decisions on Development*. Birmingham: DEC.

Butt, G. (1998b) 'Increasing the effectiveness of 'audience-centred' teaching in geography', *International Research in Geographical and Environmental Education*. **7** (3), pp. 203–18.

Butt, G. (2000a) *The Continuum Guide to Geography Education*. London: Continuum.

Butt, G. (2000b) Teaching, learning and assessment overview. In Hopkin, J., Telfer, S. and Butt, G. (eds) *Assessment in Practice: Raising Standards in Secondary Geography*. Sheffield: Geographical Association, pp. 12–23.

Butt, G. (2001a) Closing the gender gap in geography, *Teaching Geography*, **26** (3), pp. 145–7.

Butt, G. (2001b) *Theory into Practice: Extending Writing Skills*. Sheffield. Geographical Association.

Butt, G. and Lambert, D. (1996) Geography assessment and Key Stage 3 textbooks, *Teaching Geography*, **22** (3), pp. 146–7.

Butt, G. and Smith, P. (1998) Educational standards and assessment in geography – some cause for concern? *Teaching Geography*, **23** (3), pp. 147–9.

Calder, M. and Smith, R. (1993) Introduction to development education. In Fien, J. (ed.) *Teaching for a Sustainable World*. Brisbane: Australian Association for Environmental Education, pp. 116–25.

Capel, S., Leask, M. and Turner, T. (1999) *Learning to Teach in the Secondary School*. London: Routledge.

Carter, R. (ed.) (1991) *Talking About Geography: The Work of Geography Teachers in the National Oracy Project*. Sheffield: Geographical Association.

Carter, R. (1999) Connecting geography: an agenda for action, *Geography*, **84** (4), pp. 289–97.

Carter, R. (2000) Aspects of Global Citizenship. In Fisher, C. and Binns, T. (eds) *Issues in Geography Teaching*. London: RoutledgeFalmer, pp. 175–89.

Catling, S. (1978) The child's spatial conception and geographic education, *Journal of Geography*, **77** (1), pp. 24–8.

Chapman, S. (2001) Researching cross-phase liaison between key stages 2 and 3, *Teaching Geography*, **26** (3), pp. 122–6.

Chorley, R. and Haggett, P. (1965) *Frontiers in Geographical Teaching*. London: Methuen.

Chorley, R. and Haggett, P. (eds) (1967) *Models in Geography*. London: Methuen.

Clark, J. and Stoltman, J. (2000) The renaissance of geography education in the USA. In Kent, A. (ed.) *Reflective Practice in Geography Teaching*. London: Philip Chapman Publishing, pp. 238–52.

Cohen, L., Manion, L. and Morrison, K. (1996) *A Guide to Teaching Practice*. London: Routledge.

Cole, J.P. (1966) *Geographical Games*. Nottingham: University of Nottingham.

Corney, G. (1985) *Geography, Schools and Industry*. Sheffield: Geographical Association.

Corney, G. (1992) *Teaching Economic Understanding through Geography*. Sheffield: Geographical Association.

Corney, G. and Rawling, E. (eds) (1985) *Teaching Geography to Less Able 11–14 Year Olds*. Sheffield: Geographical Association.

Counsell, C. (1997) *Analytical and Discursive Writing at Key Stage 3*. Shaftesbury: Historical Association.

CRE (1989) *Code of Practice for the Elimination of Racial Discrimination in Education*. London: Commission for Racial Equality.

Crick, B. (2000) *Essays on Citizenship*. London: Continuum.

Daugherty, R. and Rawling, E. (1996) New perspectives for geography: an agenda for action. In Rawling, E. and Daugherty, R. (eds) *Geography into the Twenty-First Century*. Chichester: Wiley, pp. 359–77.

Davidson, G. and Catling, S. (2000) Towards the question-led curriculum 5–14. In Fisher, C. and Binns. T. (eds) *Issues in Geography Teaching*. London: RoutledgeFalmer, pp. 271–95.

Dearing, R. (1993) The National Curriculum and its Assessment: Interim Report. London: SCAA.

Dearing, R. (1994) *The National Curriculum and its Assessment: Final Report*. London: SCAA.

Dearing, R. (1996) *Review of Qualifications for 16–19 Year Olds*: Full Report. London: SCAA.

DES (1980) *A Framework for the School Curriculum*. London: HMSO.

DES (1981) *The School Curriculum*. London: HMSO.

DES (1988) *Advancing A levels (Higginson Report)*. London: HMSO.

DES (1989) *Discipline in Schools*. Report of the Committee of Enquiry chaired by Lord Elton (The Elton Report). London: HMSO.

DES (1990) *Geography for Ages 5–16: Proposals of the Secretaries of State for Education and Science for England and Wales*. London: HMSO.

DES (1991) *Geography in the National Curriculum (England)*. London: HMSO.

DFE (1992) *Initial Teacher Training (Secondary Phase) Circular 9/92*. London: HMSO.

DFE (1993a) *The Initial Training of Primary School Teachers (Circular 14/93)*. London: HMSO.

DFE (1993b) *Environmental Responsibility: An Agenda for Further and Higher Education*. London: HMSO.

DFE (1994) *Code of Practice on the Identification and Assessment of Special Educational Needs*. London: HMSO.

DFE (1995) *Information Technology in the National Curriculum*. London: HMSO.

DfEE (1995) *Geography in the National Curriculum*. London: HMSO.

DfEE (1997a) *Teaching: High Status, High Standards, Requirements for Courses of Initial Teacher Training. Circular 10/97*. London: DfEE.

DfEE (1997b) *Excellence in Schools*. London: HMSO.

DfEE (1998a) *Teaching: High Status, High Standards. Requirements for Courses of Initial Teacher Training. Circular 4/98*. London: DfEE.

DfEE (1998b) *The Learning Age: A Renaissance for a New Britain*. London: The Stationary Office.

DfEE/QCA (1999a) *Geography: The National Curriculum for England, Key Stages 1–3*. London: HMSO.

DfEE/QCA (1999b) *Information and Communications Technology. The National Curriculum for England*. London: HMSO.

DfEE (2001) *Schools: Building on Success. Green Paper*. London: HMSO.

Dilkes, J. and Nicholls, A. (1988) *Low Attainers and the Teaching of Geography*. Sheffield: GA.

Donert, K. (1997) *A Geographer's Guide to the Internet*. Sheffield: Geographical Association.

Dowgill, P. and Lambert, D. (1992) Cultural literacy and school geography, *Geography*, 77 (2), pp. 143–52.

Durbin, C. (1995) Using televisual resources in geography. In *Teaching Geography*, 20 (3), pp.118–21.

Electronic Arts (1990) *SIMCITY*. San Mateo: Electronic Arts.

Elliot, J. and Adelman, C. (1976) *Innovation at the Classroom Level: A Case Study of the Ford Teaching Project*. Milton Keynes: Open University Press.

Ellis, B. (ed.) (1997) *Working Together: Partnership in the Education of Geography Teachers*. Sheffield: GA.

EXEL (1995) *Writing Frames*. Exeter: University of Exeter School of Education.

Fairgrieve, J. (1926) *Geography in School*. London: University of London Press.

Fien, J. (1993) *Education for the Environment: Critical Curriculum Theorising and Environmental Education*. London: UCL Press.

Fien, J. (1996) Teaching to care: a case for commitment to teaching environmental values. In Gerber, R. and Lidstone, J. (eds) *Developments and Directions in Geographical Education*. Clevedon: Channel View Publications, pp. 77–92.

Fien, J. (1999) Towards a map of commitment: a socially critical approach to geographical education. *International Research in Geographical and Environmental Education*, 8 (2), pp. 140–58.

Fien, J. and Slater, F. (1985) Four strategies for values in education in geography. In Boardman, D. (ed.) *New Directions in Geographical Education*. Lewes: Falmer, pp. 171–86.

Fisher, T. (2000) Developing the educational use of information and communications technology: implications for the education of geography teachers. In Fisher, C. and Binns, T. (eds) *Issues in Geography Teaching*, London: RoutledgeFalmer, pp. 50–65.

Flinders, K. (1998) The new Certificate of Achievement for Geography, *Teaching Geography*, 22 (1), pp. 46–7.

Foskett, N. (1997) Teaching and learning through fieldwork. In Tilbury, D. and Williams, M. (eds) *Teaching and Learning Geography*. London: Routledge, pp. 189–201.

Foskett, N. (2000) Fieldwork and the development of thinking skills, *Teaching Geography*, 25 (3), pp. 126–9.

Fox, P. and Tapsfield, A. (eds) (1986) *The Role and Value of New Technology in Geography*. Sheffield: GA.

Freeman, D. (1997) Using information technology and new technologies in geography. In Tilbury, D. and Williams, M. (eds) *Teaching and Learning Geography*, London: Routledge, pp. 202–17.

Fry, P. and Schofield, A. (1993) (eds) *Geography at key stage 3: teachers' experience of National Curriculum Geography in year 7*. Sheffield: GA.

GA (1999) Geography in the Curriculum: a position statement from the GA. *Teaching Geography*, 24 (2), pp. 57–9.

GA/NCET (1992) *Geography, IT and the National Curriculum*. Sheffield: GA.

Gair, N. (1997) *Outdoor Education: Theory and Practice*. London: Cassell.

Gerber, R. (1984) The diagnosis of student learning in geography. In Fien, J., Gerber, R. and Wilson, P. (eds) *The Geography Teachers' Guide to the Classroom*. Melbourne: Macmillan, pp. 185–96.

Gerber, R. (1996) Directions for Research in Geographical Education: the Maturity of Qualitative Research. In Gerber, R. and Lidstone, J. (eds) *Developments and Directions in Geographical Education*. Clevedon: Channel View, pp. 131–50.

Gerber, R. and Williams, M. (2000) Overview and international perspectives. In Kent, A. (ed.) *Reflective Practice in Geography Teaching*. London: Philip Chapman Publishing, pp. 209–18.

Gerber, R. and Wilson, P. (1984) Maps in the geography classroom. In Fien, J. Gerber, R. and Wilson, P. (eds) *The Geography Teachers' Guide to the Classroom*, Melbourne: Macmillan, pp. 146–57.

Gersmehl, P. (1996) Opinion: more like a cart than a factory; understanding resistance to educational change, *Journal of Geography*, 95 (3), pp. 130–1.

Gipps, C. (1994) *Beyond Testing. Towards a Theory of Educational Assessment*. London: Falmer.

Goodson, I. (1983) *School Subjects and Curriculum Change*. London: Croom Helm.

Goudie, A. (1993) Guest editorial: schools and universities – the great divide, *Geography*, 78 (4), pp. 338–9.

Graham, D. and Tytler, D. (1993) *A Lesson For Us All: The Making of the National Curriculum*. London. Routledge.

Graves, N. (1975) *Geography in Education*. London: Heinemann.

Graves, N. (1997) Geographical Education in the 1990s. In Tilbury, D. and Williams, M. (eds) *Teaching and Learning Geography*, London: Routledge, pp. 25–31.

Gregory, D. (1978) *Ideology, Science and Human Geography*. London: Hutchinson.

Greig, S., Pike, G. and Selby, D. (1987) *Earthrights: Education as if the Planet Really Mattered*. London: Kogan Page/WWF (UK).

Grey, D. (2001) *The Internet in School* (2nd edition). London: Continuum.

Grosvenor, I. (1999) 'Race' and education. In Matheson, D. and Grosvenor, I. (eds) *An Introduction to the Study of Education*. London: Fulton, pp. 70–83.

Haggett, P. (1996) Geography into the next century: personal reflections. In Rawling, E. and Daugherty, R. (eds) *Geography into the Twenty-First Century*. Chichester: Wiley, pp. 11–18.

Hargreaves, D. (1994) *Changing Teachers, Changing Times: Teachers' Work and Culture in the Postmodern Age*. London: Cassell.

Hargreaves, D. (1998) A new partnership of stakeholders and a national strategy of research in education. In Rudduck, J. and McIntyre, D. (eds) *Challenges for Educational Research*, London: Paul Chapman, pp. 114–36.

Harlen, W., Gipps, C., Broadfoot, P. and Nuttall, D. (1992) Assessment and the improvement of education, *The Curriculum Journal*, 3 (3), pp. 215–30.

Harris, C.D., and Ullman, E.L., (1945) The nature of cities, *Annals of the American Academy of Political and Social Science*, 242, pp. 7–17.

Hart, C. and Thomas, T. (1986) Framework fieldwork. In Boardman, D. (ed.) *Handbook for Geography Teachers*. Sheffield: Geographical Association, pp. 205–18.

Hartley, D. (1997) *Reschooling Society*. London: Falmer.

Harvey, D. (1969) *Explanation in Geography*. London: Arnold.

Harvey, D. (1973) *Social Justice and the City*. London: Arnold.

Hassell, D. (2000a) Issues in ICT and geography. In Fisher, C. and Binns, T. (eds) *Issues in Geography Teaching*. London: RoutledgeFalmer, pp. 80–92.

Hassell, D. (2000b) Developing your own web page, *Teaching Geography*, **25** (4), pp. 200–1.

Hassell, D. and Warner, H. (eds) (1995) *Using IT to Enhance Geography: Case Studies at Key Stages 3 and 4*. Sheffield: Geographical Association.

Hicks, D. (1993) Mapping the future: a geographical contribution, *Teaching Geography*, **18** (4), pp. 146–9.

Hicks, D. (1994) *Educating for the Future: A Practical Classroom Guide*. Surrey: WWF.

Hicks, D. (1998) A geography for the future, *Teaching Geography*, **23** (4), pp. 168–73.

Hicks, D. and Holden, C. (1996) *Visions of the Future: Why We Need to Teach for Tomorrow*. Stoke on Trent: Trentham Books.

Hicks, D. and Steiner, M. (eds) (1989) *Making Global Connections: A World Studies Workbook*. Harlow: Oliver and Boyd.

Hillage, J., Pearson, R., Anderson, A. and Tamkin, P. (1998) *Excellence in Research in Schools*. DfEE Research Report No. 74. London: DfEE.

Hirsch, E.D. (1987) *Cultural Literacy: What Every American Needs to Know*. Boston: Houghton Mifflin Co.

HMI (1977) *Curriculum 11–16*. London: HMSO.

HMI (1986) *Geography from 5–16. Curriculum Matters 7*. London: HMSO.

Hopkin, J. (2000) Day-to-day assessment. In Hopkin, J., Telfer, S. and Butt, G. (eds) *Assessment in Practice: Raising Standards in Secondary Geography*. Sheffield: Geographical Association, pp. 37–45.

Hopkin, J. and Telfer, S. (2000) Planning for progression and assessment. In Hopkin, J., Telfer, S. and Butt, G. (eds) *Assessment in Practice: Raising Standards in Secondary Geography*, Sheffield: Geographical Association, pp. 24–35.

Hopkin, J., Telfer, S. and Butt, G. (eds) (2000) *Assessment in Practice: Raising Standards in Secondary Geography*. Sheffield: Geographical Association.

Hopkirk, G. (1998) Challenging images of the developing world using slide photography, *Teaching Geography*, **23** (1), pp. 34–5.

Howes, N. (1996) The portfolio as a key stage 3 assessment tool, *Teaching Geography*, **21** (3), pp. 143–5.

Howes, N. (2000) Long term, summative assessment and evaluation: portfolios. In Hopkin, J., Telfer, S. and Butt, G. (eds) *Assessment in Practice: Raising Standards in Secondary Geography*, Sheffield: Geographical Association, pp. 60–9.

Hoyt, N. (1939) *Neighborhoods in American Cities*. Washington.

HSGP (American High School Geography Project) (1971) *Geography in an Urban Age*. Collier-Macmillan.

Huckle, J. (1980) Values and the teaching of geography: towards a curriculum rationale, *Geographical Education*, **3** (4), pp. 533–44.

Huckle, J. (1981) Geography and values education. In Walford, R., (ed.) *Signposts for Geography Teaching*. Harlow: Longman, pp. 147–64.

Huckle, J. (1983) Values Education through Geography: a radical critique, *Journal of Geography*, **82**, pp. 59–63.

Huckle, J. (1994) Environmental education and the National Curriculum in England and Wales, *IRGEE*, **2** (1), pp. 101–4.

Huckle, J. (1997) Towards a critical school geography. In Tilbury, D. and Williams, M. (eds) *Teaching and Learning Geography*. London: Routledge, pp. 241–52.

Huckle, J. and Sterling, S. (eds) (1996) *Education for Sustainability*. London: Earthscan.

Jackson, S. (2000) Information and Communications Technology. In Kent, A. (ed.) *Reflective Practice in Geography Teaching*. London: Paul Chapman Publishing, pp. 154–67.

Job, D. (1996) Geography and environmental education: an exploration of perspectives and strategies. In Kent, A., Lambert, D., Naish, M. and Slater, F., (eds) *Geography in Education: Viewpoints on Teaching and Learning*. Cambridge: CUP, pp. 22–49.

Job, D. (1997) Geography and environmental education. In Powell, A. (ed.) *Handbook of Post 16 Geography*. Sheffield: Geographical Association, pp. 147–59.

Jones, B. (1999) Curriculum continuity in geography, *Teaching Geography*, **24** (1), pp. 5–9.

Kemmis, S., Cole, P. and Suggett, D. (1983) *Orientations to Curriculum and Transitions: Towards the Socially Critical School*. Melbourne: Victorian Institute for Secondary Education.

Kent, A. (1992) The new technology and geographical education. In Naish, M. (ed.) *Geography and Education: National and International Perspectives*. London: Institute of Education, pp. 163–76.

Kent, A. (ed.) (2000) *Reflective Practice in Geography Teaching*. London: Philip Chapman Publishing.

Kent, A. and Smith, M. (1997) Links between geography in schools and higher education. In Powell, A. (ed.) *Handbook of Post 16 Geography*. Sheffield: GA.

Kohlberg, L. (1976) *Recent Research in Moral Development*. New York: Holt, Reinhart and Winston.

Kyriacou, C. (1986) *Effective Teaching in Schools*. Oxford: Blackwell.

Kyriacou, C. (1995) *Essential Teaching Skills*. Cheltenham: Stanley Thornes.

Lambert, D. (1996) The choice of textbooks for use in secondary school geography departments: some answers and some further questions for research, *Paradigm*, **21**(3), pp. 14–31.

Lambert, D. (1997) Principles of pupil assessment. In Tilbury, D. and Williams, M. (eds) *Teaching and Learning Geography*, London: Routledge, pp. 255–65.

Lambert, D. (2001) Mind the gap – which one? Unpublished paper to UDE Geography Tutors' Conference, Liverpool.

Lambert, D. and Balderstone, D. (2000) *Learning to Teach Geography in the Secondary School*. London: RoutledgeFalmer.

Lambert, D. and Machon, P. (eds) (2001) *Citizenship through Geography Education*. London: RoutledgeFalmer.

Lawton, D. (1996) *Beyond the National Curriculum: Teacher Professionalism and Empowerment*. London: Hodder and Stoughton.

Leat, D. (1997) Cognitive acceleration in geographical education. In Tilbury, D. and Williams, M. (eds) *Teaching and Learning Geography*. London: Routledge, pp. 143–53.

Leat, D. (ed.) (1998) *Thinking Through Geography*. Cambridge: Chris Kington Publishing.

Leat, D. (2000) The importance of 'big' concepts and skills in learning geography. In Fisher, C. and Binns, T. (eds) *Issues in Geography Teaching*. London: RoutledgeFalmer, pp. 137–55.

Leat, D. and Kinninment, D. (2000) Learn to debrief. In Fisher, C. and Binns, T. (eds) *Issues in Geography Teaching*. London: RoutledgeFalmer, pp. 152–71.

Leat, D. and Nichols, A. (1999) *Theory into Practice: Mysteries Make You Think*. Sheffield: Geographical Association.

Lewis, D. (1989) Writing in a humanities classroom. In Slater, F. (ed.) *Language and Learning in the Teaching of Geography*. London: Routledge, pp. 39–58.

Lewis, R. (1999) The role of technology in learning: managing to achieve a vision, *British Journal of Educational Technology*, **30** (2) pp. 141–50.

Lidstone, J. (1992) In defence of textbooks. In Naish, M. (ed.) *Geography and Education: National and International Perspectives*. London: Institute of Education, pp. 177–93.

Machon, P. (1998) Citizenship and geographical education, *Teaching Geography*, **23** (3), pp. 115–17.

Machon, P. and Ranger, G. (1996) Changes in school geography. In Bailey, P. and Fox, P. (eds) *Geography Teachers' Handbook*. Sheffield: Geographical Association, pp. 39–46.

Machon, P. and Walkington, H. (2000) Citizenship: the role of geography? In Kent, A. (ed.) *Reflective Practice in Geography Teaching*. London. Paul Chapman Publishing, pp. 179–91.

Maddrell, A. (1996) Empire, emigration and school geography: changing discourses of imperial citizenship 1880–1925, *Journal of Historical Geography*, **22** (4) pp. 373–87.

Mahony, P. and Hextall, I. (2000) *Reconstructing Teaching: Standards, Performance and Accountability*. London: RoutledgeFalmer.

Marsden, W. E. (1992) Cartoon geography: the new stereotyping?, *Teaching Geography*, **17** (3), pp. 128–30.

Marsden, W. E. (1995) *Geography 11–16: Rekindling Good Practice*. London: Fulton.

Marsden, W. E. (1997) Continuity after the national curriculum, *Teaching Geography*, **22**(2), pp. 68–70.

Marsh, C. (1997) *Perspectives: Key Concepts for Understanding Curriculum*. Lewes: Falmer Press.

Massey, D. (2001) Geography on the agenda, *Progress in Human Geography*, **25** (1), pp. 5–17.

Matthews, M. (1984) Environmental cognition of young children: images of journey to school and home area, *TIBG*, **9**, pp. 89–105.

Matthews, S. (1998) Using the internet for meaningful research, *Journal of the Geography Teachers' Association of Victoria*, **26** (1), pp. 15–19.

Maye, B. (1984) Developing valuing and decision making skills in the geography classroom. In Fien, J., Gerber, R. and Wilson, P. (eds) *The Geography Teacher's Guide to the Classroom*. Melbourne: Macmillan.

McCarthy, M. and Carter, R. (1994) *Language as Discourse*. New York: Longman.

McPartland, M. (2001) *Theory into Practice: Moral Dilemmas*. Sheffield: Geographical Association.

Midgley, H. and Walker, D. (1985) *Microcomputers in Geography Teaching.* London: Hutchinson.

Miller, J. (1983) *The Educational Spectrum: Orientations to Curriculum.* New York: Longman.

Morgan, J. (2000a) The Future of the Geography Curriculum. In Lambert, D. and Balderstone, D. (eds) *Learning to Teach Geography in the Secondary School.* London: RoutledgeFalmer, pp. 33–8.

Morgan, J. (2000b) Geography Teaching for a Sustainable Society. In Kent, A. (ed.) *Reflective Practice in Geography Teaching.* London: Philip Chapman Publishing, pp. 168–78.

Morgan, J. and Lambert, D. (2001) Geography, 'Race' and Education, *Geography,* **86** (3), pp. 235–96.

Naish, M. (1982) Mental development and the learning of geography. In Graves, N. (ed.) *The new UNESCO Sourcebook for Geography Teaching.* London: UNESCO, pp. 16–54.

Naish, M. (1996a) The geography curriculum: a martyr to epistemology? In Gerber, R. and Lidstone, J. (eds) *Developments and Directions in Geographical Education.* Clevedon: Channel View, pp. 63–76.

Naish, M. (1996b) Action research for a new professionalism in geography education. In Kent, A., Lambert, D., Naish, M. and Slater, F. (eds) *Geography In Education: Viewpoints on Teaching and Learning.* Cambridge: CUP, pp. 321–43.

Naish, M. (2000) The geography curriculum of England and Wales from 1965: a personal view. In Lambert, D. and Balderstone, D. (eds) *Learning to Teach Geography in the Secondary School.* London: RoutledgeFalmer, pp. 11–17.

Naish, M., Rawling, E. and Hart, C. (1987) *Geography 16–19: The Contribution of a Curriculum Project to 16–19 Education.* Harlow: Longman.

Nash, P. (1997) Card sorting activities in the geography classroom, *Teaching Geography,* **22** (1), pp. 22–5.

NCC (1990a) *Environmental Education: Curriculum Guidance 7.* York: NCC.

NCC (1990b) *Education for Economic and Industrial Understanding: Curriculum Guidance 4,* York: NCC.

NCC (1990c) *Education for Citizenship: Curriculum Guidance 8.* York: NCC.

NCC (1992a) *Geography and Economic and Industrial Understanding at Key Stages 3 and 4.* York: NCC.

NCC (1992b) *Implementing National Curriculum Geography.* Unpublished Report of NCC questionnaire findings. York: NCC.

NCET/GA (1994) *Geography: A Pupil's Entitlement to IT.* Coventry: NCET.

Nichols, A. (ed.) (2001) *More Thinking Through Geography.* Cambridge: Chris Kington Publishing.

Norton, A. (1999) On the cards, *Teaching Geography,* **24** (1), pp. 25–9.

Norton, A., Hendy, W. and Watson, H. (1999) Using relief models as a teaching tool, *Teaching Geography,* **24** (4), pp. 182–5.

O'Brien, T. and Guiney, D. (2001) *Differentiation in Teaching and Learning – Principles and Practice.* London: Continuum.

OFSTED (1993a) *Geography at Key Stages 1, 2 and 3. The First* Year 1991–92. London: HMSO.

OFSTED (1993b) *Geography at Key Stages 1, 2 and 3. Second* Year 1992–93. London HMSO.

OFSTED (1995) *Geography: A Review of Inspection Findings 1993/4*. London: HMSO.

OFSTED (1996) *Subjects and Standards. Issues for School Development Arising from OFSTED 1994–5 Key Stages 3 and 4 and Post 16*. London: HMSO.

OFSTED (1997) *The Annual Report of Her Majesty's Chief Inspector of Schools: Standards and Quality in Education 1995–6*. London: HMSO.

OFSTED (1998) *Secondary Education: A Review of Secondary Schools in England 1993–7*. London: HMSO.

OFSTED (1999a) *The Annual Report of Her Majesty's Chief Inspector of Schools*. London: HMSO.

OFSTED (1999b) *Standards in the Secondary Curriculum 1997/8*. London: Stationery Office.

O'Riordan, T. (1981) Environmentalism and Education, *Journal of Geography in Higher Education*, **5** (1), pp. 3–18.

Oxfam (1997) *A Curriculum for Global Citizenship*. London: Oxfam.

Panel for Education for Sustainable Development (1998) *Education for Sustainable Development in the Schools Sector: A Report to DfEE/QCA*. London: DfEE/QCA.

Peters, R. (1977) *Education and the Education of Teachers*. London: Routledge and Kegan Paul.

Pike, G. and Selby, D. (1988) *Global Teacher, Global Learner*. London: Hodder and Stoughton.

QCA (1998a) *Geographical Enquiry at Key Stages 1–3: A Discussion Paper*. London: QCA.

QCA (1998b) *Education for Citizenship and the Teaching of Democracy in Schools: Final Report of the Advisory Group on Citizenship*. London: QCA.

QCA (1999a) *Improving Writing at Key Stages 3 and 4*. London: QCA.

QCA (1999b) *Technical Accuracy in Writing in GCSE English: Research Findings*. London: QCA.

QCA (1999c) *Revised Subject Criteria for AS and A level: Geography*. London: QCA.

QCA (1999d) *Citizenship: The National Curriculum for England. Key Stages 3 and 4*. London: DfEE/QCA.

QCA (2000) *Key Stage 3 Schemes of Work: Geography*. London: QCA.

QCA (2001) *Geography Update: Spring Term 2001*. London: QCA.

Rawling, E. (1996) Madingley revisited? In Rawling, E. and Daugherty, R. (eds) *Geography into the Twenty-First Century*. Chichester: Wiley, pp. 3–8.

Rawling, E. (1997) Geography and vocationalism: opportunity or threat? *Geography*, **82** (2) pp. 167–78.

Rawling, E. (2000a) School geography 5–16: issues for debate. In Fisher, C. and Binns, T. (eds) *Issues in Geography Teaching*. London: RoutledgeFalmer, pp. 6–22.

Rawling, E. (2000b) *Policy-Making, Ideology and the Changing Curriculum. Issues arising from a case study of school geography in England, 1991–2000*. Paper Presented at BERA conference, University of Cardiff, 8 September 2000.

Rawling, E. (2000c) National Curriculum geography: new opportunities for curriculum development? In Kent, A. (ed.) *Reflective Practice in Geography Teaching*, London: Paul Chapman Publishing, pp. 99–112.

Rawling, E. (2001) *Changing the Subject. The Impact of National Policy on School Geography 1980–2000*. Sheffield: Geographical Association.

Rawling, E. and Daugherty, R. (eds) (1996) *Geography into the Twenty-First Century*. Chichester: Wiley.

Rhys, W. (1972) The development of logical thinking. In Graves, N. (ed.) *New Movements in the Study and Teaching of Geography*, London: Temple Smith, pp. 93–106.

Richmond, J. (1986) 'What we need when we write', *About Writing* (newsletter) **2**. National Writing Project. London: SCDC.

Roberts, M. (1986) Talking, reading and writing. In Boardman, D. (ed.) *Handbook for Geography Teachers*. Sheffield: Geographical Association, pp. 68–78.

Roberts, M. (1998a) Using slide photography to promote active learning, *Teaching Geography*, **23** (1), pp. 31–3.

Roberts, M. (1998b) The nature of geographical enquiry at key stage 3, *Teaching Geography*, **23** (4), pp. 164–7.

Roberts, M. (2000a) The role of research in the initial education of geography teachers. In Fisher, C. and Binns, T. (eds) *Issues in Geography Teaching*. London: RoutledgeFalmer, pp. 37–49.

Roberts, M. (2000b) The role of research in supporting teaching and learning. In Kent, A. (ed.) *Reflective Practice in Geography Teaching*, London: Philip Chapman Publishing, pp. 287–95.

Robinson, R. (1987) Discussing Photographs. In Boardman, D. (ed.) *Handbook for Geography Teachers*. Sheffield: GA, pp. 103–7.

Robinson, R. and Serf, J. (eds) (1997) *Global Geography: Learning Through Development Education at Key Stage 3*. Birmingham: GA/DEC.

Rokeach, M. (1973) *The Nature of Human Values*. New York: Free Press.

Rudduck, J. and McIntyre, D. (eds) (1998) *Challenges for Educational Research*. London: Paul Chapman.

Rynne, E. (1998) Utilitarian approaches to fieldwork: a critique, *Geography*, **83** (3), pp. 205–13.

SCAA (1995) *Spiritual and Moral Development*. London: SCAA.

SCAA (1996a) *Consistency in Teacher Assessment: Exemplification of Standards – Geography at Key Stage 3*. London: SCAA.

SCAA (1996b) *Consistency in Teacher Assessment: Optional Tests and Tasks – Key Stage 3, Geography*. London: SCAA.

SCAA (1996c) *Monitoring the School Curriculum: Reporting to Schools*. London: SCAA.

SCAA (1996d) *Teaching Environmental Matters Through the National Curriculum*. London: SCAA.

SCAA (1996e) *Key Stage 3 Optional Tests and Tasks*. London: SCAA.

SCAA (1997a) *Monitoring the School Curriculum: Reporting to Schools*. London: SCAA.

SCAA (1997b) *Expectations for Geography at Key Stages 1 and 2*. London: SCAA.

SCAA (1997c) *Use of Language: A Common Approach*. London: HMSO.

SCAA (1997d) *Geography and the Use of Language*. London: HMSO.

Scardamalia, M., Bereiter, C. and Fillion, B. (1981) Writing for Results: A Sourcebook of Consequential Composing Activities. Ontario: Ontario Institute for Studies in Education.

Sheeran, Y. and Barnes, D. (1991) *School Writing: Discovering the Ground Rules*. Milton Keynes: Open University Press.

Sibert, P. (1998) Stretching credibility: an activity to teach map projection, *Teaching Geography*, **23** (4), pp. 196–7.

Skilbeck, M. (1976) Ideologies and values. In Dale, S. (ed.) *Curriculum Design and Development*. Milton Keynes: Open University.

Slater, F. (1980) Values clarification: some practical suggestions for the classroom. In Slater, F. and Spicer, B. (eds) *Perception and Preference Studies at the International Level*. Tokyo: IGUCGE/AIP, pp. 224–31.

Slater, F. (ed.) (1989) *Language and Learning in the Teaching of Geography*. London: Routledge.

Slater, F. (1994) Education through geography: knowledge, understanding, values and culture, *Geography*, **79** (2), pp. 147–63.

Slater, F. (1995) Geography into the future, *Geographical Education*, **8** (3), pp. 4–63.

Slater, F. (1996a) Values: towards mapping their locations in geography. In Kent, A., Lambert, D., Naish, M. and Slater, F. (eds) *Geography in Education: Viewpoints on Teaching and Learning*. Cambridge: CUP, pp. 200–30.

Slater, F. (1996b) Illustrating research in geography education. In Kent, A., Lambert, D. Naish, M. and Slater, F. (eds) *Geography and Education: Viewpoints on Teaching and Learning*. Cambridge: CUP, pp. 291–320.

Slater, F. (1998) Telling research stories, *Teaching Geography*, **23** (2), pp. 77–9.

Smith, D. (1973) Alternative 'relevant' professional roles, *Area*, **5**, pp. 1–4.

Smith, D. (1977) *Human Geography: A Welfare Approach*. London: Arnold.

Stenhouse, L. (1970) *The Humanities Project*. London: Heinemann.

Stoddart, D. R. (1986) *On Geography*. Oxford: Blackwell.

Stoddart, D. R. (1987) To claim the high ground: geography for the end of the century. *Transactions of the Institute of British Geographers*, 12, pp. 327–36.

Storm, M. (1995) Interview with author.

Sulke, F. (1999) *Letter to ITT Institutions and Partnerships from TTA*. 14 December 1999.

Tapsfield, A. (2001) *ICT in Geography Education. Implementation of DfEE Circular 4/98 (Annex B) Evidence from Secondary Geography Inspections 1999–2000*. Unpublished paper delivered at UDE Geography Conference Liverpool 27 January.

Taylor, L. (2001) Using presentation packages for collaborative work, *Teaching Geography*, **26** (1), pp. 43–50.

Teaching Geography (2001) Themed issue on Citizenship and Sustainable Development, **26** (2).

Tilbury, D. (1993) *Environmental Education: Developing a Model for Initial Teacher Education*. Unpublished PhD thesis, University of Cambridge.

Tilbury, D. (1997) Environmental education and development education: teaching geography for a sustainable world. In Tilbury, D. and Williams, M. (eds) *Teaching and Learning Geography*. London: Routledge, pp. 105–16.

Tolley, H. and Reynolds, J. (1977) *Geography 14-18: A Handbook for School-Based Curriculum Development*. Basingstoke: Macmillan.

Toynbee, P. and Walker, D. (2001) *Did Things Get Better? An Audit of Labour's Successes and Failures*. London: Penguin.

Trend, R. (2000) *Qualified Teacher Status: A Practical Introduction*. London: Letts Educational.

TTA (1997) *Standards for the Award of Qualified Teacher Status*. London: TTA.

TTA (1998) *Teaching as a Research-based Profession*. London: TTA.

TTA (1999) *Understanding Teacher Supply in Geography*. Publication 110/3-00. London: TTA.

TTA (2000) *Monitoring and Review of Circular 4/98 – Report on the Responses to the First Phase of Consultation*. London: TTA.

TTA (2001a) *Standards for the Award of Qualified Teacher Status and Requirements for initial Teacher Training (Consultation Document July 2001)*. London: TTA.

TTA (2001b) *Handbook to Accompany the Standards for the Award of Qualified Teacher Status and Requirements for Initial Teacher Training (Consultation Document July 2001)*. London: TTA.

Unwin, T. (1996) Academic geography: the key questions for discussion. In Rawling, E. and Daugherty, R. (eds) *Geography into the Twenty-First Century*. Chichester: Wiley, pp. 19–36.

Walford, R. (1969) *Games in Geography*. Harlow: Longman.

Walford, R. (1981) Language, ideologies and geography teaching. In Walford, R. (ed.) *Signposts for Geography Teaching*. Harlow: Longman, pp. 215–22.

Walford, R. (1987) Games and Simulations. In Boardman, D. (ed.) *Handbook for Geography Teachers*. Sheffield: GA, pp. 79–84.

Walford, R. (1995) Interview with author.

Walford, R. (1996) Geography 5–19: retrospect and prospect. In Rawling, E. and Daugherty, R. (eds) *Geography into the Twenty-First Century*. Chichester: Wiley, pp. 131–43.

Walford, R. (1997) The great debate and 1988. In Tilbury, D. and Williams, M. (eds) *Teaching and Learning Geography*. London: Routledge, pp. 15–24.

Walford, R. (1998) Geography: the way ahead. *Teaching Geography*. Sheffield: GA, pp. 61–4.

Walford, R. (2000) Wider issues for the future. In Fisher, C. and Binns, T. (eds) *Issues in Geography Teaching*. London: RoutledgeFalmer, pp. 296–313.

Walford, R. and Haggett, P. (1995) Geography and geographical education: some speculations for the twenty-first century, *Geography*. No. 346, 80 (1), pp. 3–13.

Walkington, H. (1999) *Theory into Practice: Global Citizenship Education*. Sheffield: Geographical Association.

Warf, B. (1999) Constructing a dialogue: geographic education and geographic research, *Professional Geographer*, 51 (4), pp. 586–91.

Waters, A. (1995) Differentiation and classroom practice, *Teaching Geography*, 20 (2), pp. 81–4.

Watson, D. (ed.) (1984) *Exploring Geography with Microcomputers*. London: Council for Educational Technology.

Watson, D. (2000) Issues raised by research into ICT and geography education. In Kent, A. (ed.) *Research Forum 2: Information and Communications Technology*. London: University of London Institute of Education, pp. 12–25.

WCED (1987) *World Commission on Environment and Development. Our Common Future (The Brundtland Report)*. Oxford: Oxford University Press.

Weeden, P. (1997) Learning Through Maps. In Tilbury, D. and Williams, M. (eds) *Teaching and Learning Geography*. London: Routledge, pp. 168–79.

Westaway, J. and Rawling, E. (2001) The rises and falls of geography, *Teaching Geography*, **26** (3), pp. 108–11.

Westoby, G. (1999) Writing for reading and learning in geography, *Teaching Geography*, **24** (4), pp. 165–8.

Wiegand, P. (1996) Learning with atlases and globes. In Bailey, P. and Fox, P. (eds) *Geography Teachers' Handbook*. Sheffield: GA, pp. 125–37.

Williams, M. (ed.) (1981) *Language, Teaching and Learning Geography*. London: Ward Lock.

Williams, M. (1996) *Understanding Geographical and Environmental Education: The Role of Research*. London: Cassell.

Williams, M. (1997) Progression and transition in a coherent geography curriculum. In Tilbury, D. and Williams, M. (eds) *Teaching and Learning Geography*. London: Routledge, pp. 59–68.

Winter, C. (1997) Ethnocentric bias in geography textbooks: a framework for reconstruction. In Tilbury, D. and Williams, M. (eds) *Teaching and Learning Geography*. London: Routledge, pp. 180–8.

Wood, P. (2001) Bridging key stage 2 and 3, *Teaching Geography*, **26** (1), pp. 40–2.

Wray, D. and Lewis, M. (1994) *Developing Children's Non Fiction Writing – Working with Writing Frames*. Leamington Spa: Scholastic.

Wray, D. and Lewis, M. (1997) *Extending Literacy: Children Reading and Writing Non-fiction*. London: Routledge.

Wright, D. (2000) *Theory into Practice: Maps with Latitude*. Sheffield: Geographical Association.

INDEX